Journalists Under Fire

Information War and Journalistic Practices

Howard Tumber
and
Frank Webster

SAGE Publications

London ● Thousand Oaks ● New Delhi

SAGE Publications Ltd
1 Oliver's Yard
55 City Road
London EC1Y 1SP

SAGE Publications Inc.
2455 Teller Road
Thousand Oaks, California 91320

SAGE Publications India Pvt Ltd
B-42, Panchsheel Enclave
Post Box 4109
New Delhi 110 017

British Library Cataloguing in Publication data

A catalogue record for this book is available from the
British Library

ISBN-10 1-4129-2406-5   ISBN-13 978-1-4129-2406-1
ISBN-10 1-4129-2407-3 (pbk)   ISBN-13 978-1-4129-2407-8

Library of Congress Control Number available

Typeset by C&M Digitals (P) Ltd., Chennai, India
Printed in Great Britain by Athenaeum Press, Gateshead
Printed on paper from sustainable resources

CONTENTS

ACKNOWLEDGEMENTS

This book could not have been written without the help and co-operation of many people. First, we are extremely grateful to all the journalists who so generously gave up their time to be interviewed. Second, we would like to thank those people who, in various ways, collaborated in this project: Marina Prentoulis for her very efficient research assistance, particularly her effectiveness in conducting many of the interviews; John Owen, Stuart Purvis and Mark Brayne for their stimulating advice at various stages of the project; Mark Wood for his support and in providing access to his colleagues; Steve Nicklin and Jan Taylor for copy editing and proofing advice; Jackie Hall Transcription Services for their work on the interviews; and Chris Priest for audio recording assistance.

Funding for the project came from the Economic and Social Research Council in its 'New Security Challenges' Research Programme. We gratefully acknowledge the ESRC's support and particularly that of the Director of the Programme, Stuart Croft, who provided support throughout the period of our research and also thanks to Gary Williams Senior Science Manager at the ESRC.

We would like to express our thanks to our publishers Sage and in particular Julia Hall, our commissioning editor for her unwavering support for the project. Thanks also to Fabienne Pedroletti our production editor, Emily Lawrence, marketing manager, Sandra Jones copy editor, Tony Sivers, proof reader and Gurdeep Mattu, assistant editor.

Finally we would also like to say thank you to our colleagues in the Department of Sociology at City University for making it such a supportive and intellectually exciting place. The International Communications and Society (ICS) group at City deserves our special gratitude.

1

INTRODUCTION: A NEW KIND OF WAR

This book is concerned with the emergence of a new kind of war and with those who report on it. We call this *Information War* to highlight a number of features of the changes that have brought about and announce this transformation. The usual presumption is that Information War is about the virtuoso new weapons that have been developed through more and more sophisticated applications of digital technologies. Some commentators refer to this as Cyberwar, to emphasise the use of smart missiles, command and control systems, and destructive fighter aeroplanes. Such technologies are largely the prerogative of the most affluent nations, especially the USA. When activated, Information War generally covers only a few weeks of 'hot' battle. Such is its overwhelming superiority that forces equipped with more conventional resources quickly collapse when identifiable and amenable to targeting. Regardless of the toughness of soldiers, irrespective of the size of armies, and despite fighting on familiar terrain, forces without sophisticated and robust computer communications systems and state of the art aircraft will crumble against those that possess cruise missiles, satellite guidance systems and stealth bombers.

It is understandable that Information War conjures technologies, at least in the first instance, so it is hardly surprising that much writing about the Revolution in Military Affairs (RMA – see Cohen 1996) over the last decade has paid almost exclusive attention to exactly these elements. Some of this can drift into a technophile's vision of war, one in which increasingly advanced technologies are all that matter. However, in this book we intend to use the concept Information War to invoke much more than technologies. For us, it also entails a series of connected social, political and economic factors.

For instance, the reliance on Information War by a relatively small elite of professional 'knowledge warriors' such as pilots and engineers rather than infantry and Marines, means that the military presence in affluent countries has receded – there are simply fewer soldiers on the streets nowadays in sharp contrast to the days of conscription that was a requirement of Industrial Wars. To this extent civilians in societies engaged in Information War are likely to be much less affected than they were during

20th-century wars, when the entire populace was often mobilised in support of the nation in struggle. War economies would then have been established, with industry and the war effort conjoined, males ordered to fight, and women sent to jobs in factories and fields. In the era of Information War, the military has adequate numbers of specialists to fly powerful aeroplanes and to operate complex missiles, and, by extension, only a few key industries such as computing and aerospace need to be closely wedded to the war capability. Information War can thereby be waged with surprisingly little direct effect on the citizens in whose name it is fought.

It matters, too, that the Cold War is now over. With it has gone the great issue that enveloped most conflicts over the previous 60 years. Moreover, the Cold War ended with capitalism triumphant over communism, so the market system has expanded everywhere, against little or no serious opposition. Deregulation, private property and profit are unchallenged principles in the contemporary world; their opposites – collectivist organ-isation, central command and top-down political control – are discredited and defeated. There will be no more wars, even proxy wars, fought between these worldviews in the foreseeable future.

Information War is waged at a time of increasing globalisation under market system principles, when issues of national sovereignty, while still pertinent, are decreasing in terms of priority. Defending the nation still can and does move citizens and their leaders, but the territorial motiva-tion is on the wane, particularly amongst those most capable of waging Information War. It would be surprising if it were otherwise, when indus-trial and financial affairs routinely cross borders in electronic form, when trillions of dollars move round the world on a daily basis. In these condi-tions, the most important matter is maintaining the free movement of capital, opening markets to trade, and ensuring stable conditions that encourage investment.

As the territorial imperative has receded, particular concern has emerged about a new variant of terrorism. This threat, while it is concen-trated in particular places, is seen to come not from given nations that make claims against others' land, but rather from networks of fellow believers who are united more by conviction and faith than by nation-hood and national aspiration. To these forces the enemy is not so much a place as a whole way of life, which is manifest in apostates who inhabit secularised, consumer-oriented and materialistic societies. It is hard to envisage negotiation with such faith-based terrorists since there is little tangible – in the form of land or home – to negotiate about.

Even though this variant of terrorism is an important feature of the world today, there are no signs of nation states disappearing in the fore-seeable future. The nation state is the major vehicle for politics, identity and order, although it has lost some ground in recent years to larger regional and even global organisations. It perhaps needs stressing that much unrest in the world comes from groups, often using terrorist methods that target civilians, with ambitions to establish their own states. Such ambition is familiar enough after decades of wars of 'national liberation'. Local terrorists who strive for the creation of their own territory – the IRA, Basque separatists, Corsican nationalists, Hamas and so on – should be distinguished from the faith-based international networks such as Al Qaeda, which have attracted enormous attention since September 11, 2001. This is all the more essential since, if policies towards them are not differentiated, there are risks of escalating the problem of terrorism with indiscriminate responses that push the two forms together.

The USA will merit specific treatment in the first part of the book, since it is by far the leading exponent of Information War and because its immense political and economic power sets it apart from all others. The defeat of communism accelerated America's rise to pre-eminence. It has also been intimately involved in all manifestations of Information War over the last 20 years. Far from evidence of a diminishment of the nation state, it is to some the epitome of the superstate that can reach and strike anywhere round the globe. Commentators have taken to identifying the contemporary United States as Empire, a contemporary version of Imperial Britain. Just how they interpret this empire varies considerably: some deplore it as exploitative and self-serving, others demand that it rules unabashedly, while still others wish that the USA would exercise its imperial strength to extend democracy and civil liberties. We address these views in a context of exceptionalism of the United States in Chapter 4 of this book.

Notwithstanding the primacy of the United States, we will insist that it is shaped by the circumstances of globalisation in ways that curtail its power. The United States is enormously powerful, but it is not omnipotent. Undeniably the USA is supreme in terms of military measure, but while it is a vast power economically and politically, global connectivity and interdependence offer some militating influence. Still more important, the United States cannot do what it will because the issue of consciousness is so hard to control even by the most powerful nations, and what people think and feel has major consequences for how they, and others, act.

Information War is different from previous wars in that, while far fewer people take part in it, and thereby there are fewer combatants who will return home to talk about their experiences, there is a massively increased media experience of Information War. In advanced societies especially, but to a greater or lesser degree everywhere, Information War commands enormous media coverage, and media are so much more extensive than ever before. Audiences follow the course of war through television especially, through rolling news, through Internet sites, through emails as well as through the more traditional newspapers and magazines.

Those who conduct such war make strenuous efforts to manage what people learn about it. Perception management is an integral part of

Information War, so critical is public opinion in such conflict. Those with Information War capability, and the United States is far and away the best equipped, are also the best positioned to exercise control over consciousness. However, so chaotic, dense and fast-changing is the information environment of war that even the USA is seriously limited in how much it can restrict what is shown round the world to suit its own perspective. America certainly has the most elaborate and sophisticated media industry. However, the Internet is beyond its control, there are news agencies other than America's own, and there are so many journalists, from many nations, that present a formidable challenge to many efforts to control what they report. Journalists themselves have their own standards that instil scepticism of the perception managers (and other sources), as well as a disposition to cover the newsworthy issue even if it is not what the media managers want. However well planned the media strategies of the military forces, conditions are so protean that images and reports of an unexpected and unflattering kind will emerge, whether they are of prisoners being sexually abused, humiliated and even tortured at Abu Ghraib jail in Baghdad in early 2004 or of civilians killed by misdirected missiles.

Further, while the United States is undoubtedly the weightiest force militarily and the leading participant in media control, when it comes to perception management, power is not a zero sum game. The terrorist attacks on September 11 were surely chosen for their symbolic effect, launched at core sights of Western capitalist economic and military authority. And the crashes into the Twin Towers, just before 9 a.m., with an 18-minute gap between the first and second assault, were surely designed to command maximum media attention. Al Qaeda set the agenda for the world's news that day and for many days afterwards with its declaration of war, by killing so many at such targets in the heartland of American commerce and media. The whole world watched the anguish of reality television that morning, from repeated pictures of the crashing planes, to pictures of desperate victims jumping from the Towers to certain death, to the breath-taking collapse of the 100 plus level buildings. This was a media event engineered by the enemies of Western capitalism and secular cosmopolitanism epitomised by New York City. Perception management is a complex matter.

Moreover, Information War not only entails coming to terms with an extraordinarily complicated news-reporting situation, it also has to adjust to the fact that the reasons for going to war in the first place now owe much to the conditions of globalisation itself. The uninterrupted expansion of market conditions has ushered the world increasingly into a single capitalist domain in recent times, but this involves much more than economic matters. It has also encouraged the spread of a consciousness of the world that proclaims that people should share certain conditions. There is an emerging sense of global citizenship which, however imperfect its practice, exercises an important influence on the justification for – and even conduct of – war. Media reportage plays a crucial role in informing audiences of embryonic issues, of trouble spots and developing crises. Furthermore, the freedom of media, the right of journalists to be present as witnesses in conditions of conflict, is itself a key aspect of the emergent consciousness of global citizenship, and is something that vexes and frequently challenges the military and governments of the day and brings them into conflict with reporters and commentators.

We intend to highlight here the import of calls for democracy and human rights that exercise a powerful hold on consciousness today. Human rights and democratisation processes exercise a force in the globalised world of today, one markedly different from the epoch of nation states when, however deplorable were circumstances inside a country, so long as they did not threaten the territorial integrity of neighbours, then nothing would be done. Nothing illustrates this more darkly than the fate of the Jews in the 1930s, left to suffer under fascism. The Second World War saw the end of the Third Reich, but for most of the Allies it had little or nothing to do with defending the human rights of Jews: they were motivated by the territorial intrusions of Hitler's Germany. Today, a persistent reasoning behind interventions is democracy and human rights. At times we may suspect and even challenge this as rhetoric, and almost always there are additional motives involved, but it appears that these are indeed salient factors in instigating Information War.

Those who wage Information War place a premium on the media to justify their involvement, as well as to try to ensure that public opinion is committed to their side. This is a formidable challenge in today's information environment, doubly so in the chaotic conditions of actual war. It is therefore not hard to explain why military campaigners now come equipped with PR spokespeople, minders for accompanying journalists, and a wealth of training and experience in 'psych ops' and media management (Taylor 1992). The promoted significance of perception management also heightens the role of frontline correspondents. There to 'tell the public what's going on', present as an expression and representative of a democratic system, frontline correspondents are major players in the mediation of war. The reporters who put together the 'whys' and 'whats' can be crucial in the war effort. This is why they are subject to perception management from all sides, from the combatants themselves, from politicians and from their own organisations.

The job of frontline journalists is also perceived to be getting more difficult and dangerous. Boundaries between combatants can be vague, and journalists find themselves on the receiving end of missiles from 'their' side and may be targeted for kidnap (or worse) because of their appearance or because they point their cameras at an inappropriate object. There are so many journalists who congregate in war zones now, often numbering in the thousands, and they come from so many points of origin, that they can be difficult to control from the perspective of perception managers. They also have access to lightweight technologies that enable them to transmit via satellite with an immediacy unimaginable even a decade ago. The Internet means that their reports are easily accessed by much bigger audiences than ever before. They can be challenged almost immediately by critics elsewhere and even by the subjects on whom they are reporting.

Thus a particular concern for us was how media correspondents handle the conditions of Information War. How do they cope with pressures from military forces? How do they manoeuvre round conflicts where there is no evident enemy? How do they manage fear and danger? What measures do they take to get access to news? How do they prepare for going on assignment? Do they use 'fixers' from the locality and if so, what is the character of that relationship? How do new technologies change their roles? What are their motivations for reporting conflict, given its strenuous demands on everything from health to personal and professional relationships? How does their professional training function in battlefield conditions? We interviewed at length more than 50 frontline correspondents including television and newspaper reporters, cameramen, television producers, photographers, staffers and freelance operatives to investigate these questions. We also examined the journalists' own reflections by reading a wide range of memoirs and autobiographies. These were frequently illuminating, reflective and invariably well composed.

Frontline correspondents[1] are an integral part of Information War. All sides of the conflicts endeavour, with varying degrees of sophistication, to influence and control what the reporters write, film or say. This is difficult to achieve, save in rather exceptional circumstances, since events in war can be chaotic and hard to predict. But it is essential for the combatants to strive for it, because Information War does not conclude with the predictable victory of the side best equipped with Information War weapons. Information War continues for very much longer than this. It continues at least until the war is no longer newsworthy and the journalists depart.

It is within this context that we set out, in Part I, our conception of Information War and the circumstances in which it has developed over recent years. In Chapter 2 we draw attention to major features of contemporary conflict, highlighting globalisation, the diminishment of the nation state, the pervasive growth and presence of media, and the emergence of new forms of enemies. Chapter 3 extends this analysis by distinguishing Information War from its predecessor, Industrial War, in ideal typical terms. Here we elaborate on core characteristics of Information War, paying particular attention to weaponry and media – factors that massively alter the symmetry of conflict and shift the experience of war from participatory to symbolic for the overwhelming majority of people. Information War, for those with the capability to wage it, is increasingly a matter of *spectacle* (Kellner 2002). Public opinion, and the associated heightened consciousness of global citizenship, can play a key role in the initiation as well as conduct of Information War. In Chapter 4 we turn our attention to the apparent exception to much of our preceding argument, the United States of America. The USA appears to run counter to our thesis, being a superstate, an imperial power, even a new empire. We agree that American exceptionalism is a vital part of the contemporary scene, with unprecedented military capability that allows it to intervene pretty well anywhere with deadly consequence. Yet simultaneously we insist that the United States is subject to pressures that limit its acting in isolation as an autonomous nation.

In Part II we focus on media at war, paying attention to frontline journalists to explore their experiences and motivations. It is largely through their endeavours that audiences, with little or no direct experiences of war today, become aware of death and destruction in often faraway places. We set out to establish how and why they undertake this work, what motivates them, and what they think about their work.

Finally, in Part III we return to questions of Information War and its connections with other social, political and economic developments. Here we emphasise the acceleration of change in a context of globalisation and neo-liberal victory in the Cold War. This, in our view, has had paradoxical consequences. On the one hand, it has added dynamism to democratising forces and, on the other hand, encouraged instability and uncertainty which, in turn, evoke a range of responses – from heightened cosmopolitanism and flexibility in some to fundamentalist assertion from others. It is in this milieu that the mediated dimensions of Information War need to be situated.

Note

1   We adopted this designation because we encountered such discomfort with and reluctance to use the term 'war correspondent' amongst our subjects, though all had covered several wars in the course of their careers (see Chapter 5).

PART I
Information War

2

WAR IN THE INFORMATION AGE

War – hostility expressed by recourse to armed conflict by more or less organised bodies of combatants – has been with us from time immemorial. It punctuates, even distinguishes, human history and contributes significantly to how people think of themselves as well as how they feel about others. But if conflict is a constant feature, the circumstances in which wars are fought, as well as their causes, have changed over time: wars between city-states were markedly different to those waged between nations; fighting with the longbow can scarcely be compared with soldiers equipped with the Maxim gun; while tank battles are vastly different from those fought from the skies. In Part I of this book we dwell on the contours and shapes of more recent transformations.

It is our contention that, over the last two decades, we have been witnessing a period of especially significant change in armed conflict – in how it is fought and why it begins – that is signalled by the concept of Information War. The 20th century was the worst by far in recorded history for damage and destruction of people and property. The 21st seems set to outdo even that bleak epoch, with ample reasons for conflict commensurate with expanding nuclear capability, and huge advances in weaponry.

The circumstances surrounding war have been transformed by the ending of the Cold War between superpowers, by the collapse of the Soviet Union, and by the triumph of the market system both in practice and in political thought. They have also been changed by the accelerated spread of globalisation, which simultaneously integrates and fragments while allowing real-time action on a global scale and promoting heightened consciousness of issues and events around the world. Moreover, war itself is changing. For those forces capable of being equipped, distinguishing features of Information War are increasingly evident. War generally involves profoundly asymmetrical combatants, and since only the relatively privileged can afford to adopt Information War, it provides enormous advantage to the likes of the USA, France and Britain. Moreover, because these nations intervene in, and even initiate, conflicts around the globe, their Information War capabilities are especially consequential for others.

However, Information War does not necessarily displace alternative forms of combat if only because most warmongers lack the resources to engage with it fully. Older and recalcitrant forms of war persist – for instance, merciless slaughter of prisoners and combatants, dispossession of property, ethnic cleansing, and the butchery, rape and torture that have accompanied the spread of barbarism throughout much of the last century. Any adequate account of the emergence of Information War needs to bear in mind the 250,000 plus fatalities inflicted between April 1992 and October 1995 in Bosnia-Herzegovina, most brought about with the rifle, pistol and knife; or the estimated 800,000 victims of the Rwanda and Burundi massacres of Tutsis by the Hutu majority who used machetes, guns and clubs to commit genocide over a few weeks in 1994. There are many other comparable horrors from East Timor to Sri Lanka, Chechnya to Georgia, and Honduras to Colombia. Modern-day weaponry is available for use in these conflicts, from Kalashnikov rifles to lightweight but deadly machine guns, from scarcely detectable land mines to plastic explosives. But most of the style of combat there is familiar, with combatants unable to adopt the full range of Information War wares.

Mary Kaldor (1999) makes the important point that brutal and brutalising means of waging war continue, but that they take place now in new circumstances. Information War is an important dimension of these changed conditions, developed by the most affluent and sophisticated forces in the world today. Inevitably it has major consequences for the rest of the world, but we are not claiming that Information War is found in every conflict zone.

Globalisation

Prominent amongst the new circumstances of war is the phenomenon of globalisation. Something of a buzzword in the 1990s, and criticised then for a lack of precision, globalisation here is conceived as a tendency rather than as a completed process. It points towards the increased integration, interpenetration and interdependence of affairs on a global scale. This is a highly uneven trend, and there remain many parts of the world unconnected to the rest – for example, places such as Somalia and Chad. While some globalisation theorists, imagining one unified world market or the growth of regions that transcend established national sovereignty, have been keen to assert the end of the nation state, it is possible to accept the tendency towards globalisation without announcing the demise of the nation state. States continue to matter; China, India, Russia and especially the United States are inordinately important features of the world today.

Though we devote attention, in Chapter 4, to the case of the United States to emphasise its exceptionally important position as a superstate, there can be little disagreement with the proposition that globalisation has encouraged 'time-space compression' (Held et al. 1999). Despite the great migrations of populations that occurred in the 19th and early 20th centuries, as Irish, Italians and Jews sailed to the USA, it is since 1945, and especially since the 1980s, that more massive migrations have become evident (Castles and Miller 1998). Add to this the phenomenon of mass tourism and hugely expanded business travel and one readily appreciates the import of 'mobilities' today (Urry 2000). When it comes to informational matters – whether in the form of business instructions and contracts, trading in stocks and shares, organising a conference or vacation, or broadcasting the Olympic Games – this movement is almost instantaneous, such that globalisation can mean real-time engagement across the world.

Globalisation was hastened by the dramatic collapse of communism in 1989. The fall of the Soviet Union and the neo-liberal enthusiasm that ensued accelerated globalisation as formerly closed societies opened their doors to investment, to privatisation and deregulated businesses. China, home of 20 percent of the earth's population, while remaining a nominally communist society (albeit an authoritarian regime), has nonetheless welcomed ties with the rest of the world, and has opened its gates to globalisation. The remarkable extension of the European Union to include nations such as Estonia, Hungary and Poland is testament to the globalisation trend whereby state borders are removed, trade barriers taken down, and the free movement of citizens allowed. Currency flows now move electronically round the globe, airlines offer scheduled flights to anywhere where there is a viable market, and corporate brands are offered and developed everywhere apart from the most impoverished places. Along with the establishment of an infrastructure of information and communications technologies, such developments push towards a situation where globalisation may be regarded as the capacity to make decisions on a planetary scale in real time – anywhere, anytime. In this respect globalisation impacts on the level of the corporation that has headquarters in New York, design facilities in Paris, and manufacturing capacity in Hangzhou while plotting a worldwide marketing strategy for its product in Los Angeles and London. It also affects the individual traveller who accesses his/her bank account to release funds while thousands of miles from home, maintains contact with colleagues via Internet cafes, and talks to family on mobile phones when reaching another destination.

Globalisation of Culture

Most discussion and debate about globalisation has revolved around economic and political matters. The capacity of corporations to move production from country to country while maintaining day-to-day oversight of their operations, has led to considerable concern about the prospect of

uring jobs being transferred to areas of cheap labour in South ᴉa, the Philippines or even the Czech Republic. The opening ntres in Asia servicing UK customers of British businesses has , similar comment and concern. The considerable difficulties involved in distinguishing precisely what is a national corporation when it operates worldwide with many overseas locations, moving capital at will while pricing across national frontiers where maximum advantage is to be gained, create anxiety about globalisation (Dicken 1998). The capacity for a government to exercise leverage over the economy when financial institutions are trading unceasingly in electronic funds without much concern for territorial borders is diminishing (Friedman 2000).

If these economic and political dimensions of globalisation have come to the fore in recent years, the cultural features of this tendency should not be neglected. Ranging from media (including film, music and television), fashion, cuisine, religious practices, familial customs and shopping habits, culture is an especially complex issue as the domain in which meanings are produced, transmitted and interpreted. However diverse and intricate culture may be, globalisation is exercising an enormous effect on this realm of the symbolic. Globalisation contributes speed and ease of movement of cultural expression, dense webs of interconnected relationships, manifested by brands that are recognised round the world.

Most importantly, globalisation of media, notably television, brings a common symbolic environment across the world. Almost everyone shares a symbolic sphere which achieves ready recognition irrespective of location. How these symbols are received and understood, indeed how long they are remembered, are of course different and complicated matters, but the fact remains that these exemplify a worldwide symbolic environment.

Media are key carriers of culture. They are crucial forces in creating a fast-moving and enveloping cultural environment, but they do not monopolise cultural content. Products, services and people themselves, as well as institutions all carry, spread and inflect symbolic messages. Commentators who see only media when they think of culture easily understate the import of lifestyle, migration and the conditions of everyday cosmopolitanism.

It is important to qualify generalisations about the globalisation of culture. A substantial literature (e.g. Schiller 2000) suggests that globalisation is primarily a Western project. The instances above come largely from a Western milieu, where music is dominated by the USA and Britain and where Hollywood contributes a hugely disproportionate share of the world's movies. Much about globalisation reflects Western power and wealth, the dominance of the American star system, Western pre-eminence with regard to news agencies, and the West's ability to parade its cultural forms on a world stage. This is ensured by the West's

technological superiority in communications and thr(
predominantly originating in North America and West(
media now straddle the globe and content moves aci
immediacy and on a scale without precedent, these cul
from and within Western metropolitan centres out to per

While flows of culture undeniably come predomi:
centres of power and wealth, they do not emanate :
direction. The considerable migration of cheap labour and oppressed
minorities from poorer areas to affluent metropolitan areas presents a
countervailing trend to cultural flows that move chiefly from centre to
periphery. Located in metropolitan cities, where their symbolic weight is
increased by location and their concentration of numbers, they can confront majority culture with a powerful sense of otherness – in language,
styles of dress, food preferences and opinions. They bring alternative
forms of belief, habit and even appearance, to the homes of the major
exporters of culture.

When it comes to media, the same point holds. While media corporations and technologies are overwhelmingly Western, there also exists a
pan-Arabic satellite system, numerous Arabic television stations, a news
organisation Al Jazeera operating out of Qatar since 1996, and Bollywood,
the Indian cinema phenomenon that produces literally hundreds of films
from the sub-continent every year, many of which are exported to the
West. Moreover, if these examples illustrate the dangers of over-emphasising
that information flows are uni-directional, it is important to acknowledge
Jeremy Tunstall's (2006) observation that most media programming is
intended for consumption by indigenous populations. The huge popu-
laces of India, China and other countries experience, most of the time,
local programmes that address their more direct interests in their own
languages. This does not negate the reality of globalisation, but it is an
important qualification to the argument that globalisation overwhelms
the rest of the world with Western imagery. The picture is not of a one-
way flow but rather appreciable interchange, and while there has been a
worldwide expansion of media in recent decades, much of that growth
has occurred in poorer nations, where the populations have gained access
to television services, especially those that offer programming framed in
their own nation's terms. Even where programmes are imported – such as
the Olympic Games or the World Cup – national broadcasters provide not
only commentary, but also selected events framed for their domestic
audiences. News supplied by Western news agencies is similarly shaped
by more local concerns.

The media explosion of recent decades, unevenly developed across the
world, has led to huge amounts of information available today. Anywhere,
anytime 24-hour news services, entertainment programmes, radio talk
shows, Internet access, cable and satellite stations are readily available.
While there is little dispute that the media are mostly owned and

lied by Western organisations, offering predominantly Western ays of seeing, there are many instances of countervailing messages produced, transmitted and received. Al Jazeera, for instance, a small organisation competing for attention with major news organisations such as CNN and the BBC, is nonetheless received across the world by audiences with appropriate cable connections or Internet links. Not surprisingly, perhaps, its major audiences are in the Arabic countries where it claims to be viewed by upwards of 35 million people, but English language versions are also readily available across the globe. In the case of Internet adoption, it would be too crude to conclude that this is exclusively a Western phenomenon with Western priorities underpinning it. For example, in absolute terms Chinese Internet users are the second largest group in the world, with some 60 million adopters, far ahead of the United Kingdom and Finland and Singapore, which are usually regarded as leading Internet societies. Such a sizeable Chinese group, with a capability to access others' information and to communicate routinely through email connections, constitutes a large part of the world's Internet community and is set to increase its share. Today's media audiences can glean information about issues and events which is often counter to what one might presume is a 'Western interest' and, in turn, metropolitan viewers and listeners gain access to information about events and issues, places and people, of which they would otherwise be ignorant.

Media, Globalisation and War Reporting

If there are elements of the media today which, because of their ubiquity and accessibility, are beyond the control of at least narrowly conceived state or regional interests, there are certain features of media and war that we wish to highlight here. The first is that news media are drawn, almost irresistibly, to cover war for several reasons. One is the obvious appeal of newsmakers towards the drama of conflict. Conflict situations are likely to achieve a good deal of attention from the media, and war is the most likely to get extensive coverage. The enormously high stakes, the life and death character of war, ensure that it is a priority for most news media. Moreover, factors such as the scale and intensity of the conflict, its location, where the participants come from, as well as its strategic implications, help it to guarantee media attention. Some conflicts achieve relatively little coverage. The paucity of exposure of drawn-out conflicts in Somalia and Angola in recent years is indicative of a lack of interest by Western news organisations coupled with difficulties of production logistics. Media fatigue with regard to news coverage means that wars that continue over time receive less coverage as the news from that source becomes 'old', even though the killing and destruction may persist. The conflict in Chechnya illustrates this point. News coverage from there is generally slight and reported in a world-weary manner as an intractable conflict. Nonetheless, the imperative of war as newsworthy persists and increases the likelihood that it will receive attention. The coverage of Chechnya soared during the siege of a school in Beslan during September 2004 that resulted in the deaths of more than 330 people, mainly children. Its drama proving irresistible to media organisations everywhere.

When war erupts, or when it is sensed that war is about to break out, the world's media swarm to the trouble spot. The bigger the conflict, the more consequential the fighting, and the more involved the major powers, then the more media will attend. For example, an estimated 2,000 journalists converged on the Balkans in 1999 during the Kosovan conflagration when NATO forces went into action against Serbia. Not far short of double that number of journalists set off for Iraq in 2003, when the United States and its 'coalition of the willing' moved to overthrow Saddam Hussein. More than 500 went directly with the military forces as 'embeds', but the majority were there as either freelancers, stringers or with media organisations but unattached to armed units (unilaterals). The output of journalists in these circumstances can be prodigious, whether in reports to newspapers, in photographs or video film, or in contributions to the web logs that sprang up during the conflict. A good deal of 'copy' is filed in particular languages for particular places, and in addition more emerges into a wider public realm from the media raid of other media output. News is also circulated through academic and agitational networks which cull, translate and highlight pertinent items for diverse audiences and interests.

Many of the journalists positioned behind and with the military forces are restricted in what they can and perhaps are willing to report. Embeds, by and large, provided stories supportive of the invading forces during the Iraq War and, while many of the reports contained factual pictures and stories of rolling tanks and sand-storms, they allowed no sense of the wider campaign precisely because the journalists' particular logistical position (and possible attachment to the troops) made this impossible to achieve. Yet such is the volume of reportage, so diverse and so numerous are the correspondents who come from many points of origin, that in the ensuing 'information blizzard' (Keane 1998) that accompanies large-scale armed conflicts, it is to be expected that some unanticipated and disturbing accounts will emerge. Military authorities and government officials will not be able to process all reports to ensure that they are 'on message'. So, from Iraq, video footage of dead American and British soldiers, first shown on Al Jazeera, was quickly available. Moreover, film of civilian casualties and of stretched hospital staff desperately trying to cope with the injured was highlighted by some journalists and widely circulated. In

Chapter 4 we observe how little of this, and of other disturbing reportage, seemed to penetrate the United States during the 2003 war because of what we term 'American exceptionalism'. However, the general point holds: the very presence of so many and of such disparate types of journalists drawn to war situations, the sheer volume of reportage, and the unmanageable character of so many aspects of war, ensure that undesirable stories will somehow reach the audience despite the actions of the military and politicians to prevent it.

A second feature of media and war is the combination of the ethics of journalism and journalists' cultivated cynicism towards sources of information. The cynicism of journalists, can sit uneasily with talk of ethical codes. Nevertheless, it remains the case that amongst the most revered journalists covering war – the role models for aspirant journalists, those who achieve widespread commendation and awards from their peers – are those with reputations for seeking the 'truth'. One thinks here, for instance, of the late James Cameron's and Bert Hardy's reportage for *Picture Post* of the ill-treatment of prisoners from Korea in the 1950s; Seymour Hersh's exposure of the My Lai massacre in Vietnam in the late 1960s; William Shawcross's dispatches from Chile pointing the finger at US involvement following the Pinochet coup in 1973; John Pilger's accounts of Cambodian atrocities in the early 1980s; Robert Fisk's 30-year history of filing reports from Northern Ireland, Lebanon and Afghanistan; Maggie O'Kane's reports from the Balkans in the 1990s; Suzanne Goldenberg's fearless accounts of the situation in Israel during 2001–2 for the *Guardian* newspaper; or John Simpson's defiantly independent reports for the BBC from Iraq where he was wounded and one of his team killed in 2003.

Truth is often blurred in the fog of war, as Phillip Knightley (2000) wrote in *The First Casualty*. Knightley himself and many other war journalists, as our interviews reveal, testify to an ethic of resistance to manipulation of news in warfare. Despite deliberate distortion, bias and media manipulation on the part of sources, there is an ethic imbued into at least the better journalists that their mission is to 'tell it like it is', no matter how difficult that may be and no matter how unpopular this may make them with government and military. Some journalists, for example like John Simpson, the BBC's World Affairs Editor and a veteran of 34 wars, refused to go to Iraq as an embed, insisting that he and those like him 'didn't want to be beholden to the very people whose actions we were obliged to report on impartially' (Simpson 2003, p. 361). There is something here of a heroic ideal that cannot easily be matched in practice. To be fair to some of the embedded journalists though, many wanted to report the military campaign at first hand and resisted attempts to be manipulated from their military hosts.

Chris Ayres of *The Times* newspaper found himself embedded with the Marines on the frontline during the 2003 invasion of Iraq. He vividly reminded us of difficulties of being a journalist with professional ideals that could be put into practice. He found himself in circumstances where he was 'absolutely terrified beyond belief' since 'I just thought that there was a fair chance that we'd die, or get captured'. Listening to Ayres recalling that it was 'absolutely terrifying' when he was separated from the main group of Marines during a sand-storm and several Republican Guard tanks approached with deadly intent, one can understand how difficult it can be to practise effectively the journalist's craft.[1] Yet even in these conditions, a journalist such as Ayres felt able to draw on his 'professional values', even taking comfort from 'doing something very normal and familiar . . . writing a story that makes you feel a lot better about the absurd situation you're in'. Ayres is a young reporter, propelled into war reporting from a background as a business journalist who happened to be in New York the morning of September 11. But his views are echoed in the recollection of veteran war correspondent Martin Bell who, when wounded at Sarajevo in 1995, became 'almost too scared to go out' (1995, p. 218). But of course Bell overcame his fear and produced much admired reportage on the bloodiest war in Europe for 50 years.

A good number of journalists are injured and even killed when reporting from war zones. To operate in such places requires an ethical calling. There are plenty of other ways in which a journalist may make his or her living, even if they remain within the business. War zones are inherently hazardous locations. Not all journalists are equally at risk, and fear may be disproportionate compared with actual risk of death and even serious injury. Local journalists are much more in danger than the internationally affiliated, and civilians caught in the wrong place are much more likely to be killed than the correspondents for the International News Organisations. Nevertheless, journalists *are* killed and injured while doing their jobs, and there is a perception amongst many of them that things are getting worse (Tumber and Palmer 2004, pp. 36–47).[2] We discuss this in more detail in Chapter 9. War reporting undoubtedly has its rewards, but an ethical calling is an important element of many respondents' motivation and preparedness to risk life and limb.

The cynicism of journalists covering war comes from several sources, not least the experiences of the reporters in conflict situations, where they are likely to receive sharply conflicting – sometimes sincerely held – accounts of events. The main cause is the efforts of combatants to 'perception manage'. Since the Vietnam War, the notion that it was an uncontrolled media which led to American withdrawal gained ground amongst powerful figures in political and especially military circles. Beginning with Robert Elegant's (1981) bitter *Encounter* article, 'How to Lose a War', the conviction that media were important to war but not to be trusted, has informed military and political 'planning for war'. With regard to the UK's activities in Northern Ireland and ever since the Falklands War in 1982, there has been a marked preparedness to 'handle' journalists, with 'minders' allocated, military spokespeople carefully groomed, and 'unfriendly' reporters held at bay. The strategy of 'embedded' reporters, a big theme of the Iraq invasion in 2003, was nothing new in this respect, and there was a clear strategy of controlling the flow of information on the part of the military authorities. So self-conscious and developed is this process of perception management that it is possible to believe that the outcome in terms of media coverage is ordained – a one-way flood of items gathered away from the battlefield, at locations chosen by the military, and from handouts issued by the Ministry of Defence's PR staff. In certain circumstances, this may indeed be the case – coverage from the Falkland Islands during the conflict between the UK and Argentina, accessible only by military transport, and with the media reliant on military technologies to get their messages through, is one such example (Morrison and Tumber 1988). It appears, too, that most reportage offered by the embeds in Iraq in 2003 was largely supportive of the units they were with (and by extension the overall military enterprise), and did little to inform the public of either the course or consequences of the war, even if on occasion it could capture its chaos and confusion.

As we show in Part II, journalists by and large went along with the policy because it was regarded as superior to the alternative of exclusion from the action, even though sharing the conditions of the soldiers brought an understandable empathy with the troops. Nevertheless, what the efforts to manage war coverage by those who wage it have achieved is to bolster the scepticism of reporters. It makes a cynical profession still more cynical when it notes the attempts of the military and official spokespeople to ensure that the media are 'on side'. In turn, this bolsters journalists' disposition to treat *all* sources sceptically, an important factor in what and how they report from the war zone.

Recent history, moreover, has weakened the sense journalists might have that they are reporting for their side, that they are *de facto* extensions of the military effort. If, for instance, journalists are foreign nationals, then it is likely that moral claims from the military for their allegiance to that military's own country's soldiery will be severely weakened. Again, if journalists today are positioned on the receiving end of bombardment from their own country's forces, by no means uncommon in recent decades, then it is to be expected that they will report in different ways than if they were following behind their own troops. The contrast with earlier generations of reporters is marked. For instance, Richard Dimbleby was the BBC's foremost correspondent during the Second World War, but, as his son recalls, he went to war in British military uniform and was 'unashamedly and proudly partisan' (Dimbleby 1975, p. 176), thinking 'things simple enough: Britain was at war; the BBC was at war; he should try to help win the war' (ibid.). Journalists today often feel allegiances to military efforts and interventions, but what has been reduced is the claim of 'my country right or wrong'.

Together, these factors – pervasive media availability, the attraction of news agencies to war situations, professional ethics amongst journalists, and their entrenched scepticism – suggest that, however urgent and sustained the efforts made by combatants to control and contain coverage, there will always be 'seepage' in what is reported. What gets covered and how it is reported are necessarily variable and hard to control with any precision.

The military attempt a range of strategies to ensure that they get appropriate and acceptable messages reported about their activities, from long-term cultivation of contacts in the media, to the granting of privileged access to favoured reporters, to aggressive physical threats towards journalists who get too close to situations the military do not want them to see. Journalists frequently comment on these strategies and they are acutely sensitive towards them, not surprisingly so in view of the numbers of correspondents injured and even killed while doing their jobs. One strategic option available to the military is total exclusion of reporters from the battle scene. This may be considered and occasionally tried, but it contains a fatal flaw in democratic nations. Today, wars are almost invariably waged on grounds of the moral and practical superiority of democratic societies, key elements of which are the presence of a free press and the right of citizens to know what is taking place in their name. When military forces exclude the media, their actions fly in the face of democratic principles and threaten the war's claims to legitimacy. More than that, this act of exclusion is usually met by accusations of military wrongdoing and can lead to damaging allegations being reported on the grounds that there must be something bad going on if the media are excluded. For instance, in April 2002 the Israeli Defence Forces (IDF) denied access to journalists when they entered Palestinian areas of Jenin and Nablus. The IDF said that they were only in pursuit of terrorists, but their massive military forces and the banning of reporters from the scene led to rumours and accusations that a massacre of defenceless people was taking place. It transpired that a massacre did not take place, but since journalists were not there to witness the fighting, such charges were given credence. This exclusion of journalists resulted in sharp criticism of the Israeli state – something to which the IDF's treatment of journalists contributed immeasurably.

Another example involved the attack of US forces on Fallujah in occupied Iraq in April 2004 following the murder and mutilation of several American contractors. Little is known about what happened there since most journalists lacked access. The US forces made no provision for reporters at a time when the risks of kidnap or attacks on non-Iraqis were considerable. Home-made videos, some local journalists' accounts, and second-hand stories from people who had been in Fallujah recently were all that the excluded media could obtain. Not surprisingly, when rumours leaked out of large-scale civilian deaths and of disproportionate and vengeful US force being applied, these were widely reported round the world. The conclusion that it is generally a mistake for military forces to exclude the media, however bothersome their representatives may be, is hard to avoid. For just this reason, military forces rarely try to keep journalists right out of conflict zones. Instead, they try to manage them.

One might add the salutary case of the military forces' exclusion of selected journalists from Iraq in the summer of 2004. An uprising in the city of Najaf, led by fighters loyal to the cleric Muqtada al-Sadr, resulted in fierce battles. Because Najaf is the home of a holy Shia Muslim shrine, any attack on the militants positioned round it was immensely sensitive, yet the rebellion had to be confronted if the occupation forces and the provisional government were to maintain authority. A response from the then provisional government of Iyad Allawi, possibly prompted by America whose air power and weapons were spearheading the attack, was to ban Al Jazeera from the country and all journalists from Najaf itself, apart from those embedded with US forces. Pointedly, reportage from Iraq was then framed in terms of the prohibition of journalists as indicative of the failure of a major motivation for the invasion itself. The clampdown on journalists was an assault on democracy, the very thing the Americans and their allies had pledged to establish in Iraq. As the front page of the *Independent* newspaper put it, such prohibition of the media was 'reminiscent in its own way of the Saddam Hussein regime' (16 August 2004). The presence of journalists is doubtless a nuisance to fighting men, but exclusion of them readily undermines the legitimacy of the military involvement itself.

The difficulties for the military and politicians in managing the news can be further illustrated by two examples. First, the series of photographs of Iraqi prisoners being abused and humiliated in the Abu Ghraib prison late in April 2004. The images of hooded prisoners, of a man stretched out in a crucifixion-like pose while his hands are connected to electric wires, of leering US guards, of naked Iraqis in sexually demeaning poses, of mocking female military police smirking at Iraqis' genitals were taken with digital cameras probably by low-level personnel. The effect was to undermine core justifications for the overthrow of the Saddam Hussein regime and was the last thing the victorious military and Bush administration could have wanted. There were hundreds of exposures readily transmittable through wireless connections to friends, associates, and even media organisations. The miniature format of these cameras, and the ease with which large numbers of images can be electronically disseminated, means that, however hard the authorities try to control information flows, the likelihood is that some will get through. Once the Abu Ghraib pictures were presented in the media, an escalation of negative stories was inevitable. The treatment of terrorist suspects held at Guantanamo Bay was revisited, Senate and House Hearings were instigated, suspicions of US behaviour by the International Red

Cross and Amnesty International were publicised, and questions arose about the legitimacy of the entire Iraq operation (Hersh 2004a and b). The photographs became 'the image of the war' anguished the *Washington Post*, and the photograph of the hooded man with outstretched arms connected to electric wires reproduced worldwide as 'this war's new mascot' (5 May 2004).

A second pertinent instance is the relatively new presence of Arab News agencies, notably Al Jazeera, since the mid-1990s as news gatherers and disseminators on television and the web to global audiences. After 9/11 Al Jazeera obtained several video messages from Osama bin Laden that it promptly showed on its news television. These reports were almost immediately picked up by Western media because they were so obviously newsworthy. However much they were edited and inflected, nothing could take away the fact that in front of viewers' eyes the West's number one enemy was palpably alive, unrepentant and continuing to threaten courtesy of a media outlet beyond the control of those in pursuit of Al Qaeda's best-known member.

During the Iraq War of 2003, and throughout the occupation and continuing civil unrest, Al Jazeera, despite being regularly attacked ideologically by the US,[3] produced numerous reports and pictures markedly different from those shown by the CNN, NBC, BBC and ITN. For instance, the claim by British forces that there was an uprising against Saddam Hussein from Shi'ites in Basra, widely reported in the UK, was flatly (and correctly) rejected by Al Jazeera correspondents inside the town. Al Jazeera showed pictures of the bodies of American and British troops killed in action and also displayed Coalition prisoners seized by the Iraqi forces. These were widely viewed on Arabic (and other) television channels. Moreover, though they were not shown in either the United States or the United Kingdom, knowledge of their display in itself was a story, as were the expressions from outrage of the British Prime Minister and from the US President. Further, the images remained accessible to anyone wishing to look on the Al Jazeera and other web sites where they were presented in English. Despite the desire to restrict what viewers can see of war, the character of today's media environment makes it very difficult for combatants to control reportage.

The Porosity of the Nation State

One needs to factor into the preceding discussion the influence of globalisation on the nation state. Despite globalisation, the world's major nations remain intact and of enormous consequence. However, what globalisation has brought is a porosity of the nation state, in which there are constant flows of activity, carrying economic decisions and migrations of people. In the symbolic realm, globalisation has made nations markedly less self-contained and exclusive than ever and less able to contain the information that people receive and transmit. At one level, this is owing to technological change. With cable and satellite televisions, computer communications facilities and the Internet readily available, it is increasingly difficult for nations to restrict the amount and type of programmes and information their populations watch and send. The emergence of bloggers from within war zones, even the everyday exchange of email in real time between people in one country and those in another that may be under attack, offer different perspectives on war. For instance, during the NATO bombing of Serbia in 1999 – the 'first web war' (Seib 2004, p. 16) – people in Britain received email accounts of the attack from Belgrade, while throughout the invasion of Iraq in 2003 one blogger, Salam Pax, recorded what it was like to be on the receiving end of intensive bombing (http://dear_raed.blogspot.com).

States without Enemies, Enemies without States

A further element of globalisation is its effect on economic matters. It was after the collapse of communism that globalisation, already advanced and in motion, accelerated, on the back of neo-liberal ascendancy. It brought with it a tendency for the world to be regarded as the core economic unit – whether in terms of dealing in foreign exchanges and investment, organising production, or marketing products and services. Though this process is far from complete, this tendency announces the declining significance of territorial boundaries between nations.

One consequence of this is the stimulation of what Anthony Giddens has termed 'states without enemies' (1994, p. 235). If there is large-scale crossover of ownership of capital across frontiers, real-time decision-making across borders, high levels of business and tourist migration, and increasing open markets and heightened trade around the globe, then there is a declining propensity for nations to go to war with one another over territory. For several centuries war has been conducted primarily about land and the resources that accompanied its seizure by one side or the other. If it is the case that territory is no longer of such compelling importance, at least for the most prosperous regions, then it follows that states are less likely to have enemies with whom they might fight. The Stockholm International Peace Research Institute lends support to this view, reporting, for instance, that in 2001 there were 24 major armed conflicts in which more than 100 people died, only one of which – between India and Pakistan – was interstate (SIPRI 2002).

One might suppose that this heralds an era of world peace, but there are negative effects of globalisation that can stoke conflict. This is evident in the toxic mix of increased inequalities on a global scale, with the poorest getting, if anything, poorer; evident too in the change induced by heightened competition, marketisation and technological innovation; and in the spread of a consensual cosmopolitanism amongst those who most readily participate in the world economy and benefit from this involvement. The advantaged peoples with access to capital and high-level education may thrive in a world of flexibility, movement and restlessness, enjoying all the benefits of a credit card culture. But the excluded, uprooted and marginal can find it deeply disconcerting and even threatening. The globalisation that demands that people change their ways as a matter of routine, abandon their cultures and take on more cosmopolitan forms, embrace the apparent egalitarianism that comes with an ability to pay, and adapt to market behaviours which insist on the primacy of money in relations, may be met by the poorest and least well situated with hostility and apprehension (Garton Ash 2004).

According to several important commentators (e.g. Barber 1995), this situation provides fertile ground for the strengthening of fundamentalism of various sorts.[4] It may take many forms – from born-again religion to neo-fascism, from literal readings of the Bible to fervent communism, from an escape into asceticism to the embracing of Deep Ecology. On occasion it may also find outlets in militant zealotry which can feed into terrorist organisations and action.

It is in these circumstances that the concept of 'enemies without states' (Giddens 1994) emerges, where fundamentalists resist the 'Great Satan' of globalised and secular capitalism in the name of absolutist creed that may even disregard national borders. This is the milieu in which the Al Qaeda network is situated. The enemies of globalisation and the market society are prepared to use the most advanced technologies to wreak destruction in the name of upholding primitive certainties. This was evident in the attack on the Twin Towers and the Pentagon on September 11 in which more than 3,000 people died; in the killing of hundreds of tourists in a Bali nightclub in 2002; in the massacre of 191 civilians in Madrid when commuter trains were blown up in 2004; and in the London bombings of July 2005 in which 52 people were killed. There is great apprehension that such zealots may one day be able to gain access to Weapons of Mass Destruction (WMD). This is a de-territorialised and networked enemy posing serious problems for the state's conduct of war which, traditionally, was conducted against other nations in the defence of its own country.

Elsewhere there are instances of fundamentalist creeds that urge 'ethnic cleansing' of 'aliens' in the name of a mythic nation in which everyone shares and upholds certain tenets. This form of terrorism, one that aims for establishment of its own nation, remains the most prevalent. It has been evident in recent decades in places as diverse as Northern Ireland, Corsica, Spain, Chechnya, Turkey, the Balkans and Palestine. It can be appallingly costly in terms of loss of life, but it represents a concern to establish a national territory – a place of one's own, often ethnically defined – which remains a powerful force in the world.

Globalisation certainly influences the aspirations of these local struggles, but their locus in particular places should not be underestimated. By the same token, it can be an egregious mistake to categorise this sort of terrorism as the same as the international terror of Al Qaeda.

Globalisation has made media pervasive and difficult to control effectively by the nation state, even in circumstances of extreme and dramatic conflict. A globalised world is increasingly one of 'states without enemies' and 'enemies without states'. This poses serious challenges to traditional reasons for the waging and conduct of war. Transnational enemies such as Al Qaeda cannot readily be overcome by invasion of another country.

This is the context in which questions are asked of media and journalists. In the circumstances in which the media are more extensive and beyond control of the nation state, while national boundaries and consequent reasons for waging war (and harnessing the media to that end) are diminishing, then what is the motivation for reporting disputes? To gain a better understanding of this, we draw a distinction between Industrial and Information War, which is the focus of attention in the following chapter.

Notes

1   Ayres abandoned his embedded position shortly afterwards. According to Ayres (2005) his satellite phone was confiscated because the Iraqis were using Thurayas to track US positions, so he could not send copy.

2   Conditions in Iraq for journalists deteriorated so dramatically after the fall of Baghdad in April 2003 that they found it virtually impossible to work. Veteran Jonathan Steele (2004) found in Iraq 'the worst working conditions I have had to face' in 40 years of foreign affairs reporting, with 'only Chechnya coming anywhere close'. Peter Beaumont (2004), though conscious that Iraq 'is the biggest story in the world and there is a terrible obligation to cover it', felt also that it was 'becoming a story too dangerous to cover'. As early as June 2004, Jeremy Bowen complained that journalists 'have become targets' in conflict zones, making the job harder than ever. By October that year *New York Times* reporter Dexter Filkins (2004) wrote that, with 'violence all around', we 'can no longer do our jobs in the way we hope to . . . if we can't leave the house, the pictures from Iraq, even with the help of fearless Iraqi stringers, almost inevitably will be blurry and incomplete'. *Wall Street Journal* correspondent Farnaz Farsihi (2004), in an email to 40 friends that was picked up by other media, baldly confessed that her 'most pressing concern every day is not to write a kick-ass story but to stay alive', so acute was the threat to life that reporting was impossible:

> 'I am house bound. I leave when I have a very good reason to and a scheduled interview. I avoid going to people's homes and never walk in the streets. I can't go grocery shopping any more, can't eat in restaurants, can't

strike a conversation with strangers, can't look for stories, can't drive in anything but a full armoured car, can't go to scenes of breaking news stories, can't be stuck in traffic, can't speak English outside, can't take a road trip, can't say I'm an American, can't linger at checkpoints, can't be curious about what people are saying, doing, feeling. And can't and can't.'

This was the major reason why, when a major US assault on Fallujah took place in November 2004, there was next to no independent reporting. Reports came only from the handful of journalists embedded with the Marines (themselves in hazardous circumstances), and these were highly constrained in what they could report. Consequently, it was several weeks after the event that the scale of physical destruction of Fallujah began to be made known – and the numbers, still less identities, of Iraqi dead and injured were never reported.

3 In 2001 during the invasion of Afghanistan, Al Jazeera's offices in Kabul were 'accidentally' bombed by US warplanes.

4 We take fundamentalism to be an expression of certainty in an uncertain world – it is an insistence that some things are not subject to change or challenge, that there are some absolutes of morality, behaviour and belief (Bauman 1997).

3

FROM INDUSTRIAL WAR TO
INFORMATION WAR

Industrial War

Industrial War developed in tandem with the industrialisation process itself, though it was never reducible simply to matters of technique or technology. It is not easy to date its beginnings precisely. Nef (1950), for instance, traces the commencement of mass armies using industrially produced weapons to the Napoleonic era, while other scholars (e.g. McNeill 1982) suggest that the American Civil War was an especially significant event in its formation. However, disputes about origins aside, it is generally agreed that Industrial War came of age during the Great War of 1914–18, when 'the integration of large-scale science and technology [was recognised] as the principal medium of industrial (and military) advancement' (Giddens 1985, p. 237). Industrial War maintained and continued to develop distinguishing characteristics until at least the late 1970s, despite the creation (and use at Hiroshima and Nagasaki in 1945) of nuclear weapons that threatened annihilation of the human race. Industrial War continued to find expression in the destructive Iran–Iraq battles of the 1980s, though by then Information War was well formed and beginning to displace Industrial War in the most advanced parts of the world.

We can identify the major features of Industrial War, in ideal typical ways, as follows:

- *War was conducted, for the most part, between sovereign nation states and chiefly concerned disputes over territory.* The modern world was created in a context of nation states, the formation of which is usually traced back to the Treaty of Westphalia in 1648. Market systems were formed and industrial advance took place within a milieu in which countries pursued their self-defined interests and placed emphasis on protection of their borders. Often this required alliances with other nations, but the principle of territorial sovereignty was paramount. Countries created armies to establish, to expand and defend their territories. In the late 18th and 19th centuries these militias were often small and frequently supplemented by mercenaries, but as industrialism and nation states developed, these grew in size and increasingly came from within the nation's borders.

■ *Mobilisation of large elements and sometimes entire populations to support the war effort*. This involved major changes in the labour force, including women taking over many industrial and agrarian occupations to release men of fighting age. There was, for instance, 'digging for victory' in the UK in the Second World War, in which ordinary citizens endeavoured to be more self-sufficient to support the war effort, and a related increase in the perception of civilian populations as targets by combatants. This latter factor helps to explain the enormous growth in civilian casualties of war during the 20th century, dramatically illustrated in the 50 million deaths during the Second World War of 1939–45, most of them civilians (Mazower 1998).

■ *Sustained efforts to dovetail industrial production and the military struggle*, often involving quasi-nationalisation, within a strategy of 'total war'. Thus, during the greatest 20th-century confrontations, major industries such as railways, shipbuilding, engineering and energy were organised directly by political and military committees charged with commanding the war economy. The stronger the industrial nation, the more assured it became of prevailing over the enemy (P. Kennedy 1988).

■ *Participation, by historical standards, of huge numbers of combatants*, generally involving the conscription of a majority of males between the ages of 18 and 34. Concomitantly, when these massed forces were put into action, mass casualties were sustained. The Battle of Waterloo (1815), in which the level of casualties reached 45,000 over three days of fighting, was recalled for much of the 19th century for its momentous losses. The first day alone of the Battle of the Somme, 1 July 1916, far exceeded these losses.

■ *Strenuous efforts to plan the war effort*. This extended from government take-over of industries such as transport and energy – deemed essential to the war effort – through to elaborate and detailed military strategies drawn up by high-ranking commanders who decided centrally how best to deploy their forces and then direct subordinates to implement that plan.

■ *Harnessing media to assist the war effort* by laying emphasis on the national interest in moral and material terms. This involved nurturing strong media commitment in support of the fighting forces and implementing, where necessary, national powers (e.g. the D Notice censorship system in the UK) to direct information. It was not difficult to ensure that media gave strong support to the war effort of their own nations. Ever since civilian reporters began to cover conflict (during the Crimean War in the mid-19th century) there have been bouts of tension and resentment between military and media personnel (Knightley 2000, p. 28). However, in Industrial Wars for most of the time correspondents wore uniforms of their own side and possessed a strong commitment to the superiority and rectitude of their forces.

Self-censorship was routine and worked very effectively: thus former Second World War reporter Richard Collier recollected:

> There was no written rulebook, but most often the warcos carried the rulebook in their heads . . . Thus there were no cruel, ignorant or ambitious commanders – perish the thought! There were no cowards in the armed services. It went without saying that all infantrymen were wonderful. Sicily, and later Italy, teemed with nubile girls, but it also went without saying that all infantrymen were chaste. There was no such thing as fornication. The war effort took pride of place. (Collier 1989, p. 146)

Information War

Over the past generation we have been witnessing the unravelling of Industrial War, to be replaced, in an incremental but accelerating manner, by what might be termed Information War. There is a tendency to conceive this in somewhat narrow technological terms, notably so in discussions of the *Revolution in Military Affairs* (RMA) (Cohen 1996). This conception evokes radical changes in military technologies, from the 'digital soldier' to the latest technologies involving drones, satellites and computer-drenched weapons of bewildering complexity. Enormous advances in technologies have been made for decades now, notably in aeronautics and electronics-rich weaponry, though applications from computer communications have also come at an unprecedented rate since the late 1980s. In this sense the RMA is part and parcel of the digital revolution. Information can now permeate all dimensions of war, whether as satellites that surveille the enemy and make pinpoint accuracy possible, as computers and their programs which record and assess military and material requirements rapidly and across vast distances, or as smart weapons that 'fire and forget', finding their way to targets on which they have been fixed whatever counter attempts are made. Information, always important in war, is no longer merely a matter of intelligence about an enemy or about resources. It is now ubiquitous, integral to and incorporated into weaponry and decision-making.

Central to this Cyberwar are developments in command, control, communications and intelligence (C3I) technologies, the pursuit of a first-rate system of one's own and identification of vulnerable points in the enemy's C3I capability. Ultra-sophisticated C3I networks can provide an enormous 'information advantage' in warfare, locating enemies, disrupting their operations, and attacking with high-powered but precise missiles. The information advantage provided by a communications network, adopted against Iraq in 1991, that ...

> . . . linked satellites, observation aircraft, planners, commanders, tanks, bombers and ships, enabled the allies to get around ... OODA (observation, orientation,

decision and action) loops at breath-taking speed in a continuous temporal outflanking. A completely new air tasking order – a list of hundreds of targets for thousands of sorties – was produced every 72 hours, and updated even while the aircraft were airborne. Iraq's radar eyes were poked out, its wireless nerves severed. (Morton 1995)

Awesomely complex information intercept, analysis and communications systems are institutionalised in the US National Security Agency (NSA) and the UK Government Communications Headquarters (GCHQ) (Bamford 2001), while the jamming or deceiving of enemy radar and the disruption of command and control networks is a vital tool for well-equipped armies, navies and air forces (Berkowitz 2003).

The reality and significance of RMA cannot be overestimated, but we would conceive Information Warfare in broader terms than just the technological. Its principal distinguishing features are discussed below.

Knowledge Warriors

Information War no longer requires the mass mobilisation of the population (at least not inside the major powers, where an important aim is to wage 'clean war' in which their own population will be left unscathed). Conduct of war will rely on relatively small numbers of professional soldiers, pilots and support teams. This represents a shift in the military towards what have been called 'knowledge warriors' (Toffler and Toffler 1993), a term which underscores the centrality of personnel adept, not in close combat or even in riflemanship, but in handling complex and highly computerised tools such as advanced fighter aircraft, surveillance systems and guidance technologies.

This changing character of the military machine is consonant with what Shaw (1991) describes as 'post-military societies', where war-fighting institutions have moved to the margins of society and have taken on more specialised and technically demanding roles. This also resonates with what Edward Luttwak (1996) has called a 'post-heroic' military policy, where overwhelming force is used on an enemy chiefly through bombing while few, if any, casualties are risked from one's own side. The prominent role of knowledge warriors in Information War means that the possessor of appropriate capability will always prevail over an identified enemy that is forced to rely on the commitment, training and even experience of its soldiers.[1]

Instant Wars

Following the collapse of the Soviet Union and the reduction of the attendant threat of a collision of nuclear powers, the expectation is that future conflicts will be what Manuel Castells terms 'instant wars' (1996, pp. 454–61). These will be brief encounters, with active operations lasting only for days or a few weeks, in which the United States (or NATO and/or UN approved forces) is victorious by virtue of the overwhelming superiority of its military resources. So long as an enemy can be identified, isolated and located, then such is the asymmetry of Information War that it will be destroyed in quick time.

The Gulf War of 1991, the Balkans War of 1999, the Afghanistan battles of 2001, and the 2003 Iraq War, each of which lasted between just four and eleven weeks, exemplify this. In the 1991 Gulf War the Allied Forces were insuperably better equipped and prepared than were the Iraqis, and the consequences were evident in the brevity of the campaign and in the respective losses: 300 or so on the American and British side, between 30,000 and 60,000 on the enemy's. It has been estimated that Iraq endured more explosive power than was delivered during the whole of the Second World War (Mandeles et al. 1996, p. 24).

In 2003, the USA's bombing campaign of Iraq, consciously and accurately titled *Shock and Awe*, and the lack of an Iraqi airforce to offer any resistance, led to a victory inside four weeks, with a few score allied casualties (many from 'friendly fire') and unknown Iraqi military deaths as soldiers were pulverised from the air before they could even begin combat. When asked about Iraqi casualties, the US Commander Tommy Franks observed that 'we don't do body counts' (of the enemy). Not surprisingly, then, estimates of Iraqi losses varied widely, most suggesting between 15,000 and 35,000 military deaths (Conetta 2003), though a cluster analysis undertaken in September 2004 by a team of researchers from Johns Hopkins University, based on death rate measures, suggested 100,000 excess Iraqi deaths due to the war (Roberts et al. 2004). Securing the occupation has been much more problematical for the USA and American casualties escalated through 2003–5 precisely because many advantages of Information War had to be given up as the occupying troops got up close to the Iraqis.

The history of the assault on Serbia during 1999 played out in comparable ways. There was extreme reluctance to commit ground troops from the NATO alliance (and especially from the Americans themselves) for fear of suffering casualties against which domestic opinion might rebel. Accordingly, NATO fought the war entirely from the air and, though a few aircraft were lost, there were no fatalities inflicted on the allies by the Serbian forces. It appears that sustained air attack was sufficient for NATO to prevail, though knowledge of advanced preparations for a ground invasion in early June 1999 may have hastened Serbia's capitulation. In marked contrast to NATO emerging unscathed, intensive bombing of Serbia left between 5,000 and 7,000 dead. Similarly, following the terrorist attack on New York and Washington in September 2001, the United States went to war against the Taliban in Afghanistan during the final months of that year. Despite the anxieties expressed beforehand, the war was rapidly brought to an end with the loss of 14 US servicemen and little soldier-to-soldier combat.

There appears something of a pattern as regards perceptions of these wars. At the outset there is considerable anxiety about the opposition to be faced. In the build-up to battle, apprehensive accounts appear in the media and there is speculation of the struggle lasting months and even years. Thus during the Serbian, Afghan and Iraqi crises there was considerable reference in the media to Western soldiers forced to fight in strange locations, lacking experience of combat, and without the determination to overcome battle-hardened and fanatical warriors who would be fighting on their own terrain and equipped with heavy armaments. During the first days and weeks of the campaigns typically this apprehension would find expression in stories of loss of life, captured soldiers or unanticipated setbacks. But then capitulation would quickly follow, the enemy routed by the devastating and unrelenting missile onslaught against which resistance proved impossible.

Leading-edge Industries

Information Warfare does not require either the mobilisation of the citizenry or of industry for the war effort. It relies instead on capturing only leading edges of industrial innovation for military purposes – for instance, electronic engineering, computing, telecommunications and aerospace. To this extent, Information Warfare represents a reduction in the militarisation of society. The days of Industrial War, when the heavy engineering plant would be converted to making tanks and other forms of armour, are receding. They are being replaced by specialist projects in niche realms, involving a reduced workforce.

Flexibility of Response

Information War requires meticulous planning for flexibility of response, in contrast to the much more elaborate and cumbersome plans of the Industrial Warfare period. Today, enormous volumes of information, along with the intelligence from sophisticated software incorporated into weapons themselves, feed into complex planning for war which prioritises, as the British Defence Ministry put it, 'mobility, flexibility, and rapid reaction'. A recurrent theme now is that the military should have flexibility to 'swarm' into troubled regions, to converge at speed from various points to attack enemies that are also likely to be dispersed themselves (Arquilla and Ronfeldt 1997). Game theory, simulations using sophisticated video facilities, and the production of systems are integral elements of Information War, as is the necessity to plan on the basis of the 'certainty of uncertainty' (Oettinger 1990). There are many examples of this capability, from the presence of AWACs (Airborne Warning and Control Systems) planes that monitor huge areas in detail then pinpoint targets for precision attacks from backup forces, to the capacity of air command in Saudi Arabia to deliver devastating B52 strikes to Afghanistan within 19 minutes of receiving co-ordinates from special forces on the ground.

Experiences of War

The removal of the civilian population to the margins of the day-to-day conduct of Information War, and the reliance on knowledge warriors, has profound implications for the experiences of war. Without mass mobilisation, the general population has little direct involvement with Information War, even when this is undertaken in its name. In former days, mass mobilisation for war meant that soldiers and sailors were routinely seen on the streets moving to and from their stations and ships. Mass participation also meant that, after the fighting, there were huge numbers of people with wartime memories, able to talk to friends and family about their direct experiences (though doubtless much would be hidden too). In the epoch of Information War, few of us encounter the fighting forces, so there are no means by which we may receive direct knowledge of the experience of war.

Instead the general population has a very much-expanded second-hand, vicarious experience of war through massively increased media coverage of conflicts. When war is in the offing, and when it breaks out, media provide saturation coverage, round-the-clock reportage directly from the scene. In Information War the fighting units are at the margins of society, while media coverage is massive, providing a most important and intrusive dimension for the wider public's experiences of war (cf. Seaton 2005).

One example of this returns us to the notion of 'post heroic' war mentioned above, in which minimal casualties are anticipated. In Information War conditions, whenever a soldier is lost from one's side, or whenever a plane is shot down, domestic media will give this extensive coverage not least because of its rarity. Coverage of these deaths comes in several variants, but what is common is that each casualty is noticed and named, recorded as an individual with family and friends, as coming from a particular place. Often the victim will be photographed, perhaps in uniform, at school, even with a wife or girlfriend. Precisely because each loss is acknowledged in this personalised and lengthy way, such losses cannot be sustained for too long before public demoralisation and opposition begins to demand an end to the fighting. This is an important aspect of the changed experiences of war. It lends support to the argument that, in conditions of Information War, the public needs to be mobilised as spectators rather than as participants (Ignatieff 2000), which is an extremely difficult task.

Perception Management

It follows that those who wage Information War devote great attention to 'perception management' for the population at home and, indeed, round the world. This is especially pressing in democratic nations where public opinion can be a vital factor in support for war. Anti-war protesters in Western societies popularly carry posters claiming 'Not In My Name', a vivid illustration of the key role that public opinion plays both in initiating and, perhaps even more important, sustaining Information War efforts. In view of this, what is especially remarkable about the invasion of Iraq in 2003 was the massive worldwide opposition to it, expressed dramatically in mammoth demonstrations during February and March of that year. The peace protest in London, for instance, was composed of around one million marchers, the biggest ever demonstration in British history, and one dwarfing such landmark campaigns as those for universal suffrage and women's rights. It made the famous anti-Vietnam demonstrations of 1968 appear miniscule.[2] There were large protests across Western Europe in Rome, Madrid, Berlin and in the Far and Middle East. It is testament to the confidence of the invading forces in a rapid victory, and also to the strength of their convictions, that the invasion went ahead anyway. As we now know, the military objective was rapidly achieved, but the battle over public opinion remains as the conflict in Iraq continues and the justifications for it are still disputed.

Further, there is apprehension on the part of the military and government that the public will react to vivid pictures of the wrong sort. There is severe anxiety about the display of bloodied bodies of innocent civilians rather than 'precision strikes on legitimate targets', or, as occurred in April 2004, the media reproduction of photographs showing Iraqi prisoners in Abu Ghraib being abused by American guards. In the United States there was particular fear that body bags containing servicemen's cadavers from Iraq would sap domestic support for the war there. This explains the US military's policy of bringing home the bodies of those killed while on duty in secrecy and at night, with no photographers allowed, it also accounts for their acute embarrassment when pictures were obtained by newspapers of flag-draped coffins in a cargo plane (now available at www.memoryhole.com).

Inevitably, acute concern about domestic public opinion impels military leaders into careful rehearsal and management of information from and about the war, whilst at the same time making assiduous efforts to avoid the charge of censorship. This would, after all, diminish the 'free media' claim of the democratic state and would undermine the persuasiveness of what is reported. Perception management must therefore work to combine ways of ensuring a continuous stream of media coverage that is positive and yet ostensibly freely gathered by independent news organisations. In the early days of the Iraq invasion in 2003, in the face of massive public opposition, this sensitivity towards negative opinion accounted for the war leaders' interpretation of their own societies' tolerance of internal dissent as indicative of the democratic freedoms for which the war needed to be waged – so that those oppressed by Saddam Hussein could enjoy such freedoms too.

Coverage of the Gulf War in 1991 revealed especially effective perception management, since it achieved massive media attention yet was antiseptic in substance (Mowlana et al. 1992; Taylor 1992; Bennett and Paletz 1994). As one *New York Times* reporter reflected some years later:

> The [1991] Gulf War made war fashionable again ... Television reporters happily disseminated the spoon-fed images that served the propaganda effort of the military and the state. These images did little to convey the reality of war ... It was war as spectacle. War as entertainment. (Hedges 2002, pp. 142–3).

However, coverage of the Second Gulf War (2003) has not been so straightforward, especially outside the United States. In the previous chapter we reviewed several of the reasons why this should be so: professionalised and diverse reporters, the relative ease of communication from the war zone due to satellite technology and the Internet, the rather chaotic circumstances of 'information blizzard', and so on. Illustrations of reports and images that cause headaches for perception managers are easy to find, particularly where conflict continues well after initial military triumph. It can be a photograph of a distressed child, reports of discontent amongst combatants, the killing of an innocent bystander by our side, or tales of abuse of prisoners by their guards. Such bad news stories can readily amplify into fears of 'another Vietnam', calls to 'get the boys home', and angst about 'what are we fighting for?'.

Rather than revisit these cases, we want here to make some observations about the spate of video beheadings that began to appear in the spring and summer of 2004. These powerfully show how difficult perception management has become. Al Qaeda or associated groups such as one led by Abu Musab al-Zarqawi seemingly produce the videos. The content varies somewhat, but they typically show a victim, dressed in an orange jump suit, seated and bound in front of four or five standing men whose faces are covered. One of these reads out a statement denouncing the West, then the prisoner is beheaded with a large knife while the men chant glorifying Jihad ('*Allahu Akbar*'). The severed head is then held aloft, to the camera, for display.

Though there are earlier reports of videos being made by Chechen rebels against Russian occupiers,[3] they came to prominence with the gruesome torture and killing of Daniel Pearl, an American journalist on the *Wall Street Journal*, in 2002. They have since been made intermittently elsewhere, especially in Iraq, where the beheading of American contractor Nick Berg in May 2004 commenced a spate of such video productions that has included as victims other Americans, Koreans, Bulgarians, Italians, Pakistanis. In August 2004 12 Nepalese catering workers in one fell swoop. Several of the victims were also Jewish, a factor seemingly more likely to lead to the killing of the prisoner (several Muslim hostages, for example from Turkey, were released from their captives though threatened with beheading).

In terms of Information War and attempts at perception management, recorded beheadings are clearly aimed at frightening, intimidating and demoralising those involved, even if indirectly, in the invasion and its aftermath. There have been some reports of workers and their employers pulling out of the region after assessing this risk. Some of these videos no doubt seek to resonate with anti-Semitic sentiment, particularly amongst audiences that resent Israel. The recordings are also loaded with symbolism, notably in the evocations of suspected terrorists held, and roughly treated, as US prisoners at Guantanamo Bay and other jails, with the same vivid orange clothing, the supplicant position of the prisoners, and in the contemptuous dehumanisation that comes from removing their heads.

They are also extraordinarily terrifying forms of video. For those who have not viewed them, it must be said that they are real and real-time executions, made with a macabre amateurism, but with horrendous screams and involuntary body noises as throats are sawn and heads cut off.[4] In an epoch accustomed to ostensibly graphic murders in a range of movies and television programmes, these videos are disturbing in altogether different ways. They are the most repellent and stomach-churning media productions the present writers have ever witnessed. They are unmistakably real, impossible to confuse with the most 'realistic' scenes from any movie. They are cruel, pitiless, intensely personal (a human being is murdered before one's eyes), and there is palpable agony on display as a defenceless man's life is extinguished in a particularly barbarous way. Of course, they are highly newsworthy for precisely these reasons.

The executioners make these videos available to Arabic news agencies such as Al Jazeera and also mount them directly on militant Islamic web sites. Western and other media record them from these sources but for reasons of ideology, respect for the victims and audience sensitivities, the videos are edited and framed in ways of which the killers would not approve. Major British and American television networks use stills rather than video footage and the sounds are removed. Despite this doctoring, they are not what perception managers from the military and government sides like to have shown, since these videos compel attention and inevitably raise questions about the purpose of involvement in the war. Videos that show the victim desperately pleading for his life and appealing to politicians to save him by doing what the terrorists demand, precede the videos of the beheadings. These spark a round of news reports that seek out government opinions, testing for vacillation and looking for signs of negotiation taking place. There are also stories of anguished parents and anxious friends, fearful for the prisoner who has been given a limited time to live. For British audiences especially this process was vividly portrayed in Kenneth Bigley's desperate appeal to Prime Minister Blair in September 2004, a plea reprised by charity worker Margaret Hassan a few weeks later. Both were murdered by their captors shortly after the videos were transmitted, amidst saturation coverage. This is hardly the sort of media content that perception managers would desire, though they do aid the demonising of the enemy.

Al Jazeera, often attacked in the United States as a conduit for terrorism, refuses to show such videos in all their gore. It reports them, and shows longer extracts than Western news agencies, but Al Jazeera is unwilling to run the videos on the terms of terrorists. However, these videos are launched on the Internet, through militant sites, where they may be accessed and seen unedited at various locations. These can be found in a few minutes by any competent searcher, downloaded and placed on other web sites. For example, the US-based site, ogrish.com, that specialises in hard-core pornography, bestiality and ghoulish photographs of accident victims, advertises an extensive list of these video executions and related materials, the display of which is defended by the for-profit Ogrish on First Amendment grounds.

The sites that allow access to the beheading videos rank amongst the most popular whenever an execution makes the news (http://50.lycos.com). In the top ten most sought after locations, alongside pictures of Harry Potter and Britney Spears, are the on-screen decapitations of American contractors Paul Johnson and Nick Berg. They also precipitate massive Internet chat and blog commentary. Their ready availability, in unedited form, is a distinguishing feature of today's information environment. Perception management is no longer the monopoly of one side in a conflict, and such disturbing images will find media outlets, and access onto the PCs of highly dispersed audiences.

Human Rights, Democratisation and Media

The media are needed for more than reporting acceptable news from battlefields and cognate areas. They are also central players in justifying war itself, especially so in democracies. The public may only be spectators in Information War, but interventions need to be legitimised and, in today's world, this is considerably more difficult than it was in the period of Industrial War. Then, the nation at war could, in the national interest, harness national media to its war ends. This legitimisation is important because withdrawal of public support means that the fighting forces can be weakened in their efforts. But the need to gain public support in democratic societies is also a key point of entry for consideration of 'human rights regimes', for the spread of what has been called 'cosmopolitan democracy' (Held 1995). And this is, necessarily, something in which media are involved, not merely as conduits for opinions of military or government leaders, but as agencies that examine and explore the democratic bases for interventions from outside. This was a distinguishing feature of media during the Iraq War of 1991, the Kosovan War of 1999, and the Afghanistan intervention of 2001. It was noticeably under-employed during the Iraq invasion of 2003, where major themes were the 'war against terrorism' and the alleged threat of WMD, although there was much made of liberating Iraq and building democracy in that country.

The role of the media in Information War does not commence with the eruption of open conflict. They are usually present well before this stage and can play a key role in 'shaming' regimes by exposing poor human rights records and in instigating intervention in certain areas (Boltanski 1999). In an appreciable, uneven and hard-to-measure manner, there has developed an increased sensitivity towards, and awareness of, human rights and their abuses around the world (Held 1995; Robertson 1999). Globalised media can play a significant part in this, even if that involves little more than bringing issues to public attention (Seib 2004).

The spread of concern for human rights is connected to a wide range of factors, though media are always intimately and integrally implicated. The spread of news reportage and television documentaries is crucial, but so too is the massive growth of foreign travel, as well as the activities of transnational organisations and social movements such as Amnesty International, UNICEF, Human Rights Watch, the Red Cross and Médecins sans Frontières (Brysk 2002). These do not act with a single purpose, and neither do they develop or transmit messages of a uniform kind. However, they do help to engender a sentiment of the inviolability of the individual, and that human beings have universal rights – of freedom from persecution and torture, of religious toleration, of self-determination, and of access to basic resources such as food and water. They may also stimulate processes of democratisation which, even if imprecise, evoke notions of a vibrant civil society, contending political parties, free and fair elections, a free press, impartial civil servants, and legitimate legal authorities and due process (Held 1996; Whitehead 2002, pp. 6–35). Doubtless it will be argued that this commitment is vague, inconsistent and often inchoate. It has to be conceded that this is so and in substance things are highly variable. Nevertheless, it does not necessarily weaken the commitment, which can, in appropriate circumstances, lead to calls that 'something should be done' – whether about starving children, victims of disasters, or even about oppressive military aggressors (Norris 1999).

One of the more heartening features of the last 30 years has been the steady growth of democratic states, defined minimally as those allowing elections between competing parties. In Europe in the early 1970s, for instance, Spain, Greece and Portugal were ruled by militarised autocracies and the east of the continent was under communist dictatorship. Today all of Europe is democratic, the three nations mentioned above are thriving members of the European Community and all the former Soviet satellites are now independent states. Even Russia, if imperfectly so, is a more open society than it was 15 years ago. Across the world today the majority of states are democracies, 30 percent of them becoming so only in recent decades (Diamond 2003). Furthermore, the extension of democracy, and of democracy as a human right, finds expression increasingly in international law, treaties and discourses (Held 1995).

Connected processes of accelerated globalisation, which itself plays a key role in heightening awareness of human rights, and the collapse of communism have weakened nation states and encouraged a more global orientation in which universal rights are more important than hitherto. There has been a perceptible 'alteration in the weight granted . . . to claims made on behalf of the state system and . . . to those made on behalf of an alternative organising principle of world order, in which unqualified state sovereignty no longer reigns supreme' (Held et al. 1999, p. 69). Martin Shaw identifies 'globality' as a distinguishing feature of our age, one where there is increasingly a 'common consciousness of human society on a world scale' (2000, pp. 11–12).

The conception of 'global citizens' (Urry 2000) is such that, while the world may more and more be regarded as a single market, it may also be seen as a society with rudimentary but common expectations of behaviour. Such universalism is far from achieved, but the trend towards it represents a significant break with established practices, where emphasis has been placed on the territorial integrity of nations (Wheeler 2000). Appalling things might be happening to citizens inside a nation, but to date it has been exceedingly difficult to envisage other governments (so long as their own borders and/or interests were not threatened) intervening out of concern for victims within another's sovereign territory. Even today international forces are not inclined to invade others' national frontiers.

Global interventions in the name of humanitarian and democratic principles are far from commonplace nowadays. For example, there was a period late in 1993 when, after losing 18 military personnel killed in Somalia by local militias who then dragged American bodies through the streets, the then President Bill Clinton withdrew United States forces from there and vowed not to put them at risk again. Since the USA is the most militarily powerful force, any refusal on its part to become involved in the affairs of other nations usually means that action will be taken by no-one else; consequently the local militias that are most ruthless and best armed will prevail. The most telling instance of non-intervention, when timely involvement might have been effective in saving many lives, took place in 1994, when hundreds of thousands of Tutsis were massacred by Hutus in Rwanda in little more than 100 days while appeals from UN personnel on the ground were denied (Power 2002, pp. 329–89). It is even arguable that NATO's involvement in Kosovo would not have happened but for saturation coverage given to the horrific history of Bosnia in the 1990s.

At the same time, neither the NATO involvement in Kosovo during the spring and early summer of 1999, nor the British entry into Sierra Leone in 2000, can be explained satisfactorily in terms of the strategic, still less territorial, interests that dominated military decision-making in the days of the supreme nation state. These latter have of course by no means disappeared, as repeated 'realist' advice testifies – to stay out of areas where ancient ethnic hatreds prevailed and where no self-interest was evident. This philosophy was articulated by Secretary of State James Baker, with regard to the dismemberment of the former Yugoslavia and the mainly Serbian slaughter of Bosnians, when he pointed out that 'we [the USA] don't have a dog in this fight'. Since there have been suggestions that anti-Islamic feeling, and even Islamophobia, has motivated Western involvement in Iraq especially, it is perhaps important to remember that the Kosovan intervention was to assist Muslims who were being attacked and dispossessed by Serbian forces. With regard to Sierra Leone, this tiny nation has scarcely any significance on the global stage, but ten years of internecine struggle, the displacement of almost 50 percent of the 4.5 million population, and the practice of the Revolutionary United Front to use child soldiers and routinely mutilate those who crossed its path, persuaded the Blair government in Britain to order troops into the country to intervene so that the bloodshed would be stopped.

However, strategic interests have by no means disappeared but they have weakened in the face of the pressures of human rights and democratisation. Thus the attack on the Taliban forces by the United States was presented not only as an assault on forces supporting the terrorists who carried out the bombing of the Twin Towers on September 11, 2001, but also as a rejection of those who denied basic human rights to women especially.

The abject circumstances of the Jews, persecuted for centuries but especially so over an intense period inside Nazi Germany and during the Second World War by the Third Reich, is an especially clear instance of the former extreme unwillingness for outsider nations to become involved in others' internal affairs until their own borders, or those of their allies, became threatened. Total war was waged to counter German territorial aggression rather than to resist the genocidal policies that were being implemented inside the Axis nations. Telling evidence for this is the well-documented reluctance of the Allies to give sanctuary to large numbers of Jewish refugees just before and even during the war, as well as the refusal to bomb extermination camps despite knowledge by the early 1940s of the 'Final Solution' policy which had already resulted in the slaughter of millions of Jews (Wasserstein 1979; Lacquer 1980; London 2000). Ignorance of what was happening to the Jews cannot, therefore, be offered as an explanation for the Allies' lack of concern about their fate, since information about systematic mass murder came from diverse sources: those who wanted to know, could do so. The fact is that the Jewish genocide was given low priority by the Allied forces.

It is an egregious mistake to imagine that this was a war to the finish against fascism that had set out to exterminate Jewry and others unacceptable to the Nazi *Übermenschen*. The Second World War certainly was an anti-fascist campaign, but it was entered into because the Nazis and Axis countries invaded territory and/or acted aggressively towards the Allies by seizing Polish territory. The Jewish anguish scarcely registered in the minds of most countries, or indeed most people, at war. In fact, German protestations in the early 1940s, that everything was the fault of the Jews so that Aryan nations such as Britain and Germany should not be fighting amongst themselves, were stifled in the UK for fear that this would resonate with anti-Semitism and weaken the war effort (Seaton 1987; Griffiths 1988). The word Holocaust was not recognised until the late 1960s (Novick 2000). The Final Solution was never a central concern of the Allied forces nor of its publics. That the Second World War has come to be seen in some quarters as one to save the Jews is an interpretation that only began to be heard a generation after its end.

Václav Havel (1999) articulated the changing situation when he voiced support for the NATO engagement in Kosovo on the grounds that 'the notion that it is none of our business what happens in another country and whether human rights are violated in that country ... should ... vanish down the trapdoor of history'. Tony Blair (2001) made the same case for intervention to bring down the Taliban regime in Afghanistan. Evoking the 'interdependence [which] defines the new world we live in', Blair defended intervention on grounds of democracy and human rights:

When Milošević embarked on the ethnic cleansing of Muslims in Kosovo, we acted. The sceptics said it was pointless, we'd make matters worse, and we'd make Milošević stronger. And look what happened: we won, the refugees went home, the policies of ethnic cleansing were reversed and one of the great dictators of the last century will see justice in this century. And I tell you if Rwanda happened again today as it did in 1994, when a million people were slaughtered in cold blood, we would have a moral duty to act there also. We were there in Sierra Leone when a murderous group of gangsters threatened its democratically elected government and people.

One cannot be blind to the fact that nation states remain important and that realpolitik concerns will remain uppermost when it comes to questions of intervention of forces from outside (Hirst 2001). In this light, it is hard to imagine outside intervention in China in support of democratising forces: for although that nation is a police state par excellence, it is also in possession of nuclear weapons, the world's biggest standing army, and mighty military resources. Nonetheless, it is still the case that Information War must unavoidably be concerned with much more than strategic or territorial interest. And a key feature of these elements is the spread of a universalism which denies the right of nations to do as they will inside their own borders. Media coverage of events and issues, as well as the efforts of other agencies, actors and campaigners, ensure that nations cannot easily hide from outside scrutiny. Again to quote Havel (1999), it would 'seem that the . . . efforts of generations of democrats, and the evolution of civilization, have finally brought humanity to the recognition that human beings are more important than the state'. Mendacious nations will continue to disguise territorial interests by adopting the language of human rights and democracy, but the fact that such countries feel this is a useful legitimating strategy is itself testament to the spread of discourses which, while national borders are of decreasing importance, may lead to interventions by transnational communities. It is the same drive which led to the holding of General Pinochet in Britain between 1998 and 2000 and his subsequent prosecution in Chile, as well as the working of the United Nations War Crimes Tribunal in the Hague that has led to the conviction of numerous Serbian and other war criminals, including Slobodan Milošević.

It has to be said that the invasion and occupation of Iraq in 2003 by American and British forces does not readily accord with this account. The USA led a pre-emptive strike against Iraq on grounds that Saddam Hussein was preventing United Nations inspectors from verifying that he had abandoned Weapons of Mass Destruction (WMD). The UK government went along with this reasoning, emphasising that Iraq had to be forced to comply with UN resolutions demanding inspection. Britain also, like the Americans, strongly suggested that Iraq did possess WMD that it was prepared and able to deploy within 45 minutes.

While acknowledging that attempts to legitimise the 2003 war promoted the issue of WMD, the apprehension about WMD being developed inside Iraq and perhaps getting into the hands of terrorists was tied intimately – by Tony Blair (2004) – to the spread of what he called a 'global community' which upheld democratic values and human rights principles as 'common rights and responsibilities'. It was his judgement that terrorists' refusal to recognise the universality of these principles, and their willingness to use and to seek WMD, meant that the pre-emptive action of the attack on Iraq was justified, as is the continuing pursuit of terrorists. It is quite possible to question Blair's reasoning, not least since he himself conceded that it was a judgement of risk based on the record of Saddam Hussein in torturing and murdering thousands of his own citizens as well as his record of previous use of WMD. There was no evidence that Saddam Hussein had or intended to have any relations with Al Qaeda, though Blair judged that such a 'rogue state' possessed of WMD might make such an alliance in the future, at which point pre-emptive action from Britain and the United States might be too late to prevent their deployment. Perhaps Tony Blair miscalculated here, and his intelligence briefings were inaccurate and even misinformed, but his apprehension should be noted. Furthermore, his appeal to democratic and human rights in support of his reasoning ought also to be acknowledged. This is consonant with our view of there being a heightened concern for these matters in the world today.

Conclusion

We have argued here that changed circumstances make the practice of Information War significantly different from that of Industrial War. Naturally there are continuities through time, but diminished nation states, more global connections and flows, and the pervasive character and immediate access of media rank high amongst these differences. While media penetrate deep into everyday life and thereby inescapably impinge on consciousnesses, they ought not to be seen merely as conduits of a government and military machine in times of war. On the contrary, whatever the efforts that are made to ensure effective perception management, the media are a good deal more complicated and play a more ambiguous part in both the conduct and the initiation of Information War. In this regard an increase in significance of human rights and democratisation discourses is surely worthy of special note.

Notes

1   It remains the case that even defeated enemies generally face occupation, at which stage infantry do become important on the ground and, by this token, are vulnerable then to attack by sabotage, ambush and other forms of resistance.
2   The Vietnam march mobilised less than 5 percent of the numbers of the 2003 protesters.
3   These are also readily available on the Internet, e.g. http://stream. thewetlandsinc.com/hap/chechclear.asf
4   The Nick Berg killing, for instance, lasts for over 40 seconds – that is, the video is some 5 minutes, while the real-time killing, from entry of the knife to severance of the head, is 40 seconds of anguish and extreme terror.

4

AMERICAN EXCEPTIONALISM

In the preceding chapters we have made the case for how globalisation is leading to a more complex and difficult to control information environment, is cultivating a global consciousness, and is encouraging concern for global citizenship. We have also suggested that this has consequences for the initiation and handling of conflict. There is one obvious problem with this account – the United States of America. This surely is an immensely important nation state, the most powerful state ever in human history, with unprecedented military might and wealth. The USA may even have claims to being a superstate, such are its awesome power and resources. Further, the United States has demonstrated, time and again, a willingness to act in its own interests around the world, bringing forth charges of its being an empire – a state capable and willing to advance its interests wherever it so deems. Most recently the USA showed this when it invaded Iraq in 2003 as a pre-emptive measure against what it perceived to be a threat to its interests, against virtually the entire world's wishes. Britain joined in the attack, and contributed 40,000 or so personnel, but few imagined that the USA would not have acted unilaterally had it felt the need. Accordingly, we need here to square the case of America with our general argument.

In this chapter we shall be looking at features of American history and its characteristics to account for its particularity as well as to suggest ways in which even the USA is shaped by globalisation. As a preliminary, however, we need to clarify our argument about the nation state. Globalisation matters enormously in the world today. Yet this globalisation takes place in a world of nation states, of varying significance and size. This process may empower nations to act more determinedly as nation states and yet restrict their capacity to act independently in pursuit of their own interests. Globalisation has not brought about the end of the nation state, though it has globalised the circumstances in which the nation operates, limiting them in some ways though presenting opportunities in others. In this development the United States has been globalised as a nation state with enormous capacity for reach and influence, though even it has found itself constrained by globalisation in important ways. Thus the United States could attack Iraq in 2003 with the huge military force at the disposal of the world's pre-eminent nation. Yet it could not achieve legitimacy for this action, and indeed met with serious dissent from within the United Nations and the opprobrium of a good deal of the world.

Robert Cooper (2004) distinguishes between three kinds of states. *Post-modern* states are those that relinquish much of their sovereignty for mutual benefit in this integrating world, for instance members of the European Union. *Pre-modern* states are failed states often cursed with civil conflict and corrupt government, for instance in Congo or Chad. *Modern* states are those such as Russia, China and America that continue to protect their territories and interests in a manner familiar from the previous century, albeit in a context of globalisation. This is a helpful way of acknowledging differences between states in the world today, one that allows us to appreciate increased integration at the same time as we may see the continuing salience of older divisions. Yet Cooper's typology is somewhat linear, failing to appreciate the mix of aggrandisement and diminishment of nation states that can come with globalisation.

Drawing on the thought of Michael Mann (1986; 1993), we would identify four analytically separate dimensions of power in this globalising world – military, economic, political and cultural – the effects of which can be contradictory. In terms of military power, the United States is unassailable. Economically, too, the USA is a massive force, testament to which is the dollar as a *de facto* world currency, though there are threats from the European Union (Kupchan 2002; Todd 2004) and, in coming decades, from China (Frank 1998). Distinguishing with precision a distinct American economy in an epoch of global trading and transnational corporations is a formidable task. Politically the United States does play a disproportionate role around the world, notably in organisations such as the United Nations, the World Bank and the International Monetary Fund. However, because this power is exercised in a world of nations whose significance is amplified by the enormous appeal of nationalism, the USA finds there are limits to its political power. It meets resistance to its political ambitions from amongst the other 190 or so nation states and must negotiate to maintain hegemony. The final dimension of power, ideology/culture, is especially problematical for America and central to our concern in this book with media and war. From around the world the USA encounters a great deal of resistance to American values, lifestyles and especially policies which are frequently countered with critical visions – whether from the Pope or Islamists, Conservatives in Britain and Gaullists in France, or radicals in Venezuela. They may even be contested from within, as for instance in Michael Moore's 2004 cinema documentary *Fahrenheit 9/11*, a box office success of a distinctively American populist kind, in which he opposed his country's invasion of Iraq. As Jean Chalaby (2005) observes, the United States is undeniably pre-eminent in the realm of media, but this is a far cry from its being capable of persuading the rest of the world to share its beliefs and interpretations of events.

What is important to convey here is that the world has globalised, but that this has occurred in a world of nation states and that the results, perhaps most conspicuously with regard to the United States, simultaneously may increase and decrease what a nation can do. In considering the relations between nations and globalisation, it should also be emphasised that the state is crucial to a good deal of everyday life. The nation state provides the structure for the delivery of welfare, legislation, law and political representation. With the state being the organisational framework for so much of contemporary life, it is not surprising that people struggle to create states suitable to their needs and aspirations. This struggle is the motivating force behind calls for devolution from established states as well as for the construction of supra-national governance arrangements that are appropriate for a global era. Given the often-contradictory expectations placed upon them, it is hardly surprising to find that states are both coveted and resisted in many parts of the world. For instance, there are not many nation states that are more than a few centuries old, many are very new (e.g. those formed from the former USSR and Yugoslavia, and the newly reconstituted Germany), and a great number of established states are strained by breakaway movements that desire their own state (e.g. in Northern Ireland, Spain and Corsica). States are important structures but in almost all there is fluidity and tension.

The nation state must be able to engender feelings of 'we' if it is to function effectively, and most people do identify with their country, even if it is not much more than rooting for their representative at the Olympic Games. However, this identity can also be divisive since it may require an outsider to clarify his or her own belonging. National antipathy can readily descend into something much worse than mutual mild hostility between football fans. National identity has been intimately tied to ethnicity in most countries as states came to be founded on ethno-nationalist bases. The nation state, in conception, generally presumes an 'in' and an 'out' premised on ethnic, racial or religious affiliations.

Any adequate account of 19th- and 20th-century Europe reveals an intense level of ethnic cleansing throughout the period (in France, in Germany, in Poland [Smith 1998; Mazower 1998]) which draws attention to the dark union of ethnicity and nation. Yet it is also the case that people nowadays – after years of high-level migration, travel and cosmopolitan consumption – manifest multiple identities, such that the nation has less of a hold than it did a generation or two earlier. Today identities appear to be more layered, hybrid and complex than they once were, especially in the advanced societies and major urban centres. Clearly, this is differentiated by age, education and class – the white working class in the British provinces expressing a more intense nationalism than, say, the professional metropolitans in London. Consider, too, recent campaigns in Britain to create separate assemblies for Scotland and Wales, in which nationalist feelings have co-existed, often uneasily, with identities of Britishness.

Nonetheless, civic nationalism, whereby one is included as a citizen regardless of race, ethnicity or religion, appears to be making headway, while ethnic nationalism is increasingly regarded as a symptom of under-developed and peripheral regions. This, too, is intimately connected to globalisation, ethnic nationalism surging most often where people find difficulties adjusting to the pressures and upheavals that come with the triumph of much more extensive and intensive market relations (Robins and Webster 1999).

American Exceptionalism

It is in a context of this continuing presence of and need for nation states amidst ongoing globalisation that we intend to examine features of the United States. An analysis of distinctive characteristics of the USA will enable us to better appreciate its pre-eminent position in a world of nations, why it acts as it does, as well as to recognise limits to its powers as a nation state. We seek, in short, to highlight the paradoxical character of the United States today, at once an empowered nation state with par-ticular features and proclivities attendant upon this, and yet simultane-ously a country inhibited in how it may act by globalising tendencies.

American Military Supremacy

Perhaps the most remarkable feature of the United States today is its supremacy as a military power over all other nations. The United States alone accounts for almost 40 percent of world military expenditure, and it commands the largest and most sophisticated weaponry available. Its military budget exceeds by far that of any other nation; the expenditures of the next dozen nations combined come nowhere near America's bud-get, which is ten times that of the British (itself a leading military force). With the end of the Cold War, the United States stands alone as a military superpower, with the resources and reach, as well as capability, to attack and prevail over any threat. With some 1.4 million personnel in its armed forces, the United States does not command the world's largest army (e.g. China is more than twice the size, and Russia and India have similar numbers), but its technological and expertise advantages are massive.

The United States' military presence is worldwide: it has about 700 bases located in excess of 100 countries (C. Johnson 2004), the C3I (Command, Control, Communications and Intelligence) network to knit them together, and an air force and missile facility to rapidly attack any identified enemy. Globalisation of military affairs means, for the most part, Americanisation. The USA has a worldwide presence, co-ordination and massive capability to strike as a national force wherever it deems necessary. It is precisely because the United States possesses such incomparable military power across the world that so many interventions involve the USA. Almost alone of nation states, it can intervene anywhere and with confidence that it will prevail against resistance.

All the leading examples of Information War technologies are available to the USA. Indeed, they are pioneered and adopted by that nation. As the International Institute for Strategic Studies (IISS 2002) observes, US military strategy increasingly emphasises that it uses to maximal advantage its technical capabilities, especially since its coverage spans the globe. Thus it must be able to hit targets with 'decisive action with rapidly deployable and agile stealth forces', the efficacy of which will depend on the military exploiting the 'benefits of fusing information and firepower' such that there will be an intimate link between networking of 'sensors and shooting'. In such ways the 'ubiquitous employment of microprocessors throughout military systems, remote sensing technologies, advanced data-fusion software, interlinked but physically disparate databases and high-speed, high-capacity communications networks [will] enable the precise application of force against the most important enemy targets' (IISS 2002, pp. 232–4).

Militarily the USA is beyond challenge and it has total control of sea and space. On land, too, it is supreme, until it feels it must occupy territory and quell domestic populations, at which point it may become susceptible to attacks that can lead to significant losses. America's relatively small numbers of combatants can mean that, if it is required to patrol vast areas of the world, the country can become overstretched from too many demands made on it, especially where troops are required on the ground. Nonetheless, the USA is the only state capable of acting unilaterally in the post-Cold War situation. Should it identify a threat to its interests – as for instance it did with regard to Iraq in 2003 – it is able to strike pre-emptively because of its dominant military strength. The USA can do this secure in the knowledge that no other state can offer a serious military response to its power.

America's military supremacy is of enormous significance, but this does not mean that it meets no resistance. Michael Mann (2003), for instance, identifies 'weapons of the weak' such as the Kalashnikov rifle, suicide bombings, and even highjacked passenger aircraft when flown into skyscrapers. Still more sobering are the efforts of some nations to develop nuclear weapons, or perhaps primitive nuclear devices (so-called 'dirty bombs'), as a negotiating tool or worse. Often quoted in this regard is the Indian Chief of Staff, who, when asked what were the lessons of the first Gulf War, replied: 'Never fight the United States without nuclear weapons' (quoted in Bobbitt 2002, p. 14).

The United States' number one military position has contributed to a spate of writing, chiefly critical (e.g. Harvey 2003; Johnson 2004), arguing that it is in fact an imperial power, though it may deny this even to itself. Those who approve of it being an empire, such as historian Niall

Ferguson (2004), urge that the United States be unapologetic about it. The strategy of 'pre-emptive strike' articulated by the Bush administration between 2002–5 gives credence to the view that there are those who may share this outlook.

A more benevolent version of American empire comes from Philip Bobbitt (2002). This argues that we stand at a point of epochal change since wars between nation states over territory and about ideologies, that fuelled the 'Long War' of 1914–90, are ended. What has replaced these are varieties of the 'market state'. The United States is the 'entrepreneurial market state', one committed to free markets, human rights and democracy and unwilling to tolerate their absence in other nations on grounds of territorial sovereignty. Pre-emptive military invasion from the United States might, in these terms, be regarded as an action of the 'market state' determined to bring to disadvantaged nations what it already enjoys. There is an echo of this in Michael Ignatieff's (2003) conception of 'Empire Lite', an 'imperial rule for a post imperial age'. Here the US intervention to overthrow Saddam Hussein in 2003 was justifiable in that it had become 'the last hope for democracy and stability alike'. Cooper's (2004) advocacy of a 'new kind of imperialism, one acceptable to a world of human rights and cosmopolitan values' offers much the same sentiment.

There is undoubtedly some affinity here with our argument that the spread of global consciousness encourages concern for democratisation and human rights. While the upholding of democracy and human rights principles on a world scale ought logically to be led by global institutions such as the UN, the demands of mobilisation and military requirements mean that the major national force, the United States of America, is generally the decisive agent of intervention, even if acting in the name of supranational values. The NATO-led (with US military predominance) defeat of Serbia in 1999 to stop ethnic cleansing was an instance of intervention for humanitarian ends.

However, one year after the invasion of Iraq, during which there had been about 1,000 American troops, and many more Iraqis, killed in civil unrest, widespread resistance to the occupation, and few signs of the establishment of democracy, Michael Ignatieff (2004) himself had second thoughts about support for the war. His (and Bobbitt's as well as Cooper's) argument can readily be charged as 'a theory doing imperial service' (Mann 2003, p. 11).

The USA was the only force capable of defeating Saddam Hussein and effecting 'regime change' quickly. Moreover, the case for military intervention on humanitarian grounds was compelling in view of 20 years of murderous totalitarianism. This argument was, however, rarely made. The USA was mobilised to attack Iraq in 2003 chiefly because it was alarmed by the spectre of terrorism following 9/11 and frightened by terrorists' potential access to WMD (weapons of mass destruction). The United States was prepared to act unilaterally because of these fears. Just why this happened leads us to consider other features of American exceptionalism.

Experience of War

The terrorist assault on the Twin Towers in New York City and on the Pentagon on the morning of 9/11 was a dramatic event. It claimed 3,000 lives, and the Manhattan incidents were televised in real time. The pictures and sound were deeply disturbing as people were able to watch a truly terrible event unfold. It was also a powerful example of terrorism in the global era, an assault planned thousands of miles away largely by Saudi Arabian malcontents living outside their own country, co-ordinated across three continents, yet which managed to seize civilian airliners and turn them into awesome weapons.

The United States was bound to respond to this attack. Its invasion of Afghanistan, where Bin Laden and his associates, who were responsible for the aeroplane highjackings, were being protected by the Taliban regime, was a predictable response. But this attack also led to a radical shift in US policy and action. After it, a 'war against terrorism' was declared, and a strategy of 'pre-emptive attack' on perceived threats was adopted. The Bush government announced that it would attack what it perceived as threats wherever it felt its national security so demanded, that other nations were 'either with us or against us' in this 'crusade', and that it would act unilaterally should it need to, since now George Bush was a 'war president'. In 2002 the military budget, already enormous, was raised and is set to continue to grow until 2007. The invasion of Iraq in 2003, prepared for months, was a logical follow-up to the Afghanistan invasion.

Yet one needs to ask why the USA responded in the ways that it did, ways that were resonant of an old-style nation state. The USA understandably would take the lead in any moves against international terrorists since it had suffered grievous loss and it was the major military force in the world. But it did not have to respond in the hawkish ways that it did. It could have worked resolutely for international co-operation in pursuit of the 'enemies without states' in Al Qaeda, tapping the wellspring of sympathy for the US that followed 9/11. It could have determined to treat the issue as a matter of criminality rather than as a declaration of war that called for a response in kind.

The neo-conservatives in the US administration were an important factor in this route not being followed, but there seems to us to be a still deeper reason. This leads us to enquire about the traumas of war in the United States. The point we wish to make here is that many nations have experienced losses in and out of war, often much more grievous than on 9/11. These always lead to a response, but what sort of response varies considerably, depending on conditions and outlooks in the stricken nation.

It is important to register the intensity of the shock of 9/11 inside the United States. America had previous experience of terrorism within its borders, notably with the Oklahoma bombing that killed 168 people in April 1995. But this had turned out to be a domestic assault perpetrated by a Christian fanatic, Tim McVeigh, and at least one associate. There was also the explosion in the World Trade Center on February 26, 1993, undertaken (probably) by Al Qaeda in which six people were killed. But 9/11 was a much bigger attack on Americans. It was also perpetrated by outside forces. It impacted enormously not only because it was unexpected by the vast majority of citizens, but also because the United States had long perceived itself to be internally invulnerable, a safe haven from external enemies. Most other countries, at one time or another in their histories, have been bombed, invaded and even occupied by outside forces. For many countries these are recent memories, whether of enemies at war or terrorist acts from Red Brigades in Italy, the Irish Republican Army in Britain, or secessionists in Russia. The United States, however, had little or no experience of such things. The immediate point of reference for 9/11 was, significantly, 7 December 1941, the date of the unannounced attack on the Pacific Fleet at Pearl Harbor in which some 2,400 men were killed in Japan's declaration of war on the United States. The response to 9/11 was equally outraged and militaristic.

Exceptionally small numbers of Americans have been either killed or maimed or even directly involved in war, something that served to increase the shock of 9/11. To understand the US response it is necessary to appreciate that the country's experiences of war casualties are remarkably limited. During the 20th century many nations have lost between 5 and 20 percent of their total populations through war, and one group, the Jews, underwent the genocide of 70 percent of their European members during the Holocaust years. Other non-nationals such as Kurds, Romanies and Armenians also suffered appallingly. Deaths of civilians and soldiers have numbered in the millions, from countries as diverse as Germany, France, Russia, Turkey, Ukraine, Japan, China, Poland, Vietnam, Cambodia and Korea. Against this, one might set the fact that the United States lost virtually no civilians to war over the last century. Moreover, it is astonishing to realise how few American combatants in war were killed relative to other nations and to its own population. Indeed, the number of Civil War (1861–5) dead, some 600,000, still exceeds that in all other American wars combined. The United States lost some 400,000 combatants during the Second World War (about the same as the UK, which has five times fewer population), but as historian David Kennedy (1999, p. 856) observes, 'few Americans had been touched by the staggering sacrifices and unspeakable anguish that the war had visited upon millions of other people around the globe'.

When one sets the losses of other nations from war against the hold in American memory of participation in Vietnam when it lost about

55,000 men in over a decade, one may begin to better understand the profound shock of America at 9/11. War experiences have made those who have suffered particularly badly from it, such as Germany and France, eager to avoid military entanglement (Kagan 2003), cautious even while determined in their response to terrorism. The United States, a nation relatively unscathed by war, was viciously attacked on 9/11 and many Americans appeared to feel themselves in serious danger. If the psychological effects of 9/11 were disproportionately high, so, too, may have been the response of a nation quite beyond military challenge.

Patriotism

It is often observed that the United States evidences significantly more patriotism than other nations. Americans are prouder of their country than the rest of us are of our own. Large majorities affirm this regularly in opinion polls, very many fly the Stars and Stripes outside their homes, and they pledge allegiance to the USA daily in their schools. Patriotism has been encouraged by American involvement in war. Thus the USA emerged from the Second World War suffused with the glow of victory, warmed by its having sustained relatively few human losses in that battle, and enjoying a booming economy that grew at about 10 percent each year and left the Depression a distant memory. Patriotic cohesion was consolidated by participation in this major conflict that Americans widely perceived to have been successful because of their timely entrance. Patriotism ebbs and flows depending on issues and events, and pollsters rarely ask their subjects what they mean by the word. Yet the singularity of American commitment to their country remains striking. The 9/11 assault heightened this already high degree of national identification and this in turn contributed to America's vigorous response to terrorism (*Economist* 2003).

The American Dream

But America's exceptionally high levels of patriotism cannot be explained solely by its involvement in war. The United States, as is often remarked, is a nation founded on ideals rather than on a common history and/or ethnic affiliation. In this regard the USA stands in contrast with, say, Britain, where, after the 1707 Act of Union, a national identity was forged not on the basis of ideas, but by Britons being Protestant, by recurrently fighting outsiders, and by rule over colonies whose people were manifestly different (and inferior) in colour, culture and languages (Colley 1992). In the United States, ideals of liberty, individualism, egalitarianism and democracy have been refrained from the time of the Declaration of Independence in 1776, through Abraham Lincoln's Gettysburg Address in 1863, to Martin Luther King's speech at the Lincoln Memorial one hundred years later. Phrases ring through the ages: 'all Men are created equal', 'government of the people, by the people, and for the people', and 'I have a dream that one day this nation will rise up and live out the true meaning of its creed'. Campaigners for change have often drawn upon these ideals to complain that America has failed to match its aspirations. In short, the USA is founded on ideology rather than on a particular heritage (Lipset 1996; Barber 2003). A consequence is that to be American is at least as much a matter of embracing ideals as it is of having a particular religion or skin colour. Conversely, to be 'un-American' is not just to be foreign; it also comes close to being a denier of life-guiding principles.

We would emphasise that the American ideals are not mere abstractions. Though there are huge inequalities and injustices in the United States, visitors from as far back as Alexis de Tocqueville quickly sense and comment on its openness, opportunity and 'can-do' ethos, and on the easy familiarity of American citizens towards others. More than this, the United States is a nation of migrants, most of whom have fled economic and political oppression. Whether from famine-struck Ireland, Nazi Germany or anti-Semitic Russia, the migrant experience has given extraordinary testimony to the American ideals. Large numbers of them have lived out the American Dream. Some of this success can be manifested in vulgar materialism and hucksterism and in what outsiders may see as excessively competitive and over-familiar behaviour. But such critics too readily ignore these vital aspects of the United States, the power of ideals combined with the immigrant experiences that realised so much of the ideology. It is this, far more than Hollywood movies or rock music lyrics, that is the major element of America's 'soft power' (Nye 2002) around the world. It inspires and attracts many who are otherwise deeply antipathetic to US policies.

It cannot be surprising, in view of all this, that the United States, heterogeneous though it is in so many ways, felt acutely challenged by the terrorist attacks on September 11. The assault was on both its ideals and its practical accomplishments. With the US wounded so grievously, one may understand, if not condone, its behaviour in hitting back so very decisively.

American News Media

American media are the most technologically advanced and economically advantaged in the world. And, as the world has globalised, so too has the US media business. This is so much so that globalisation here can seem to be Americanisation. Driven by commercial imperatives, the US media are entertainment oriented, escapist and diverting, producing content that combines maximum popularity with least cost. Schiller (2000) has argued that these media are an extension of American corporate power, the sales arm of an economic empire that traverses the world, the purpose of which is to transform audiences into consumers of American brands – such as Nike, McDonald's and Levis – and American lifestyle. The American media industry can even, in these terms, be harnessed to persuade audiences abroad of the rectitude of State Department policies. Accordingly, globalised American media perform a key role in protecting the economic and political interests of the United States by ensuring ideological domination.

This approach addresses questions of power with regard to media production and distribution, but it is also limited. It does not acknowledge that commercial criteria can fly in the face of ideological requirement. Currently, for instance, United States broadcasting companies have been undergoing significant localisation of programme content precisely because they have found that audiences do not appear keen to watch limitless amounts of American content (Chalaby 2005). A further criticism of this approach to US media is that it fails to appreciate fully that audiences around the world, even when receiving American content, filter this through their own national (and other) imagery. Further, the appeal of America is much more substantive than media messages, being manifest more persuasively in the wealth, opportunities and openness of the USA and the achievements of the millions of migrants who found their way to its shores.

However, we wish here to make some observations on American news media, especially as regards their coverage of the Iraq War of 2003, particularly because of what they revealed about America itself. It is widely agreed that US news coverage from the Gulf was highly partisan, US-centric throughout, and framed by a conviction that the US military forces were fighting a just war. There was a range of support for the war from US media, ranging from the careful tone of the *New York Times* to the hectoring, strident and ultra-patriotic broadcasts of Fox News. But all the US news organisations backed the US mission in Iraq, from editorial line to report content. During the summer of 2004 at least two newspapers, the *New York Times* (26 May)[1] and *Washington Post* (12 August),[2] apologised to their readers for their poor standards of reportage, especially during the period of build-up to war in 2003 (Massing 2004a and b).

What should be stressed here is the singularity of the US news media. There were dozens of other news organisations covering the Iraq invasion, and some 20 broadcast news companies were in Baghdad at the time of the invasion. What is evident is that US coverage was distinctive in its largely uncritical and sanitised coverage. For instance, it showed few civilian casualties of the war, though pictures were available from other sources. US reporters, especially the embeds, depicted little of Iraqi suffering. The much-trailed military strategy of *Shock and Awe* was uncritically reported, with little mention of the death and destruction this would bring down on human beings. In contrast to the huge coverage of the accuracy of missiles, nothing was said about what effect this could have on the Iraqi soldiers, on whom many of these missiles precisely rained from B52s. Leading government and military spokespeople were treated deferentially by reporters whom one might have expected to ask searching questions. Enormous coverage was given over to the diverting drama of 'Saving Private Lynch' in April 2003, the story of a young female military member who had been wounded and captured by Iraqi forces. Even the news frame of the US media was euphemistic, preferring 'Operation Iraqi Freedom' to the 'Invasion of Iraq' that was favoured by most other reporters.

There were many reasons why this was so. US reporters were behind the lines of their own troops and could not easily get to the other side. For the most part they could not speak Arabic so could not get to local informants, and they were heavily dependent on government and military spokespeople. Perhaps more important, American journalists were victims of US military and government perception management, particularly due to the constraints that were placed on the embeds. Proximity to the action was traded against reporting as the military so desired. As Doug Kellner (2004) notes, 'on the whole the embedded journalists were largely propagandists'. Mental embedding appeared to accompany physical embedding with the US forces.

This explanation for the US news media coverage of the Iraq War will be familiar enough to students of news construction. But it fails to account for the singularity of the American coverage. It is crucial to grasp that 'US news organisations gave Americans the war they thought Americans wanted to see' (Massing 2003). The decisive factor was the perception by journalists of the American people, and this in turn was necessarily a matter of the self-perception of journalists themselves. This focused on the US as a righteous people facing unprovoked attack after 9/11. Saddam Hussein readily fitted in with the vision of the inhuman enemy who has to be destroyed. Americans' exceptionally high degree of patriotism, the after-effects of the first major attack on US people on their home territory, and their self-perception as a virtuous people contributed to news coverage that was distinct from other reportage of the Iraq War. Revealingly, Fox News, unapologetically populist, dismissive of liberal qualms, and a cheerleader for the war, saw its ratings rise during the conflict. It remains now the most popular cable and satellite news channel in the United States, though scholars and professional journalists deplore its bias and partisanship.

We can only speculate on the consequences of this limited range of news coverage. It may have encouraged a degree of insularity amongst American audiences, though doubtless class, geographical location and education would differentiate this. It reflected the views of its audiences as much as it shaped them. It certainly did not help to enlighten audiences that are known to be poorly informed about overseas matters (and who also travel beyond the USA but rarely – only about 15 percent of Americans have a passport). However, what we do know is that this US news coverage of the Iraq War, whatever its worldwide availability, was contested and resisted pretty much everywhere (Hertsgaard 2003), something that speaks volumes for the limits of the world's most powerful country to persuade others of its own interpretation of events.

Conclusion

One can acknowledge the might of the USA as a superstate, one that manifests particular characteristics as a result of its history that can result in paradoxical actions and perceptions. However, America is also a state in a world of nation states that globalisation both aggrandises and limits. The USA is undoubtedly the dominant military power in the world today, boosted by a capacity to strike anywhere it so determines. But the USA is only one nation state from almost 200, certainly the pre-eminent one, but to an important degree *primus inter pares* because each state has a voice of its own, and interconnections encourage a mutuality that defies acting alone. When it comes to politics and ideology especially, there are serious limitations on what the United States can achieve on a world scale. There is certainly little evidence that America is capable of convincing the rest of the world that it should endorse its outlook. On the contrary, the spread of nationalism around the globe means now that US efforts unilaterally to subjugate other nations to its will, even if these are well intentioned, are sure to be resented and frequently actively opposed.

Furthermore, while the United States does have formidable media that, by and large, parade its version of events especially in news coverage, these fail to persuade beyond American shores. Instead, during and following the Iraq War of 2003, there has been massive anti-American protest across the globe.

Notes

1 In an Editor's Note on page A10, the *New York Times* declared: 'We have found a number of instances of coverage that was not as rigorous as it should have been.' It continued 'Looking back, we wish we had been more aggressive in re-examining the claims as new evidence emerged – or failed to emerge.'
2 *Washington Post* media critic Howard Kurtz wrote that editors resisted stories that questioned whether Bush had evidence that Saddam was hiding weapons of mass destruction: 'The result was coverage that, despite flashes of ground-breaking reporting, in hindsight looks strikingly one-sided at times.' Assistant Managing Editor Bob Woodward said in the story: 'We did our job but we didn't do enough, and I blame myself mightily for not pushing harder. We

should have warned readers we had information that the basis for this was shakier than many believed'. Pentagon correspondent Thomas Ricks said: 'There was an attitude among editors: Look, we're going to war, why do we even worry about all this contrary stuff?' Executive editor Leonard Downie Jr. said: 'We were so focused on trying to figure out what the administration was doing that we were not giving the same play to people who said it wouldn't be a good idea to go to war and were questioning the administration's rationale.'

PART II

Frontline Journalism

5

WHO THEY ARE
AND WHY THEY DO IT

'My newspaper calls me a war correspondent when I'm covering a war, and when I'm not covering a war, they don't.' (Ross Benson, *Daily Mail*)[1]

'I don't really consider myself to be a war correspondent', explains James Meek.[2] 'I think there aren't very many real war correspondents anymore . . . there are journalists whose specialism is war and that's all they do [but] there aren't many people like that.' Most journalists covering conflict share this view. They do not consider themselves 'war correspondents', but journalists who report on war. It is a subjective distinction, yet although we discovered many of them had covered numerous conflicts, there was a widespread reluctance to designate themselves war correspondents. To some it seemed presumptuous, even ludicrous, while others found the title restrictive and outmoded in the present era.

David Williams[3] of the *Daily Mail* emphasises the breadth of his work:

'I'm a journalist . . . I think some people glory in the term "war correspondent". Yes, you cover the conflicts, but I do much much more than that. I'll be covering the news side of the next Olympics, I covered the last four or five Olympics on the news side, so I wouldn't term myself a war correspondent. Yes, if there is a major conflict, the chances are that I will be sent there but I'm far more than just a war correspondent.'

These journalists tend to travel out to conflicts for relatively short periods of time and then return to their home bases. This is different from the 'old'-style foreign correspondents who may be assigned for up to three years in a particular country or region (see Morrison and Tumber 1985). This type of foreign correspondent appears to be a dying breed.

For Brian Williams[4] of Reuters the changes are evident:

'There is a big difference between going and covering something for a month or six weeks or even a couple of months, and actually living there for a year and seeing the seasons change. It's a different type of person. More and more people just fly in and fly out. In Vietnam, you lived there, you lived every second of every day in the war. I think it's more serious type people who cover it now.

I'm not saying necessarily that they do better stories but I think sometimes maybe they don't touch the people as much as the older correspondents used to. When you live right in the midst of everybody you feel the story a lot more than when you're remote from it.'

Jonathan Steele[5] of the *Guardian*, who has spent his working life writing foreign reports, feels that frontline correspondents are 'expected to be much quicker, much more newsy, much more dramatic, therefore less analytical, less laid back, less descriptive than a good writer is in creating an atmosphere gradually rather than coming with a bang. It has changed our trade and that's a bit of a loss'.

For Peter Sharp[6] of *Sky News*, it is becoming a younger person's game:

'It's much more psychologically demanding than it was when I joined. You joined ITN, you had three bulletins to hit and that was it, and no lives. And if you were abroad you'd file, get that piece to an airport, which would be taken somewhere to put on a satellite and that's it. And they probably couldn't even phone you anyway. So the demands of the job have grown and it can be really brutally exhausting. Nineteen-, twenty-hour days, three or four days in a row. I was out there when they picked up Saddam and I can't even remember much about it: we just worked from Sunday through 'til Wednesday and it was 50 lives, which is what you'd expect. Sky's getting much better now at putting enough people in the field, because if they sent you out with a producer, who couldn't do lives, and a cameraman, who couldn't do lives, and you, that's a team of three. You'd be dead in three days. You just wouldn't be able to keep going. So there's much more thought to "Let's send out an editor and a cameraman and a producer and two correspondents and maybe another producer". It's more expensive, but it's the demands that you have to fulfil – it's 24–7.'

Although not based permanently abroad, many of those to whom we spoke viewed themselves, as Rory Carroll[7] put it, 'more a foreign correspondent who occasionally covers conflict' and could be rather dismissive of 'war junkies' (cf. Steele 2002), as they called those who did nothing but follow war.[8] The BBC's Gavin Hewitt[9] elaborates:

'If somebody described themselves to me as a war correspondent, I would instinctively mistrust them because I think if you specialise in covering wars, almost by the definition you lose connection with ordinary life and ordinary people. War, thank goodness, is abnormal. It is something that happens when all else fails. And I have met people who just go from one conflict to another. And often they're very damaged people and they're damaged principally because they cannot disconnect themselves from the unreality of war. And war, I think, delivers great highs to those who are covering it, partly because of the risk, the thrill of escaping danger. But it is an unreal existence . . . to my mind, the very best reporters who cover wars are those who cover them with a certain degree of reluctance, and that connects them to most ordinary sane people's view of war that, at best, it is a painful necessity . . . The idea of being a war correspondent is not a term that I would want to be used about myself.'

Hewitt's view is not unique. Many journalists covering conflict view with a certain disdain those calling themselves war correspondent. It is seen as self-glamorisation that is to be avoided. ITN veteran Colin Baker[10] is blunt: 'I don't like being called a war correspondent. I'm just a correspondent who's been to war . . . and when you go and watch people die, who gives a shit what your title is?' Thus very few describe themselves as war correspondents or their jobs as war corresponding – the only concession for use of the title might be when they are actually in a war situation and scarcely anyone we talked to described themselves as a 'dedicated' war correspondent.

Caroline Wyatt[11] of the BBC, for example, currently based in Paris, describes herself as a foreign correspondent who also covers wars:

'I haven't been placed in a war zone as a job, so I've not been placed in Israel, I've gone there to cover things that have happened in Gaza. I went to Kosovo to cover the war while I was based in Germany. I went to Iraq in '98 for Operation Desert Fox, and then I was based in Iraq. I stayed with the military for the last conflict there – and in Kuwait for about a month before it started. I'll cover where the BBC sends me but equally they'll send me to go and cover an earthquake. It's anything foreign, and it might be a war but it might be a humanitarian disaster.'

Uwe Kroeger,[12] a reporter for German television ZDF, paints a similar picture of being based in a region as a foreign correspondent and being sent to cover a conflict when it broke out in that same area. Many journalists expressed a desire *not* to be classified as war correspondents. They were concerned about being painted as 'war junkies', unsavoury obsessives who move compulsively from one conflict to another (although many of these journalists have covered several wars themselves and success in one assignment readily leads to a career in reporting from conflict zones which then makes them liable to identification as war correspondents). Jane Kokan,[13] a freelance journalist, describes herself 'as an investigative journalist. That might take me to war zones, to countries exiting from war, but it's not like I jumped from one war zone to the other'.

Eschewing the term is not confined to reporters, as demonstrated by photographers, such as Sean Smith[14] of the *Guardian*:

'I'm not a war photographer. I'm not actually sure what it means. I've covered a number of jobs which have been in conflict areas; I don't think that makes a war photographer. If you're a journalist who happens to be taking pictures rather than writing, you're documenting human life in just a slightly unusual situation.'

Motivations

'Covering a war is, in my experience, a job that a lot of people want to do because it seems, or may appear, to be the glamour part. Foreign corresponding has a glamorous ring to it. The reality, when you get there, is that 90 percent of the people really don't want to know about it. The first set of bullets that goes off, they all want to go home. Of the remaining 10 percent, 2 or 3 percent are completely mad, they think they're working for Special Forces and they tend to get themselves into terrible trouble. And the people who do it for any period of time tend to be fairly straightforward.' (Ross Benson, *Daily Mail*)

Undoubtedly there is an excitement and glamour associated with the work of the frontline correspondent. They are a core constituent of what Andrew Marr (2004, p. 327) describes as an 'unacknowledged aristocracy of journalism'. Wars can make great stories – often more compelling than any others. For many journalists there is an element of addictiveness to the lifestyle, one that brings an intensification of emotions. Although there are some low points, 'When it goes well', as Luke Harding of the *Guardian* admits, 'it's the most exciting thing in the world.'

Following a meeting with mercenaries whilst travelling through conflict zones, Anthony Loyd (1999) suggested there was little real difference between them and others who go to war voluntarily:

Men and women who venture to someone else's war through choice do so in a variety of guises. UN general, BBC correspondent, aid worker, mercenary: in the final analysis they all want the same thing, a hit off the action, a walk on the dark side. It's just a question of how slick a cover you give yourself, and how far you want to go. (p. 54)

Alongside, and sometimes in place of, a stress on excitement, many war correspondents refer to the social value of their work. 'Truth-seeking' and a sense of making history are primary motivations, leading to the elevation of the occupation as a vocation. As Maggie O'Kane[15] of the *Guardian* comments:

'I did some very good work as a war correspondent because I believed passionately in the role we had to play, and I believe that particularly in Bosnia, we had a role to contribute in ending the war and enforcing a halt, which in the end journalists did contribute to, and I'm very proud of that. So there's an element which makes it definitely a vocation. The second thing is that it's a hugely exciting way to live your life, which is seen as adventure and fun, and you can't deny that.'

Other journalists spoke of the 'need' to be at the heart of events – compelled to be present at moments of history. For some such as Yannis Behrakis,[16] a photographer with Reuters, the initial motivation was one of adventure, a way to keep away from the routine. But then it became a mission:

> 'I show people what is happening in remote places, what they know only from movies or books . . . a message to people in nice and normal places, that the earth is not too big and things are happening maybe away from your home, but one day it might come here, so don't open the door . . . It sounds romantic, but you need some romantic thoughts in order to do this job.'

Many journalists talk of being at the front row of history. Orla Guerin[17] of the BBC describes her early days reporting for RTE at the time of the breakup of the Soviet Union, the collapse of the Communist Party, the fall of Gorbachev and the rise of Yeltsin:

> 'You would wake up every morning thinking what amazing, jaw-dropping historic thing is going to happen today, and every single day something would happen that you just couldn't possibly have predicted. And it was a very privileged position to be in, particularly as a young correspondent – I was 23 at that point – to be involved in this extraordinarily tumultuous period.
>
> And it was a great privilege to be reporting for RTE because Ireland is a small country, and people pay attention and are very interested in news and current affairs. So you literally did have the feeling that you were witness for many more people who were back in Ireland. And that's always a great privilege as a journalist, to know that you are reaching an audience. And at the BBC, which obviously has a far bigger reach around the world, it's a great privilege, and also at times a very great responsibility, because you know that very many people are listening to you.
>
> There's no doubt that it's an amazing experience as a journalist to see history being made, and that's something that's very tempting for us all. Covering conflict is in many ways one of the most compelling areas of journalism, and most people who do it want to keep doing it – it's rare that you find somebody who goes and covers a conflict or a war and who says "I don't want to do that again". It's normally the opposite – people are compelled to come back and do it again. And you want to feel that you're getting at the truth, because that's not always obvious in a war.'

Similarly David Zucchino[18] of the *Los Angeles Times* stresses his need to be present at history in the making:

> 'I love being in the middle of things that are happening and being there. It's very exhilarating and very exciting and very rewarding to be at the centre of historic events. To me, there's just nothing more important than doing that. And particularly in the modern world, so much of what's happening that is significant and important is happening in war zones.'

The desire to be present at historic moments necessarily means that there is an element of risk inherent in the occupation whether it is in gathering the story, or editing the material, or transmitting it back to their news organisations. While the physical and psychological welfare of all journalists is to some extent at risk, war/foreign correspondents face the most severe conditions and demands. The identification with their specific practice is therefore reinforced.

Jeremy Thompson[19] of *Sky News* describes how logistics can cause the most problems. Even a correspondent as experienced as Thompson feels a degree of apprehension, seeing it as an essential ingredient of the trade:

'In war I think you should always be apprehensive. I'm always apprehensive. If you're not apprehensive, if you don't wake up with butterflies about a big story that's breaking around you, then you shouldn't be doing it. And if you go into a war zone and you don't feel frightened, that is the time to get out, because you should feel frightened. So if you don't feel it, then you've been there too long, so get out.

Occasionally in a violent situation, you will feel real fear, but it's more of an excitement apprehension, whether you're up to the mark, whether you can crack the job, whether you can do it, whether you can get all the bits and pieces of the story you want, rather than a fear of failure. It's often the logistics as much as anything. And whether you'll be able to get enough bits to tell the story visually. That was more the pressure than it is now, where quite often it's not about gathering the pictures, which is what I've done for most of my life. It's more now about getting to a place and going live and picking up the pictures as a secondary thing.

That in a way is the subtle transition into the 24-hour news channel world, where the emphasis is on the live reporter being somewhere, being at a scene and describing it. And pictures in a way are slightly secondary to that. Whereas, before it was the gathering of the pictures and the great package that you all aspired to. Was your package better than the BBC's package, or ITN's? That's what you strived for. And now it's getting there first and being on first.'

Journalists try to grab the attention and sentiments of their audiences in order to make them aware of conflicts around the world. This personal commitment is enhanced when journalists see themselves as 'witnesses' to atrocities and gross injustices. The public is perceived as more or less ignorant about world affairs, and the journalist-witness has to open their eyes to the world's brutal reality. As Kim Willsher[20] of the *Mail on Sunday*, who covered the conflict in the former Yugoslavia, relates:

'I wanted to be covering what was the main story of the day. . . . you want to bear witness to what has happened. I felt that there was an obligation. I wanted to tell the story of the people who were suffering in this way. I certainly didn't get any thrills out of the danger . . . I was never reckless, and neither were my colleagues. It was a case of covering a historic event, a world story, and making sure that people in Britain knew what was going on. At the time, there was a lot of misinformation about this war. There was a lot of feeling that each side was as bad as the other. And as always happens in war, it's the innocent civilians – the women, the children and the elderly – who get caught up in it and who suffer the most. And I thought that it was important that these people were heard. I don't wish to sound pompous or arrogant about it, but you hope that by opening people's eyes to what is happening, that maybe something will be done to stop it from happening. If enough journalists are telling the story, the politicians will see what's happening and will actually do something to stop it continuing.'

The prioritisation of the moral and ethical duties of the journalist towards the public and the world in general is part of the professional values framework within which contemporary journalism operates.

Willsher is not alone in citing Bosnia as an example to illustrate a front-line correspondent's motivations. The experience of reporting from the former Yugoslavia had a profound effect on many journalists. Maggie O'Kane believes that, particularly in Bosnia, reporters had a role to con-tribute in ending the war and enforcing a halt to the fighting. However, as well as elevating the correspondent's role to that of a vocation, she also views the lifestyle as a hugely exciting, albeit a possibly escapist, one: 'Somebody said to me that sometimes when I'm in the field all I have to do is get from A to B, there's no electricity, there's no poll tax, there's no moany wife. I mean it's an escape.'

James Meek of the *Guardian* refers to excitement and spectacle but also to a flight from triviality:

'The superfluous anxieties, concerns and obsessions of fashion and income and status and personal relationships with your family and your friends and your colleagues – all these things just disappear. It's not that you're pushing them away, you know they're there, but they become distant. And that works not just for journalists but for the people that you encounter in these situations. Whether the romantic idea that there is some special wisdom to be found talk-ing to people who are involved in a war is true or not, I'm not sure . . . but certainly any relationship in these circumstances and any occurrence does seem more intense. And perhaps the reason it seems more intense is because people aren't making small talk.'

Such sentiments help explain the difficulties faced by journalists in making the transition back to 'ordinary' life – scarcely surprising when one learns of their experiences (see Chapter 11; also Feinstein 2003).

Some journalists contrast their work experiences and 'ordinary' life. For instance, Tim Lambon,[21] cameraman with *Channel 4 News*, outlines the intensity of his working life compared with life back at home:

'You come back and you get a bill from the gas board or a letter from your bank saying that you're overdrawn and it makes you extraordinarily angry. You want to say to them, listen I've just been in a place where people are trying to kill you, and you're worried about my being overdrawn. Give me a life . . . The interesting thing about the combat experience is that it is so completely intense. You can be alive one moment and dead the next. Only things that really matter, matter, and there's a lot of irrelevancies which you don't want to have to deal with basically. But, you come back and you slide into it. You have to deal with the bills and the bank and whatever.'

Adrian Monck[22] candidly observes that reporting war is …

'… the sort of life where you can go away for a few months and come back for a month, hang out with the family, and then when life gets too boring then you'll return, you go somewhere exciting and your adrenaline level shoots up again. That's . . . another part of the life that becomes very attractive.'

A sense of responsibility and obligation mixed with excitement are commonly cited as motivating forces. Jon Swain[23] of the *Sunday Times*, a highly experienced journalist, explains:

'It [the work] is different. It's good to have ripples in your life. I think the job is worthwhile. I think these events are important to report, and every so often – not often enough, but every so often – you can make a difference, you can get events noticed. You can embarrass governments.'

The human story is a common theme among frontline journalists. Many see their role as telling stories about people's lives and the effects of government decisions on ordinary folk. John Sweeney[24] of the BBC and the *Observer* newspaper explains how he tries to make the victims of conflict comprehensible to his readers and viewers – to make them alive as human beings:

'If I was going to do a story in Sudan at the moment, I'd try and find a kid who looked a bit like an African version of Wayne Rooney who's playing football and I'd then tell his story. What you need to do is to try to make them into Peters and Pauls and Johns and Mikes and Daves; or Sarahs and Kates and Angelas and Annes and Ruths. You need to close down those barriers. You need to make them people who are not just depositories of agony, who are interesting and funny, and who in a different light, in a different world, in a different environment, wouldn't just go "Oh my God! Oh my God! Oh my God!" but would say "Christ, what an awful colour in your bathroom". And the more you do that, certainly in newspaper terms, the more interesting they become. If you read the Amnesty International Report after a while, you just get bored silly don't you?'

The photographer John Downing[25] sees himself as the eyes of his readers:

'If you go inside hospitals, you can always find injured children. You know there are pictures there. You're trying to get it back to the people, how horrendous it is, war. My special knowledge makes me the eyes of my readers; they can't all be there but I can and I can try and show them what's happening the best I can.'

Another photographer, Jerry Lampen[26] of Reuters, paints a similar picture of his motivations.[27] He states that he is trying to show people what is going on in the world and also on occasions to raise consciousness:

'In Gaza, I managed a couple of times with my pictures to raise a lot of awareness of what is going on there and that is really what I want to do. It's not that [with] one picture we could change the whole conflict. No. But if I can reach a couple of people, then for me it's succeeded already.'

For freelance photographers, getting the 'right' picture can be difficult. How, for instance, do you balance drama with representativeness? Chip Hires[28] explains the dilemma:

'Most people have little impact on changing anything. And just showing really what happened without dramatising it more than it was already, while trying to give a proper balance on the situation, is hard to do in a still picture. The more dramatic pictures are the ones that are more likely to get published, so you're always looking for a good picture. But the balance is, is it an honest picture at the same time? It's honest in the fact that unless you set it up and organised it, it's honest – but at the same time, is it representative of really what's happening? And that's really hard to do.

And then put it into context. It's up to the editor back in the office to decide that it's worth publishing or he chooses this one over another. All that is so arbitrary. There are so many things out of your control. You're just one little link, one little cog in the machine. If you have an assignment with a magazine, you can talk to the editor of the magazine and really discuss it, but working for an agency is more removed. He [the editor] publishes it or he doesn't publish it, and you have absolutely no input.'

Many frontline journalists use examples to illustrate how they feel they can make a difference. Jon Swain, for example, relates how an incident reported on in Kosovo – for which he won an award – led to a philanthropic gesture:

'I described a little girl whose arm was almost severed by a shell splinter and her arm had to be amputated with a pair of pliers without any anaesthetic. And then she had to be carried back across the mountain. She was 5. But a woman in Argentina, a very rich woman, read the story, which was reprinted in the Buenos Aires Herald . . . She gave half a million dollars to the World Food Programme on condition that they found this girl, to give her a prosthetic arm. I found the girl in the end, and she was given a prosthetic arm.'

The desire to bring home the horrors of conflict or disaster to viewers and readers can sometimes lead to news organisations starting a campaign. In such situations it is clear that journalists may feel that they can make a difference. Possibly it prevents them from feeling that they are purely voyeurs. Tom Stoddart[29] paints the picture:

'You can't really sit in a hospital and see a child who's had his leg blown off [and not be affected by it] . . . . Of course it does make a difference. That's when you make good pictures – when you have a reason for doing it. When you're angry. When you're frustrated. That's when the pictures are good. Not just when you're filling a hole in a magazine. When you really have something to say, it's more valuable.'

But it is not everyone who can do this – it is skill, nerve and experience that characterise the best. Mark Wood, Chief Executive of ITN, sums it up:

'It's performing in a situation where operationally things may be difficult, just getting the cameras in, getting the picture, getting the satellite dish working and getting the stuff out and keeping calm . . . . Staying in control in difficult circumstances is probably the most important of long-time journalistic skills.'

And it is the experienced ones on whom the big news organisations rely most. Brian Williams of Reuters, for example, went on his first trip when he was 23 years of age to Vietnam and describes it as very exciting. This is hardly surprising, given that it was the biggest story of the time. Once a journalist has covered one war, then more assignments may follow and a career begins to be built:

'You've always got the choice to say no, but it can sometimes become a bit of a vicious circle: you've covered one war, then you've covered two wars, so they'll say, "he's great, he's good at covering wars, he really knows how to look after himself. Oh we've got another war, he can go there". There's no problem about saying no. I was saying no no, I've had enough, but like most people I think, it is like a little bit of a drug – you're covering a war, you're free, you're not in head office, you're outside, it's physical and mental, it's a front page story.'

Another very experienced journalist, Jeremy Thompson of *Sky News*, sees an increase in pressure with the transition to 24-hour news:

'You're asking a hell of a lot of reporters these days, putting a great deal of responsibility on their shoulders to report accurately and fairly under pressure and live. It is a huge thing, and people will make mistakes – luckily not too many – and you try and correct them as quickly as possible. I see very few major mistakes. People might get names wrong and stumble over some things, but I'm amazed at how good the youngsters are these days at assimilating a story.'

Brian Williams, though, believes that employers should consciously put people into different environments so that they do not become locked into being a permanent frontline reporter (and thereby turning into the 'war correspondents', even the 'war junkies', that so many of our interviewees resisted).

Whilst employers need to be aware of the physical and psychological stresses of their journalists (see Chapter 11), a sense of inner compulsion is a characteristic of many experienced correspondents. The escape from boredom and the adrenalin generated from an assignment may ensure the return to danger. Jane Kokan outlines the scenario:

'Some people think we have a death wish. I haven't got a death wish but once you've experienced a war zone and you've survived and brought back a good story, you want to go back and you want to tell more stories. I've worked in offices before where you work nine to five and it can be kind of boring sometimes, so I think there is that tenseness. Life moves a bit faster and it's more exciting and you're doing real reporting. You're not just sitting behind a desk and a computer; you're actually out in the field. And there is a perception that you're doing real journalism. Then there's the risk that you could be kidnapped or shot. You just don't know what's going to happen.[30]

The late Ross Benson of the *Daily Mail* believed there was a psychological type that could cope with life as a frontline correspondent:

'You're not there as a war junkie or a tourist, you're there to do a job of work. Back in the '80s when I was doing it, I was away from England probably six to eight months of the year. I would meet the same people wherever I went; the guy from the *New York Times*, the guy from the *Washington Post*, the guy from *The Times* of London, it tended to be the same people moving around. And if I can give you a comparison, I once asked the head of Ford what they looked for in a driver, which seems a fairly straightforward question. He said the first thing they do is psychological tests and I said "What do you mean, psychological test? Don't you want to know who goes fastest?" He said "No," and I said "Alright, well, you've got Ayrton Senna, three times world champion and Nelson Piquet, three times world champion; Ayrton Senna lived like a monk and Nelson Piquet had five mistresses and three illegitimate children, or was it the other way round?" "So there's no comparison between the two." He said, "No, no, no, that's personality. What we are looking for in the psychological tests is how you react under pressure, you know, your back tyre bursts and suddenly the car is going all over the place, most people throw their hands up in horror and the car crashes. Those two boys would keep working right until the last minute, do you see what I mean?"'

In war correspondents there is a similar kind of mentality. They have to remain focused and cannot afford to be overcome by homesickness.

But even if these journalists possess these attributes, questions remain as to why they do it. Some experience their own tragedies. Anton Antonowicz[31] of the *Daily Mirror* outlines the story of one woman reporter he met in Baghdad:

'They talk about tough girls, and some of the women are remarkable. I'm 53, but you see young girls in their 20s doing the job and you think how the hell can they do it? [One reporter] worked for a Spanish newspaper, a remarkable girl, terribly thin, looked awfully frail. And one day I came down to breakfast in The Palestine [hotel] and she was crying. I asked her what had happened, and she'd just discovered that two friends of hers, two Spanish journalists, had been killed. They were with the embedded troops, and they'd been killed by accidental fire, at the airport. The year before, her husband had been killed in Afghanistan. He was a television journalist. What is it that makes somebody who has lost the man that she most loved in the world, come out to Baghdad to carry on doing it? Now is that some kind of personal journey that she's on? She discovers two more friends are dead, and she's still there in the middle of all this, as though she's some kind of spectre walking through death. Is that a psychological need on her part, or is it something that she feels she has to do as a journalist? Because if she doesn't have that kind of intrinsic need and belief that what she's doing is right, then how can she make any sense of all these deaths that are happening around her? I mean that's a novel.'

Julian Manyon[32] of ITN, one of the most experienced television journalists around today, believes that journalism is essential for revealing abuses and misdeeds:

'I would say I'm one of those people who began to do the job because I believed in it. And almost 35 years later I'm still doing it, at least in part, because I preserve a degree of belief in its relevance and importance and that's what I get my satisfaction from. It's very easy to knock journalists and journalism and it's quite true that our profession does flagrantly do things which really would reinforce the cynicism of the public – when stories turn out not to be true or information or interviews have been bought, instead of honestly obtained. But on the other hand, all I would say is that it's very difficult now, in the year 2004, to imagine a world without journalism and, for example, foreign journalism. Unquestionably, had journalists not been present in Iraq over the last year, far worse abuses would have been carried out by various elements of the armed forces than have taken place and have obviously been made public in the Abu Ghraib prison, for example. Unquestionably, anything that is away from the light of day in the field of conflict and foreign affairs festers and produces abuses and it still remains the job of the journalist to try and dig things out and to publicise them. And a world without this taking place would be a pretty sorry place. In fact, you would return to the values of the Middle Ages.'

Julian Manyon's words reveal a force of conviction about his work. What we found amongst the journalists we interviewed, if often shrouded in avowals of cynicism and world-weariness, was a *passion* for their vocation. At one level this meant maintaining a level of concern for fellow humanity experiencing distressing circumstances that many journalists thought was an ingredient of good reportage. Barbara Jones[33] of the *Mail on Sunday* felt 'very strongly that you shouldn't get hardened because the minute that you are so tough that things don't even upset you, then you might as well give up because how are you going to write about it with feeling?'. A similar ethos is evident in Jon Swain's admiration of James Cameron's capacity to 'write compassionately but without sentimentality', as it is in Colin Baker's insistence that if journalists 'have no heart . . . there's no sensitivity', hence 'unless you shed a tear and feel moved . . . then I don't really want to hear what you have to say or what you write'. Bill Neely echoes these sentiments: 'You can get tremendously involved in war reporting. It's not something that you can just dip into and not be affected by it.'

David Zucchino was keen to stress the need for compassion alongside the passion:

'There's always that gnawing fear that you're somehow profiting from the misery of others because so much of what's reported, particularly by war and foreign correspondents, is tragedy and terrible things happening to people. You're very much an intrusion in their lives at a very difficult moment and you have to walk a fine line between compassion and objectivity when you're in these situations. You're barging in on people and asking them questions when something very very disturbing has happened to them or to someone they know. And you know – and they know – that tomorrow, you'll be onto another story but they'll be left for the rest of their lives to deal with that. You have to keep that in mind and be sensitive to people, be respectful, keep your distance, be compassionate, sensitive about how you deal with them and what you ask them. When I can, I like to go back – a day later, a week later – and follow up and see what happened, when things are less emotional and less stressful.'

At another level this passion is revealed in the commitment to being there, the drive to bear witness to the unfolding of significant events. Janine di Giovanni of *The Times* made this point, when she argued that the motivation might spring from the fact that one is a witness, in the middle of history (di Giovanni 2001: 8; see also di Giovanni 2003). The imperative to be 'where the action is' so as to 'tell it like it is', exercises a powerful hold over many journalists. It is recognisable in Gavin Hewitt's acknowledgement that 'one of the things that drives people . . . is to be there at the heart of events . . . to be there . . . when the Berlin Wall comes down . . . to be there when American troops enter Baghdad'. It is evident again when Julian Manyon recounts being 'again consumed by interest and passion for this [Chechnya] story'. Manyon combines this passion for the story and for humanity when he advises that 'without that passion . . . at least a degree of it, journalism becomes a rather sterile and tedious occupation because we're not . . . writing insurance reports about boats that have sunk . . . we're telling the story of the people who went down with the boat, if I can put it that way'. And it is manifest in Colin Baker's sentiments:

'I've always thought that if I go away somewhere, I am being trusted to report what I see . . . How can you balance something when you're watching a village of Muslims being wiped out in Serbia? . . . You report from the heart and you report what you see. That's the best you can do . . . Today you still have journalists who to me have no heart, and there's no sensitivity. I want people who sometimes wear their heart on their sleeve. I want them to go and get deeply involved, and tell me how moved they were or how disturbed they were by what is happening. I'm not interested in what the official press releases say. I want people who go beyond that and that's the way I've grown up and the traditions I've grown up with.'

This is a passion that keeps many of these journalists at the job, though it may compel them to witness horrors and sup with the devil.

Notes

1   Ross Benson, who died in 2005, covered conflict in Nicaragua, El Salvador, The Falklands, Afghanistan and Iraq.

2   James Meek is a *Guardian* journalist who has covered the Gulf Wars, the Chechen conflict, and Afghanistan in 2001. He won the Foreign Reporter of the Year award at the British press awards in 2004.

3   David Williams of the *Daily Mail* has reported from conflict areas including Chad, Sierra Leone, Tiananmen Square, Beirut, both the Gulf Wars, Afghanistan, Chechnya, Angola, Congo, Rwanda, Indonesia, Timor, Sri Lanka, Georgia, Russia, Colombia during the drug wars, the Falklands, and the Balkans including stints in Bosnia, Croatia, Kosovo and Serbia.

4   Brian Williams has worked for Reuters in Vietnam, Israel, Lebanon, Afghanistan, India, Pakistan, Sri Lanka, and Iraq.

5   Jonathan Steele of the *Guardian* has reported from Nicaragua, El Salvador, Zimbabwe, Mozambique, Angola and Afghanistan amongst other places.

6   Peter Sharp of *Sky News* worked in Zimbabwe up to its independence before moving to ITN and running the bureau in Johannesburg. He has subsequently covered conflict in Eastern Europe, Ethiopia, Sudan, Bosnia, Afghanistan and both Gulf Wars.

7   Rory Carroll was covering the trial of Saddam Hussein for the *Guardian* in October 2005 when he was abducted by gunmen and held for 36 hours before being released.

8   Pedelty (1995, p. 30) in his study of foreign correspondents in El Salvador, argues that most frontline reporters are 'neither the die-for-the truth adventurists they would have us believe, nor the lobotomised barflies of solidarity discourse'. The truth, he states, is much more complex, and in certain ways, more disturbing. We would tend to agree.

9   Gavin Hewitt of the BBC has reported from many conflict areas including Iran, Afghanistan, Iraq, Nicaragua, El Salvador, Honduras and Lebanon.

10   Colin Baker of ITN has worked in many conflict areas including Cambodia, Rwanda, Ethiopia, South Africa, Brazil, Peru, Colombia and Somalia.

11   Caroline Wyatt has covered the Middle East, Kosovo and Iraq for the BBC.

12 Uwe Kroeger was based in Johannesburg, covering Africa for ZDF, the UK as bureau chief based in London, Southeast Asia based in Singapore and is now bureau chief in New York.

13 Jane Kokan has reported from many conflicts including the Balkans, Chechnya, Algeria and the Sudan.

14 Sean Smith is a photographer with the *Guardian* who has worked in Iraq, the Middle East, Chechnya, Georgia and Bosnia.

15 Maggie O'Kane worked in Bosnia, Afghanistan and other conflict areas for the *Guardian*. She now runs *Guardian* films.

16 Yannis Behrakis is a photographer for Reuters who has covered conflict in Chechnya, the Middle East, Somalia, Afghanistan, Sierra Leone and both Gulf Wars.

17 Orla Guerin covered the breakup of the Soviet Union and the conflict in the former Yugoslavia for RTE before joining the BBC.

18 For much of his career David Zucchino of the *LA Times* has been based in the Middle East and Africa.

19 Jeremy Thompson set up and ran the Asia bureau for ITN after which he covered the Balkans conflict and then ran the Africa bureau before joining *Sky News* where among many conflicts he has covered Afghanistan and Iraq.

20 Kim Willsher of the *Mail on Sunday* has reported from Bosnia, Afghanistan, Kosovo, the Middle East, Sierra Leone, Angola and North Korea.

21 Tim Lambon of *Channel 4 News* has worked in numerous places including South Africa, Nicaragua, El Salvador, Philippines, Afghanistan, Beirut and Iraq.

22 Adrian Monck was Deputy Editor, *Five News* until 2005. He had experience in Northern Ireland as well as Bosnia.

23 Jon Swain of the *Sunday Times* first reported from Vietnam and Cambodia. Since then he has covered numerous conflicts including the recent Gulf War.

24 John Sweeney of the BBC has worked in Yugoslavia, Rwanda, Chechnya, Kosovo, Zimbabwe, Algeria and Iraq.

25 John Downing is a photographer who has covered Bangladesh, Uganda, Sudan, Vietnam, Rwanda, Afghanistan, Bosnia and South America.

26 Jerry Lampen has worked as a photographer for Reuters in Albania, Pakistan, the Middle East and Iraq.

27 Paul O'Driscoll, photographer with the *Guardian*, believes photographers have to get closer to the action than journalists:

> 'In my experience I rarely meet journalists out in the field. And if I do meet them, they're never in the front. It's not in the nature of their business to be in the front. It's in their nature to string together a story from different sources, put together a story from different pieces of string. They can't afford . . . . to be there, right beside you. Whereas a photographer needs to illustrate what's happening and tends to have to be where it's happening, that's the closest you can get.'

28 Chip Hires has covered conflict in East Timor, Kosovo, Iraq, Beirut, El Salvador and Afghanistan.

29 Tom Stoddart has worked as a photographer in many places including Sudan and Bosnia.

30 Stephen Hess found similar traits among the foreign correspondents he interviewed in 1983 and then again in 1992. They talked of dealing with danger,

often of being scared, sometimes of being exhilarated. Hess quotes Peter Arnett stating that 'he learned to love the thrill of covering wars, for which there was no substitute' (Hess 1996, p. 58).

31 Anton Antonowicz of the *Daily Mirror* has worked in Kosovo, Afghanistan, East Timor and Rwanda.

32 Julian Manyon of ITN has covered numerous conflicts from Vietnam to the second Gulf War.

33 Barbara Jones of the *Mail on Sunday* has covered conflict in Lebanon, Sierra Leone and Afghanistan.

6

ON ASSIGNMENT

'The only thing worse than being asked to cover a war is not being asked.'
(Bill Neely of ITN quoting his colleague Terry Lloyd, who was killed in the
Second Gulf War.)

Preparation

Frontline correspondents work on short notice of assignments, making it
difficult for them to be informed about every country. Research time is
often very limited. Journalists can be told to get on a plane straight away
to cover a conflict or disaster. With the spread of presenter/journalists
reporting live from location rather than the studio this may be happening
more frequently.[1]

Freelance photographer Chip Hires vividly describes an episode when
there was no time for planning:

'If I'm doing a project, a magazine feature, I know I'm going to leave on May 25
for instance, and I know I'm going to be back on, June 30, then you have time
to do that [research]. I went to Timor the last time in '99. I was sitting in my
office at four o'clock and I was supposed to go to Canada the following day,
and they said, "Listen, there's a plane tonight at seven, we want you to be on
it". So I had a motorcycle guy who actually rushed me home. I packed my bag
and rushed to the airport and I got there within half an hour of the flight leaving. I hadn't really followed Timor very much – I knew it was a problem but I
didn't know all the ins and outs.'[2]

Because of the lack of time for preparation, journalists working for
large news organisations have an advantage in the resources available.
They will generally have local contacts on the ground that are aware of
the problems and capable of resolving many of them beforehand. Some
journalists will keep a ready kit in anticipation of a hasty departure.
Daniel Demoustier, a cameraman who has worked for ITN, has everything ready:

'I have my bullet vests, I have my helmet, I have all my first-aid kits. And then
there's all of the essentials like taking enough water, good maps, all the little

things you are used to taking with you. And good communication, of course –
a good satellite telephone is very important, even two if you can, in case you
lose one.'

Obtaining a visa can often be an obstacle for a speedy departure and, as
Anton Antonowicz observes, there are times when correspondents need
to be resourceful:

'In Baghdad last year [2003], it was very difficult to get a visa, and what they
didn't know in my case, was that I was on a black list already, banned from Iraq,
by virtue of the fact that I'd been there during the Iran–Iraq conflict, and I'd
interviewed Saddam Hussein at that stage. A long time ago now but the Iraqi
secret service, Mukhabarat, subsequently discovered that my wife is Iranian,
and for whatever reason, they thought I was a spy, even though they thought
that the piece I wrote was very well balanced. So I was supposedly on a black
list. But I got the visa last year, which, more than anything else, is a testament
to just how poor their intelligence service was, or their record keeping was. At
the airport, when I finally got into Baghdad, one of the secret service men
there, whom I had developed a very good contact with, said to me "Is this your
first time in Baghdad?" I said "Yeah, fascinating, yeah, wonderful" etc. I wasn't
going to tell him that I'd actually met the big moustache himself.'

Barbara Jones of the *Mail on Sunday*, who was relatively inexperienced
when she went to Afghanistan, describes part of her homework: 'Well the
Internet is the huge resource tool. I just printed out everything I could
find about the background to the country, the background to the conflict,
the background to British involvement, what kind of missiles and aircraft
and troops they would be sending.'

Dan Edge, a young freelancer with experience of Kashmir, Pakistan and
Palestine, also acknowledged that the Internet 'can be the most powerful
tool', especially in the 'initial research phase', adding that 'I can't imagine
how difficult it must have been to find out quality information quickly
before the Internet'. But Edge adds a note of caution about over-reliance on
the Internet, since 'you'll get a lot of crap' from a Google search, before com-
mending the use of 'excellent libraries' at work. The experienced reporter,
John Carlin,[3] reinforces this advice, warning that dependence on the Internet
was a 'path to perdition'.

Maggie O'Kane reads as many books as she can and also praises the
Guardian's 'wonderful library'. 'For a first-time conflict like Haiti, the
research people in the library are fantastic and they'd prepare you a big
folder and you'd read as much as you could and you'd buy as many
books as you could to bring with you, and you'd read them on the plane.'

Apart from using newspaper libraries, books and Internet searches,
journalists contact colleagues who have been to that country or area
previously, think-tanks, academics and other experts in Britain. The
Guardian's James Meek suggests that the autonomy of the role of frontline
correspondent begins with the homework:

'You're on your own and that's as it should be. People have to be autonomous; they have to know how to do it by themselves. If the company's going to hold your hand in your research before you leave, then what use is that for you when you get there? Because you're not going to have anyone holding your hand when you get there. You have to be able to organise and prepare and research by yourself. One of the basic skills of a journalist is finding things out. And the minimum that you want to do before you go to a conflict is to read the recent news reports from that area. Now, of course, with the Internet, there is the opportunity to learn quite a lot more. You tend to find that 90 percent of the material on the Internet is from news reports from proper news organisations, who have funded their correspondents to do these difficult and dangerous things. Most of the Internet in English about non-English places is parasitic.'

Meek also counsels about the importance of speaking various languages, not only when reporting, but also in the earlier preparation:

'If it happens that you speak the language, that's the ultimate preparation. Unfortunately, often that's not possible. I think the British media's reporting of the former Soviet Union has been greatly enhanced by the fact that most of the British correspondents who worked in the former Soviet Union, at least in the time that I was there, to some degree or another, spoke Russian and I think their coverage was so much better for that. And I think that coverage of the Middle East is so much the worse for the fact that so few correspondents speak Arabic . . .

You also want to get around to reading at least one book about the place that you're going to, but again that's not always possible. In the case of Afghanistan, everyone was reading Ahmed Rashid's *Taliban* book, and it's a very good book, very well written, very accessible, very detailed. Of course, once you get into the story, you meet more people who know it well. So you have those sources, you have the books, you have the language, you have the news reports, and you have the Internet.'[4]

Freelance journalist Antonia Francis,[5] whose aim is to spend four to five months on assignment, stresses the importance of knowing some language and culture of the place in which she will be based and is instrumental in her approach:

'I have to learn a little bit of the language once I'm there, and I think that's a basic ingredient of understanding the story. And if you don't have that, if you don't know how to get from A to B and to rely on human exchange rather than just the dollar, you can't do any work as a journalist. So I learn the language out there. I try to learn a bit on the plane, but that's not really my main goal. I always try to read a bit about the culture, but that, to be honest, is not really from my own interest so much as the . . . use it will be – because people there will be impressed . . . and it will allow me to engage further with them. So I use it as I do my dictionary of jokes – to be able to engage with people in the field.'

Other journalists (even though they may be competitors) are often a vital ingredient of handed down knowledge and reciprocal help, especially if it is a new assignment. Access to sources is paramount for all journalists. Meek explains:

> 'When you set out somewhere you haven't been before, there's an awful lot of trepidation and anxiety. But the closer you get, the more relaxed you feel. The thing you are most anxious about is not so much getting shot at, as not being in the right place at the right time – not getting the access to people you need to talk to, not being able to get to this town which is under siege, not being able to talk to the soldiers. These are the things that are worrying you. And the closer you get to the conflict zone, the more opportunities you have to talk to people, local people, people who know what's going on – and other journalists. In the first days of a conflict – in fact throughout – other journalists are always your best resource because you are each other's eyes and ears. There is competition and you do sometimes not tell people things that would be useful to them, but more often than that, you'll be chatting to each other because you know that you can help each other more than you can harm each other. You'll be in one town and somebody else will be in another town. You can help each other by swapping that information.'

When on assignment in Chechnya, the BBC's Caroline Wyatt relied on other journalists both in conversation and through their books:

> 'We talked to a lot of people, to journalists who had been there, human rights groups working there . . . to Russian journalists like Anna Politkovskaya, who spent a lot of time in Chechnya, who's very, very good and who can give you advice about where to go, what to do and how to behave, who to talk to, who you can trust, what not to do. For Iraq, there were a lot of books around. For Chechnya, there's not that many.'

Some of Wyatt's crew had been to Chechnya before and had developed contacts in the area, whereas in Afghanistan it was more of a *'leap into the blue'*:

> 'We were the second team in, so the first team had already found somewhere to live and stay with the Northern Alliance in Afghanistan in a village. It was the foreign ministry compound of the Northern Alliance. It was a mud hut with four rooms in it, and that's where the [now] foreign minister, who wasn't foreign minister [then], because he was part of the rebel group at that stage, would hold press conferences. And at first there were about ten journalists there, all BBC. By the end of two weeks after the campaign had started, there were 200 journalists living in that same compound. So we left. We had found another house by then. We were helped by another charity that was working there. For Afghanistan, we had lots of Russian maps because the Russians were the last people to be there. And speaking Russian helped, because a lot of people in the North spoke Russian and remembered the Russians quite fondly. A lot of them had been to the University of Moscow.'

It is not just journalists who are important to journalists. Experienced frontline correspondents will develop a huge base of sources over the

years and work hard at maintaining contacts despite difficulties. Marie
Colvin[6] of the *Sunday Times* explains her methods:

'When I started going to the Arab world, a lot of the reading didn't stick until I
went to the country and then suddenly I would absorb the reading like a
sponge. It's just the way my brain works. And I would call around colleagues,
call around Arab newspapers, have a tea or coffee with people and ask them
what they thought was going on there: was there anyone there who was interesting? Who were the players? You do a lot of research – both personal and
archival. Now after 15 years covering the Middle East, if you look at my
contact book, I have people I've known for years in every single country. Sadly
some of them have been killed, some of them have moved on, but I make a
point of it being a continuum. I make a point of keeping up contacts over the
years. Maybe it's just a phone call to say "How's your family?" or, "What's
going on there?". Now I do less research. That gives me more time on the
ground. . . . If you haven't been to a country, you make sure you have a
stringer. You call around your colleagues who have been there before, [to ask]
what sort of hotel to stay in, who's good, and you do a lot of reading. And over
the years, as you get more experienced, you have your own contacts. And I
always help others. If anyone calls me and says, "I've never been to Iran
before", I'll just help them out completely, because I've been helped out in
ways like that as well.'

For journalists covering conflict it is also important to have the right
equipment. Barbara Jones details what she used for covering the invasion
of Afghanistan following 9/11.

'We went out there and didn't know what to expect, I didn't take a tent but I
took a sleeping bag and cooking utensils and things like water sterilisation
tablets. And it was such a pain to carry all that because you're also carrying
your own clothing, which is going to be outdoor clothing and foul weather
clothing, and now you've also got all your electronic equipment, which these
days is getting more and not less. I mean we had satellite equipment, satellite telephones and obviously your computer, cameras. It's a lot to carry, so
you're pretty well burdened in that way.'

Most journalists will take preventive injections for hepatitis and other
diseases before leaving, while many also take prescription drugs with
them such as antibiotics and sleeping pills. Many have favourite gismos and
will compare notes with colleagues. Peter Sharp of *Sky News*, for example,
explains what is important for him:

'I always take some very good sleeping stuff like Bivibag, which is a totally
zippable thing you can sleep out in . . . or in the rain and you'll be fine. And
Thermo-vests, which are self-inflating, quite thick and very packed up. I can
remember the days we used to compare lists. "I've got a new gadget for the
list, which is very expensive, but it's an absolute must". I was the first to have
it here, it was a satellite radio, which is unbelievable, because you just plug
it down, stick the dish up, the reception's unbelievable. You can get CNN off

air – you can't see the pictures, obviously, but the signal's absolutely fantastic. And they've got these new things now called Bose headphones, which are noise-cancelling. So you flick a switch on the side of it, pull out the plugs and it creates its own sort of dead sound. You can be anywhere and you won't hear a thing, which is perfect for long car trips. We all have our toys, we really do.'

All have their favoured things, chosen to make their time away more bearable. It is all about survival in strange lands. Peter Sharp, for example, used to carry little spray tins of Evian water to wet his face. He would also carry little things to give away, such as sweets for children. In Africa he always used to have a Polaroid camera 'because you get stopped at a roadblock, in the middle of Liberia or somewhere. And some of these people had never seen a camera before, never seen their own picture. It used to work like magic. Little things like that can really get you out of a hole'.

New Technologies

Frontline correspondents have extensively adopted new technologies. The spread of the Internet, digital cameras, lightweight recording equipment, email and, perhaps above all, the availability of the satellite videophone, have had significant influences on the working practices of frontline correspondents and on their relationships with colleagues, the subjects on whom they report, as well as on wider constituents. The technologies have increasingly become more versatile, miniaturised and converged, so that recording and transmitting images and text is immeasurably easier and faster than in the days – scarcely a decade ago – when technologies were unreliable, heavyweight and cumbersome. The essential accoutrements of the frontline correspondent today may be a laptop computer, cell phone with video facilities and communications connections. Correspondents now have greatly enhanced means of finding out about issues, communicating reports and – of less obvious benefit – of being called upon to service the unceasing demands of rolling news and of their reportage being readily available to those about whom they speak or write.

The Internet provides background information on location, events and organisations. Gavin Hewitt reminds us of just how recent this innovation is, recalling that:

'When the Soviets invaded Afghanistan [in 1980] . . . I can remember writing down on a piece of paper what I knew about Afghanistan, and it was not a long list. I simply did not know very much about Afghanistan, and there was no Internet at the time whereby you could tap in the word "Afghanistan" and become an instant expert.'

But the Internet is not accessed simply so that the correspondent can mug up before setting out to work. It is also a tool for checking the veracity of information received, even for providing additional news stories. It allows, for instance, ready access to other media, so correspondents in the field can find out what colleagues are reporting elsewhere. This means that the BBC correspondent sees what his or her counterparts at NBC are covering, as well as the presentations of Al Jazeera and the *Irish Times*. Furthermore, the Internet has meant that bloggers – sometimes located in places that the journalists themselves cannot reach – can become contributors to media accounts. Julian Manyon explains:

> 'The Internet is a valuable source of information . . . I can dip into it, even in Baghdad . . . I think this is a very interesting phenomenon and in cases like Iraq before the war, very valuable . . . [It] is not just about the dissemination of information; it's also about the verification of information. By definition, if you've got a blogger in Fallujah, for example, during the American siege of the city [in 2004], it's deeply interesting to know what somebody there is saying . . . it amplifies the possible sources of information.'

It is in such ways that the Internet contributes to the transformed information environment of much conflict nowadays. It allows reports to be sent, and email to be exchanged, from a laptop to wherever, so long as adequate communications links are available. Thus even in remote parts of Africa such as Liberia, Rory Carroll found Internet cafes a 'godsend' since from them he could file back to the *Guardian*. Good-quality satellite phones can even bypass poor quality telecommunications in a given location, so the journalist may possess even better facilities than local combatants.

The Internet impacts on frontline correspondents in other ways, too. For instance, Suzanne Goldenberg points out that the Internet 'means that a reporter can be almost immediately accountable for what is published in the newspaper, no matter how far away she/he might be from the area of distribution'. Goldenberg underlines an important consequence: 'The people one is writing about can often read what one is writing, which I suppose helps keep people honest – or intimidates them.'

This ready access to what one has written by those about whom one is writing is, according to Rory Carroll, 'mostly a healthy thing'. For instance, if colleagues can be ribbed on their 'purple prose', then perhaps this encourages restraint. More of a concern might be pressure and threats that come from groups who find what has been reported about them to be disagreeable. Chris Ayres vividly recalls an attack on him (when he was working as an embed with the US Marines) from a military officer who was 'fizzing with barely controlled rage' (Ayres 2005, p. 279) having read Ayres' reports that were published in *The Times* of London a few hours earlier.

Ben Brown notes that new technologies have widened the range of those responding to reportage. Thus 'with the Internet and everything you get . . . a lot of email reaction to stories, especially if you're covering a story like Israel where both sides are incredibly vociferous . . . [and] watch like a hawk everything, every word that every reporter says'. A result, the felt, was that 'if you're somewhere like that, you're incredibly self-conscious about how you report it, and careful, just very careful. Because just one wrong bit of terminology and you can cause huge upset'.

We need to register the scale and speed of these technological innovations, amongst which the take-up of lightweight satellite videophones is of primary importance since they allow journalists to send pictures and text from pretty well any location. The transformative effect here is massive. As James Mates of ITN explains:

> 'Satellite phones make it all possible, and especially now with the handheld satellite phones and the Internet . . . cell phones seem to work everywhere. Even in the worst conflicts you often find a signal on your cell phone. Now we are able to feed pictures down telephone lines and satellite phones. You can feed pictures now on a broadband connection on the Internet . . . You can do telephone reports from anywhere . . . All these things have made 24-hour news possible.'

This can enormously empower frontline correspondents.

James Meek also draws attention to these changes, recalling the time he first went to war in 1991:

> 'I travelled into Kuwait, which was being liberated by the allies, with a notebook and a pen and a carry bag full of food that I had bought in a local supermarket in northern Saudi Arabia. I had no flak jacket, I had no helmet, I had no satellite phone, I had no medical kit. I had a gas mask which I'd picked up from the British, as a British citizen in Saudi Arabia. I had a chemical warfare suit which I scrounged from some British people in Iran and I had other little bits of the full chemical warfare suit which I also scrounged from British solders . . . That first night of moving into Kuwait, there was absolutely nothing I could do, nobody knew where I was, whether I was dead or alive. None of the journalists I was travelling with had satellite phones. There was just absolutely nothing that we could do. So we spent the night in the desert with all these oil fires over our heads in complete and absolute darkness. And then we moved on the next morning. We arrived in Kuwait City and purely by luck, CBS, the American TV station, had brought this gigantic truck with a satellite broadcasting system on it, and I was able to make a call to Scotland and file my story. And then later, when all the other journalists arrived, the biggest news organisations at that time did have big satellite phones, huge great big things. And if you begged and you pleaded and you knew somebody, then they would maybe let you make a call. That was the way in which you were filing stories in those days.
>
> The first time I was in Chechnya, I didn't have a satellite phone – the paper considered that they were too expensive, we didn't need one. I would drive hundreds of miles to find a phone from which I could file. It was tedious, it was dangerous, it was extremely annoying. But then satellite phones started to come along, and with every successful conflict they've become easier

and easier, until now you've got these Thurayas . . . I've made calls from extraordinary places.'

Jeremy Thompson feels that work was more fun in the 'old days', when journalists could 'disappear' for days on assignment:

'"I'm just going up the Andes and I'll ring you when I get back, in three weeks' time." A long time ago you'd ship tins of film in an onion bag back to London and then go down to the beach and have a few beers and wait 'til they told you they'd got it, two days later. And then satellite transmission started to fire up late '70s and through the '80s – and you tended to go out and get a story, get the pictures, do it, bring it back, edit it and then feed it from whatever the capital city of some outlandish place was. And you sat and prayed that it would work, willed the satellite to work. It was all a bit Fred Carno. But I guess it was part of the Boys' Own adventure.'

The new technology can provide a reference for recalling episodes of communicating from remote places and under bizarre circumstances. As John Sweeney informed us, 'I've used my mobile on a pong-pong boat in the South China Sea.'

Brian Williams of Reuters recalls his experience in South East Asia to illustrate the contrast between then and now:

'When the invasion of Laos took place, I was on the border there with about a dozen other journalists. There were no cell phones there. It took about four hours to get back to a base where there was a phone that I could use to give the news. Even in Afghanistan it was the same when the Russians invaded. Your biggest challenge was not getting the story but how to get the story out quickly . . . The technology has changed it tremendously. It's made your job far easier because you don't have to worry about actually getting the news out.'

Whilst new technology has increased the speed of news production, the demand for instant news can inhibit more in-depth analysis. German television reporter, Uwe Kroeger of ZDF, outlines the disadvantages of speed and the advance of technology:

'Speed is an advantage no doubt, but it can also be a disadvantage when the demand for instant news gets so overpowering that you don't have a chance to do your own work and try to find out for yourself what's going on in the little area that you're in at the moment. The worst situation is that you are chained to your hotel room with your editor, your picture editors, and your live shot is on the roof of the hotel room and that's where you operate from – your hotel room. And you depend on people to bring you video tapes and you just appear in front of a camera and tell the audience, "Ok, listen, this is happening here," without having seen for yourself what *is* happening.'

Many journalists complain that rolling news is frustrating and limiting. Experienced journalists like Peter Sharp acknowledge the changes but can see them as a challenge:

'Anyone who's been in it as long as Jeremy [Thompson] and I have, we've all had to adapt. The lessons, the basic functions and your responsibilities haven't changed that much. But in terms of the speed in getting the story out . . . you're going live before you know where the story's heading. Many, many times that happens. It's much more challenging, but you tend to get your head around the story a lot quicker if you're going live than if you're just doing a set report and a package. You've got to be able to stand up and answer questions. That's a big plus of live television. And it is very, very rewarding when it goes well, very rewarding.

It's funny – television news in a way always used to be about the pictures and your exclusive pictures and what you said and how you put the package across. In those days – and I'm talking now about the late '70s, early '80s – there really wasn't this huge global connection between various organisations. You hardly ever saw the same pictures. Now we subscribe to some of the same picture organisations that the BBC subscribe to, or ITN. So you get a very homogeneous set of images.

In those days, when I was a correspondent in South Africa, I had one cameraman, the BBC [correspondent] had his cameraman and we were fighting, shot for shot, on that particular story. I had WTN and he had Visnews. The package you produced at night, you would live or die on. It was very, very good training. Now you put a script down and London will find you some great pictures from Al Jazeera or from Fox or from someone else. Today you win by getting going live and getting your satellite up and getting yourself live on air. That's the first premise of this place. Forget the package – the package comes later. Get the pictures out and get yourself in front of the camera. And that's very rewarding but it's slightly different.'

The new technology has altered the relationship between the frontline correspondent and his or her news desk. Contact is now virtually instantaneous with a loss of autonomy for the journalist. Kate Adie (2002), for instance, observed that during the Balkan conflict in the 1990s, 'if we [correspondents] stuck to reporting the facts – the scenes we'd witnessed, the incidents we had verified – we managed to convey a limited but accurate picture of what was going on'. With satellite communications making the news desk able to contact field reporters on the spot, there came 'indications of a major shift' in practices. Adie explains:

'As we described how we'd spent four hours in a wet ditch being shot at in order to get vital evidence of ethnic cleansing . . . there'd be murmuring from London that we were at cross-purposes. Again and again there came the phrase "That's not the view from here. How we see it is . . ."' (Adie 2002, p. 8)

More positively, Peter Sharp explains how he used to receive 'feedback' from the news desk and beat the opposition:

'In the old days you'd be in some hotel in Africa and you'd go for dinner and, depending on the time difference, you'd go down to reception and you'd sit there, and the telex would chatter up around half ten, quarter to eleven London time, which could be two in the morning, your time. And then [it would] say something like, "Yeah, excellent package, ran story three, your scripts and pictures far superior to BBC. And these are your plans for tomorrow as we've discussed, you'll charter here and charter there." And I don't know why no-one else did this – I used to give three, five bucks or ten bucks to the receptionist and I'd just get copies of all the telexes that came in. They were delivered in the morning and I would look at them. And the BBC's comments to their packages were almost the same as ours, "Your script much better than Sharp's." But then I would have the advantage of looking at their whole day sheet. There was a lot of that in those days. I mean it was pretty cut-throat.'

Instead of 'herograms' delivered on ticker tape and faxes a few days or hours later, nowadays contact is immediate. As Jeremy Thompson remarks:

'We tend to have a laptop and it (herogram) comes on the top line, "good stuff". There are not many places where you can't be in instant contact with a satellite phone. I'm standing somewhere in the middle of nowhere with a satellite dish pointing at the sky and can have a normal conversation with people, so it's transformed really.'

New technology can make everything instant – 'the globalisation of pictures', as Chip Hires describes it. On occasions it can also make established freelance frontline correspondents redundant. Hires describes a scenario:

'When I used to go to Pakistan or Palestine or a Third World country, there were no local people taking pictures, or if they did, they did it for their local newspaper and they never went outside their local domain. Now they all have pretty good equipment. They have access to the Internet, they know the pictures. They all have been educated in what it takes to have a publishable picture in a Western magazine or a world magazine. In the old days, they would send someone like me to a godforsaken place, and we would take the pictures and send them back. Now they get a local guy to do it, and a local is doing it for the wire services particularly for Reuters or AP or ASP, and they have very good pictures. It's globalisation, and everyone talks about outsourcing. They don't have to pay me to fly to Timbuktu any more, because there's somebody in Timbuktu who lives there, who knows the story, who speaks the language, who has all the contacts. So except for really big stories now, you have a lot of local people doing it. Which is on the one hand good. Why should just Westerners take all the money and do all the stories and impose on somebody else? It's not good for my personal financial situation, professional situation, but it's certainly good for a Palestinian who used to make $50 a month if he was lucky, and now he can make $1,500 a month living in Gaza.'

The role of technology is also seen, particularly by news organisations, as a growing problem in the coverage of conflict and war. BBC journalist, Nik Gowing, has been ubiquitous in his warnings to news organisations and governments about the new dangers.

Today there is no escaping digital cameras – they are present at every trouble spot and capture every disaster. It is no longer just journalists who produce images and distribute them around the world. Nowadays many of the pictures that document events, such as the aeroplane attacks on the Twin Towers or terrorist bombings, are taken by private individuals. Modern gadgets such as laptops, mobile phones and radio telephones allow these images to be transmitted at lightning speed in 'real time' around the globe. This represents a huge challenge to governments. Crimes that contravene human rights laws and military attacks can hardly be kept secret anymore and this puts governments and the armed forces under enormous pressure. (http://www. britischebotschaft.de/en/news/events/nik_gowing.htm)

According to Gowing, the media's responsibilities have also changed. Today's high-speed technology means that decisions have to be made quickly. Television channels want to spread news as speedily as possible, but photographic and film material also has to be authenticated, as 'one mistake can destroy your credibility'. Forgers and terrorist organisations have also been making use of modern techniques for a long time to further their interests.

Notes

1   The rationale for broadcasters having an anchor on the spot is that it brings a different dimension to the story. It engages the viewer through a familiar face. The face that normally leads the viewer into the news is transferred to the scene of the major story. It takes the viewer into the story in a different way, making it more immediate. It also emphasises the importance of the news story.
2   At the time of the Falklands conflict 20 years ago, journalists related how they were told to go to Portsmouth immediately to board the Navy Task Force about to set sail for the Falklands. (See Morrison and Tumber 1988, ch. 1.)
3   John Carlin of the *Independent* and *El Pais* covered Argentina during the Falklands, the 'dirty war' there, then Central America during the especially bloody 1980s.
4   For work on the relationship between journalists and their sources, see Schlesinger and Tumber 1994.
5   Antonia Francis has covered Afghanistan, Nepal and Kashmir.
6   Marie Colvin covered the Middle East for ten years as Paris bureau chief for UPI. Amongst her assignments she has reported from the first Gulf War, East Timor, Chechnya, Kosovo and Bosnia.

7

WORKING RELATIONS

'If one of you was in trouble, we'd all, pretty much without exception, go and help – like when Terry [Lloyd] died, we all helped.' (Jeremy Thompson, *Sky News*)

Life on the Ground

Barbara Jones relates how the Afghanistan experience taught her how to manage in low-tech countries:

'You've got to take all your battery chargers – these are countries with no electricity. So now you've got to buy a generator or hire a generator and you're on the road. How the hell are you going to get power to your computers? We thought we might be camping out, but in fact we didn't have to camp out in Afghanistan because people were only too happy to rent us rooms – very basic places, a village home with virtually no sanitation or electricity and sleeping on a concrete floor. You couldn't get hot water unless someone boiled it over a fire and there's no sink or bath or shower. And if you were very lucky, maybe once or twice a week you'd get a bucket of hot water and a plastic container to pour it over yourself or wash your hair.'

For the frontline correspondents, reporting from a strange land, there are housekeeping duties that need to be completed. There is no such thing as an average day, but certain routines have to be followed: keeping themselves and their kit clean; maintaining electrical gear; checking into the office.

For women correspondents there are additional housekeeping problems as well as the need to prove their worth. Sara Oliver of the *Mail on Sunday* describes her time as an embedded journalist in Iraq:

'I was very lucky with the unit that I was sent to. Initially 16 Air Assault said they didn't want any women in their unit and the three women journalists who were embedded were all sent to 16 Air Assault. I think it was just a coincidence, but it gave us all a laugh at the time. And I know certainly that my unit were very nervous about the fact that they were having a woman and would it be a disruptive influence. But more importantly, would I be able to cope? I was physically very fit before I went out to the war and I had done my utmost to be familiar with all of my technology and I was determined to be as self-reliant as I could. More so because I was a girl.

One of the things that made quite a big difference psychologically was in the first few days that I was there I just walked into the shower blocks when I wanted a shower. They're not communal shower blocks, they all have their curtains, but there are a lot of men walking around naked or just dressed in their underpants. Not that I ever took off any more than my vest and shorts in front of anybody but just the fact that I was quite happy to walk into those wash blocks and get washed and go about my business, I think that surprised them all a bit. And then they felt, well, that's okay she's one of us, she's obviously not setting herself up as different, she's just saying I'm here to do my job and I'm going to go and do it as normally as I can.

And I participated a lot. I made it my business to get to know a lot of people, ranks as well as the officers, and I ate with them and sat down and talked with them in the evenings. And we all enjoyed St Patrick's Day together, which was great. It's like a sort of carnival day, even though that seems implausible. And I felt that I earned my stripes. I carried all my own equipment, I made it all work, I was quite happy living in rough conditions. And the day before we crossed the border we dug our own trenches, and I dug my own trench. It was horrible, but I did it. And I know that there was a lot of comment passed that particular day that on the one occasion when I could have sat back and said "Oh I can't possibly, it's too much for me," I got stuck in and I did my best. And my best was not found wanting, and I know that stood me in very good stead.'

Conditions can be very unpleasant for the frontline journalist and their resourcefulness can be tested to the limit at times. Barbara Jones worked as a unilateral in Iraq. She describes making camp with her colleagues in a disused airfield, having first had to justify their presence to the British Army who wanted to escort them back to Kuwait:

'We found this airfield with all these abandoned guns and tanks and stuff all over the place and litter – and these dreadful stray dogs, packs of dogs barking all night. We had little camping stoves that we all brought in from Kuwait. We had rice. We used to boil the water and then make tea with some of it and then boil the rice and cook. Of course we all got sick in the end. There were sand-storms, sand in everything and flies in everything, and these wretched dogs being around. I used to buy eggs because I find . . . it doesn't matter how poor the place is, everyone's got chickens because they're a good source of nourishment. I would hard boil eggs in the water [and] you've still got the water for your tea. You've got eggs which are clean . . . and you can carry them easily during the day, just peel them and eat them and you've got nutrition.

Of course there's nowhere to wash. We brought jerry cans with water in and petrol – you couldn't get petrol anywhere, so we tied all these jerry cans on the top of the jeep. And in fact on the third day of the war I came across this terrible situation where the ITN correspondent, Terry Lloyd, had been . . . caught in the crossfire and they'd shot the jerry cans on the top of his car and the whole thing had gone up in flames. So there's a risk involved in carrying petrol around with you. There were no bathroom facilities whatsoever, so you just went off into the desert. That was miserable. It's harder for women because you had to plan when and where you'd go to the bathroom and hope that no one else was there. I hate that sort of thing. I'm not very good at that. And we had wet wipes, you know, those wet wipes that you use for babies?'

All the women reporters mentioned wipes as an important household item. Jones describes the morning routine:

'They [wipes] were the best things of all because you wake up in the morning in your sleeping bag in the back of the jeep and you can wash yourself all over with wet wipes. And now you feel more or less human, and you can get some water and clean your teeth outside and then you can prop up a little mirror and you can put some make up on and now you're ready to go.'

Judith Matloff (2005) argues that 'the challenges confronting women are often overlooked because they're embarrassing – like menstruation and sexual harassment. Or they're inconvenient; after all, it's expensive to order a special flak jacket for the one girl on the team, or to pay for special training'.

Resourcefulness is a common characteristic of the frontline journalist and the experienced ones know how to scavenge. Brian Williams, a Reuters correspondent, describes obtaining food in Afghanistan, a country he had visited four or five times:

'I arrived there and we had a number of people in a Reuters house and most of them were saying, "Oh it's awful here, we can only get tinned food and blah-blah-blah," and I said, "I know Afghanistan has markets, has anybody been down to the market?" And they hadn't. I said, "Well listen. I'm going to go down to the market and I'll bring us all back food." And I went down the market. There's lots and lots of different food if you've got money in Afghanistan . . . and then everybody got the idea that you go to a local market. It's very important that you try to eat and live like the locals, because at the end of the day, that kind of taste of a country comes through that. It's always been one of the enjoyable things of not so much covering a war, but being in dangerous type places and hunting and scavenging, finding new customs, new food, new ways of doing things.'

Age though can catch up with the frontline reporter. Tim Lambon thinks he is near the end of the road:

'You do have to be in good physical shape, and I think that I'm coming to the end of my wars. I'm 45 now and everything's starting to give up. . . . I know that I am not in top physical shape anymore. My knees are suffering from arthritis and all sorts of problems. I just can't get up and down so easily anymore. And that's purely a matter of age, and also having abused my body for so long doing all this shit.'

Every situation and location is different of course. Typically, during the conflict in the Balkans journalists stayed either in a hotel or in a house that had been hired from the locals. In Priština and Kosovo, journalists stayed at the Grand Hotel, which, according to Bill Neely of ITN, was anything but grand. Whilst in Kigali and in Haiti, Neely and fellow journalists stayed at very good hotels and would then drive 40 minutes to the war zone. As he explained:

> 'You spend time in dreadful situations and then you drive back to your five star hotels. And then last year I was embedded with this military unit and that literally meant digging trenches at night in the ground to sleep in, doing exactly what the Marines would do. As there weren't any hotels, there was no running water. You know you crap in the desert just like the rest of the Marines. So it just completely varies.'

Jonathan Steele of the *Guardian* describes some of his time in South America as 'commuting to the frontline':

> 'You could leave your hotel in San Salvador – which was a first class hotel, with a swimming pool, pleasant living conditions – rent a taxi, drive past the government lines and road blocks. They might or might not tell you that it is dangerous to go ahead because the guerrillas are there or the Muchachos or the terrorists or whatever they wanted to call them, and you would just say "All right, we don't expect you to take responsibility, we're journalists, we'll take the risk ourselves." And you would drive forward and then you would talk to the guerrillas. You would spend a few hours with them and come back and then you might talk to the soldiers at the roadblocks or ask to speak to an officer in the headquarters for an hour or two. And then you would go back to your hotel and write up your story and relax over a drink with your colleagues in the bar.
>   But, as I said, there was this hard thing where you were almost commuting to the frontline, through various checkpoints, talking to both sides of the war, getting the sort of impression of what was happening and then reporting it in a way that none of the combatants could do themselves, so you had a privileged position; you could talk to both sides and they could only talk to one side.'

In Sarajevo, journalists staying at the Holiday Inn experienced a rather bizarre scenario in which the hotel's windows were blown out, there was no electricity or running water, but then at dinner time all the waiters would put on black ties and serve what little food was available. It was, as Lin Hilton, photojournalist, remarked 'very surreal'.

Perhaps the biggest contrast in location, which has an important bearing on the type of news reported, is the difference between those correspondents based for most of the time in a hotel and those on the road. The competitive pressures faced by 24-hour news organisations have led to a new type of television reporter nicknamed 'roof monkey'. Bill Neely of ITN expresses concern at these new phenomena and warns of the dangers:

> 'You have your hotel and up on the top you have your satellite dishes and cameras, and you have your journalist in front of the camera and they're just there all day long, talking to the camera – "And now we can go back to

Baghdad live and talk to our correspondent. What's happening there now?" And the correspondent will say, "Well, what's happening in Baghdad, is this . . ." But they haven't left the roof. They're just getting their information from other people. That's surreal. We have to be very very careful with that kind of thing because it can be a real danger. You're just feeding a beast that's all-consuming, that wants instant information, instant judgements – what happened, how did it happen. It often takes a very long time to work out how something happened. But there you are, on the roof, [and] you've got to give answers. You can't keep saying, "Well, frankly, I don't know," otherwise you'd be out of a job.'

Neely argues that there has to be a place for the journalism of discovery and discovery takes time:

'It's taking more and more time as the methods of propagandising grow, as propaganda becomes more slick and clever, as governments are aware of how information can be held back. You know it takes a lot of time to work on good, solid factual scoops. But there's a place for both. Organisations just have to be aware that, as well as the roof monkey, there is the guy on the ground ferreting away to get the story.'

The large news organisations can afford to do both. But for the so-called 'ferret', life can be tough. Ben Brown of the BBC spent time with the Mujahideen in Afghanistan at the time when they were fighting the Russians. Brown would keep fit through jogging, but nothing prepared him for his trek of six weeks as he walked from Pakistan into Afghanistan through the mountains and desert:

'We were doing 12 hours a day and I was absolutely out on my feet. We'd start in the early hours of the morning, partly in the dark, and we'd go till dusk. And then we'd stop for a couple hours in the day because the sun was so hot.'

Brown drank mainly black tea with lots of sugar for energy:

'I was absolutely shattered because it was so hard, the walking, because you're on mountains all the time and hard, hard walking. It's not a job you want. I actually drove myself to the point where I was collapsing almost. The last few miles when you come across the desert after 12 hours, I would collapse. I could only go ten paces and then I had to stop, then another ten. And I was ahead of everybody, with the outrider, and he just kept going and he'd say stay, stay and I was determined to finish it. I can't believe now that I could only walk ten paces, I was so tired. I was just trying to make it through.'

The roof monkey scenario could also reveal cultural antagonisms and rifts between reporters who head out into the field and those whom Chris Hedges (2002, p. 143) disparagingly calls 'hotel-room warriors'. Freelancer Antonia Francis is particularly critical of the situation she experienced in Kabul:

'The whole scene in Kabul was completely ridiculous. You had the Continental Hotel, one floor with the new government which was Northern Alliance members, all of whom I knew from when I was living in north Afghanistan. And all the journalists or the major corporation journalists – BBC, *The Times, Telegraph* – were on the second floor and they didn't go out. They just exchanged between them. . . . I just didn't see any evidence that they went outside or knew the history of these people, which scared me enormously. But I was forced into exactly the same mechanism because I had to get back to do a satellite feed and every three hours we were on the roof and I didn't like that kind of journalism at all.'

Despite the friendships developed in adversity, Francis feels an outsider:

'You have comradeship, and you have lots of silly jokes and lots of people who say "Ah, the last time I saw you was in Baghdad or in Beirut or blah-blah-blah." And there's a real community there. But it's a community that really does not interest me. It's bragging and it's a club for people who need to be members of a club rather than going out and doing the story properly. I don't like to participate.'

Francis believes that freelancers often have more knowledge of an area and that is where they make their mark: 'It's the freelance cameraman and the freelance photojournalist who know the story better than anybody else.'

Mark Pedelty (1995) offers confirmation of this in his study of foreign correspondents in Central America during a period of bloody internecine war. Pedelty adds that antagonism between staff journalists ('the A-team') and freelancers/stringers ('the B-team') – who are often local correspondents hired on contingent terms – needs to be understood in a wider context (p. 78). Thus, as costs rise, so news organisations may come to rely increasingly on freelancers for material, reserving full-timers for the big news occasions, thereby minimising expenditure. While it may be cheaper and more efficacious for the organisation to hire 'B-team players' for detailed and ongoing news, there are occasions on which newsworthiness deems that the 'A-team' needs to be 'parachuted' in. The BBC's Ben Brown concedes that: 'We big foot their local correspondent . . . it's the way it works.' But it also exacerbates tension between the 'big footer' and other correspondents who, he adds, 'don't like it' when they are supplanted as newsmakers.

Though it is commonplace for all correspondents to complain about restrictions placed upon them – since all insist upon independence and autonomy to do their job properly – we ought not to ignore these internal differences. Freelancers and staffers have different locations, the former having poorer resources and being less trusted by news organisations than the latter who, if better supported, are usually caught in stricter administrative controls (Pedelty 1995, p. 76). One may gauge these tensions between correspondents from the different language that is invoked. Employment status, for example, is at once identified and evaluated in separate vocabularies. Thus staffers may refer to freelancers as 'part-timers' and retain the title 'correspondents' for themselves, while freelancers and stringers prefer to refer to themselves as 'independents'.

Frontline correspondents generally work in teams and the relationships within those teams are an essential ingredient for a successful working life. Jeremy Thompson of *Sky News* stresses the importance of good working relationships:

'You end up being very close in small teams, in tight teams. It's important that you get on well together, so I've always tried to make sure that they're teams that work. And particularly when I've had bureaux, I've made sure that I've been able, where possible, to pick the right people and weed out those who haven't really worked – just the chemistry of a small team. In Africa for four years really it was just me and my cameraman a lot of the time – just the two of us – and round Asia it was just three of us.'

For broadcasters especially, team working is essential. The BBC's Orla Guerin describes her consensual method of working:

'If I'm going to go somewhere, I will discuss it with the producer that I'm work-ing with, and I'll discuss it with the cameraman or camerawoman, and we make a team decision – Do we want to go there? What's the level of risk? What's the latest information we have? Do we think the road is safe? And, if we're all happy, then we go off and we do it. It's not a case of me simply decid-ing on my own that I'm going to go, because if I'm taking a risk, other people are involved in it as well, so they also have a say.

Over the years, you develop a habit of relying on instinct, and other people's instinct is as powerful as your own, and if somebody has a very bad feeling or is very unhappy about doing something, then I won't do it. I'm not going to drag somebody against their will. Most of the time, I'm working with camera-men or camerawomen who have been doing this at least as long as I have, and in some cases for a lot longer. You reach a joint decision and it's based on consensus. And you review that all the time.'

However, circumstances of conflict can mean a reporter having to work with unfamiliar colleagues. Peter Sharp, Thompson's colleague at Sky, describes his experience during the second Gulf War:

'My role was based in Northern Iraq, and the team was going to be me, a pro-ducer, and a cameraman/editor who could do both. That was three of us. And we also had, attached to us, a sort of maverick team, which was an ex-SAS guy – who was just learning to shoot cameras not guns – and an inexperi-enced but keen editor/cameraman. And we were supposed to go into the north of Iraq, which was then going to be a very busy area of operations. We got separated – one of these horrible logistic tangles. And we never got together for the rest of the war. So now I found myself with two people I didn't know, who'd never worked with Sky, and who had very limited experience.'

Sharp found himself in Northern Iraq for well over two and half months with two people who knew nothing about the way Sky operated. It was a frustrating experience, but Sharp relates how he really admired the members of his new team and how they worked their way into 'a really, really good unit'.

But why can't the system be flexible enough to enable experienced journalists to choose for themselves the people they work with? Sharp provides the answer:

> 'It wouldn't work, because you'd be wanting to work with all the best people and the crews would be wanting to work with the best correspondents. They tried it once here and it didn't work. Of course, if you're running a bureau, you've got your team and that's it. But you do find that on the trips you go on, you tend to get people that have been on those sorts of trips and are good at them and can cope with them. Because there's a lot of coping to do. It's not just the journalists. You've got the producer who's doing the day-to-day, hour-by-hour, contact with London and saying, "Look, they want you to do this, they want you to do that". And then you've got the correspondent, who's up in front of the camera writing the scripts, the editor who's packaging them, editing the stuff, the cameraman and then at least two dish engineers, who are running this huge dish. Now that's our little unit.'

The difficulties experienced – lack of sleep, lack of food, dehydration – are considerable and wearing. Adrian Monck recalls:

> 'People [can be] very stressed. They're hard worked. There's no relaxing in these places very often . . . you can't even have a hot bath. You're in the same clothes and you smell, and it's not very comfortable. You've been like that for a few weeks, and everyone gets on each other's nerves.'

Such circumstances ensure that any tensions within the team are heightened. Peter Sharp relates his experience of a toothache in Northern Sudan:

> 'It was the worst thing that ever happened to me. I was with Nigel, the crazy cameraman, and with Richard Dowden, and I was in a lot of pain. And Nigel was a very uncaring cameraman – a very good cameraman but very uncaring. And Richard was a lovely man. I was lying on a deserted, shot-up radio station in agony. And I could hear them get up in the morning, and Richard said to Nigel, "I'm really worried about Sharpie, he was moaning through the night". And Nigel goes "Bollocks!". I found this aid organisation down the road and they hit me with cortisone and within a nano-second it had gone. It was amazing, it was just gone. And I had to sleep. I hadn't slept for days. And then I woke up and it had come back – it was a big root canal problem. And I had to fly out. I just got a charter out and had to go home. There's no way you can just cope with something like that.'

Competition and Co-operation

Camaraderie is a strong feature of the frontline correspondent's life. Practically all the journalists to whom we spoke told of the friendships built up over the years. Many retold tales of co-operation, particularly when the logistics and location were dangerous and difficult.

For Julian Manyon, camaraderie is 'one of the attractive features of the job' and it's a camaraderie that 'crosses national boundaries very strongly'. Many other journalists echoed this sentiment. Kim Willsher evokes the spirit evident in the group:

'There's less rivalry out in a conflict and more *esprit de corps* because you're all in the same dangerous situation. We would share cars, we would share hotel rooms. You turn up somewhere and there'd be two hotel rooms left and everyone would just kip down together, on the floor, and somebody would say, "Oh don't worry, you can come and sleep on my floor." Everyone is reduced to an equal and there wasn't tension between males or females at all.'

David Zucchino confirms this view:

'I've really been surprised at how well men and women work together. There's a lot of respect for women by the male correspondents. We're long, long past the days where they're seen as competitors or interlopers. Everyone just accepts any correspondent who's there, whether they're a man or a woman. People understand the risks they're taking and there's a lot of mutual respect.'

Jane Kokan describes how fellow journalists become 'your brothers and sisters':

'You're all in the same boat. Someone's missed the birth of their daughter or son, or someone's relationship is collapsing, or somebody could be going through difficult times and we're all going through difficult times on certain levels. We all don't necessarily want to be there when they're bombing the shit out of the city. The number of times I've been huddled up in basements or behind the wheel of a lorry going: "This is so stupid, I do not want to die this way." It's a weird thing to experience.'

Tim Lambon compares the journalists' relationship with one another to that of the military:

'There is a community that goes round the world. We all meet up in these bloody horrible places. The hard core of that community were the people who stayed behind in Baghdad during the war [in 2003]. We all know each other and we all love each other and we all help each other. But we hardly see each other when we come back. That happens with soldiers as well. In the military you will live, eat and sleep with somebody for months at a time, lay your life on the line for them and bleed for them. But when you get back into Civvy Street, you hardly ever see them again.'

Lambon's partner, Lindsey Hilsum, recalls support she received from fellow journalists when Lambon was arrested:

'Friendships amongst correspondents in the field are very different from other friendships in your life. People who I see when I'm in Baghdad may live in

London but I won't necessarily see them when I'm in London. I don't actually want to see them when I'm in London – that's another life. But when you get back out there again, they are your best friends and they're the ones who look after you. And when things go wrong, for example, my partner was arrested and we thought he might end up spending years in prison in Liberia. The people who helped me cope and tried to help to get him out were all my friends who had been war correspondents, who'd been in vile places like Liberia, so the moment when things go really wrong, they're there.'

Jeremy Thompson also talks about respect for each other:

'If one of you was in trouble, we'd all, pretty much without exception, go and help – like when Terry [Lloyd] died, we all helped. I went off to try and get to the Red Crescent inside Basra to go and look for bodies and hospitals. We all pulled together and everybody did what they could to try and find out what had happened. That happens, time after time.'

The more dangerous the location, the more the competitive edge tends to dissipate. In Bosnia, for example, a voluntary pool system was introduced in Sarajevo involving the broadcasters. It was organised to prevent risk and spread resources through preventing crews from rival news organisations venturing out to film the same action.

Nonetheless, the fact that reporters are competing with one another, even in circumstances that all find trying, should not be forgotten. As Dan Edge says, 'intense camaraderie between journalists . . . can flip at a moment's notice into intense competition'. Accordingly, there is a delicate balance between competition and safety. Jonathan Steele explains:

'You get very complex issues of working as an individual or working with colleagues. Everybody wants to have a scoop; that means not telling your colleagues what you're doing. On the other hand, you don't want to be taking unnecessary risks. The trouble is that you need to tell colleagues that you are going to go somewhere and that, if they haven't heard from you by a certain time, they should sound the alarm or check whether you've got back to the hotel, or just forgotten to tell them. You have to share this information. This issue of what you tell your colleagues and what you don't tell them is very complex; it depends on the story, it depends on your relationship with the other papers, it depends on who you are as a personality. Some people are tighter with information than others. Some people are more competitive than others.'

Caroline Wyatt also stresses that camaraderie and competition are intertwined. Checking up on the whereabouts of other journalists has both a safety and competitive dimension. Conditions make a difference to the degree of competition. According to Wyatt, it is much harder to be competitive when embedded with the military because of the difficulties of gaining an exclusive. Since the journalists are in the same situation, they tend to work against the common enemy by putting concerted pressure on the military authorities to provide access and information.

Although willing to accept help from others on assignment, there is a line that James Meek is unwilling to cross:

'The spirit of co-operation is stronger than the spirit of competition. Generally speaking, people are astonishingly helpful. What often happens is that people will give other people quotes. It's quite a tricky area. There was a time in Afghanistan when I was out all day, riding the roads, and somebody went to an interview with a minister and he gave me a copy of what the minister said, which was very helpful. I felt that it was all right to use those quotes . . . I included some of the quotes in my story because it was straightforward.

But there was another time when I was in a village in Uzbekistan and the next village, a few miles away, was under siege by the Russians because there were Chechen hostage-takers in the village. They'd taken a hell of a lot of people hostage and the Russians wanted to try to keep them there, capture them or kill them. That seizure went on for several days and I stayed in this village. One day other correspondents left the village and went to interview people from a hospital who had been involved in an earlier incident with these Chechens. They came back and had some quite good quotes and they offered to give me these quotes. But I didn't want them because I felt it was too much using another reporter's work. They'd spent the time, they had the enterprise, they'd gone to that place, and I hadn't done any of those things – I had stayed in the village and done other things. I just felt it wouldn't be right to make a story out of somebody else's work unless I was going to present it as theirs, and I couldn't because they were from a rival newspaper.'

If there are decisions to be made about receiving assistance, what are the parameters of providing help? There appear to be no absolute guiding principles. It seems rather that the character and degree of co-operation are negotiated in contexts, influenced by particular personalities, the resilience of previous relationships, and the specifics of circumstances encountered, all overlain by loose ethical considerations. John Simpson (2002, p. 53) adds that newspaper and television journalists differ in that 'newspaper journalism is a collaborative business, and most writers tend to hunt in packs', whereas television journalists 'travel around in small groups . . . so have no great need of company', thereby encouraging more competition and non-cooperation with other news outfits than is found amongst print journalists 'who tend to collect together in groups in the field'. Be that as it may, television correspondent John Irvine of ITN still endeavours to set some boundaries:

'There are things that it's fair to co-operate on. If, for example, you're filming the same thing and the BBC cameraman was with you and his tape broke and he needed to borrow a tape from your cameraman, it would be fair and reasonable to give it to him. Or if he'd been filming exactly the same thing and his pictures were faulty and he was having a problem, I would be honour bound to say yes, because the guy had gone through all the risks that I'd gone through to get the same story. The fact that he wasn't going to get the pictures out of his camera had nothing to do with his lack of endeavour. So I think I'd be honour bound to help him out. But if I went back to base and he hadn't bothered to go out and try to do any of the filming and he asked me for any of the pictures, of course I'd say no.'

Jeremy Thompson of *Sky News* describes an incident during the liberation of Kuwait in 1991 when he helped out a rival journalist from the BBC. They had known each other long before when they were rivals in Asia. Brian Barron was the BBC's correspondent and Thompson was ITN's new Asia correspondent.

'When I first arrived in Hong Kong we had a very civilised lunch and he said "Oh this is wonderful, welcome". He hadn't had a rival correspondent. "This will raise the profile for us both, the desks will take more notice of Asia, terrific." And then we didn't really talk for the next three years, just tried to stitch each other up.
  Years later, the day after the liberation of Kuwait in '91, I went up for the first look-see up the road, north out of Iraq, and found the bombed-out convoy of Mutla Ridge, got the first pictures of it, and thought I'd push on up to see if there were any more retreating Iraqi troops. And we saw oil wells on fire, mayhem everywhere. And we got up to the border – me, my cameraman and Robert Fisk, who I'd given a ride to – and there, standing in the middle of nowhere, was this very forlorn figure of Brian Barron and his cameraman Eric Barry whom I've known for years.
  Brian's . . . a hundred yards over there and they're just standing there by the vehicle looking a bit sorry for themselves. And eventually Brian sends Eric across to say, "Just wondered if you might do us a favour JT because we went up to try and film the Iraqis on the border there and they came out and arrested us and took our camera off us, so we haven't got a camera. Brian's wondering whether your cameraman might lend us your camera and a tape so that we could at least do a stand-up of Brian . . . on the border." So I said, "What do you reckon guys?" and they said "Well, it's up to you mate." And so I said, "All right Eric, tell Brian that I know he wouldn't do this for me, but I'm going to do it for him." And so we did and then we left Baghdad as fast as we could and got our story on air an hour before he did, which was great. They were the first pictures of the convoy on Mutla Ridge.'

Some journalists who have shared experiences, particularly dangerous ones, get together annually for a reunion. Jon Swain, for example, meets up for lunch with ex colleagues from Vietnam on or around 30 April every year, the anniversary of the fall of Saigon.

'I suppose it's like veterans from D-Day . . . We end up telling the same old stories every year. I think it's quite important actually. And next year [2005] is going to be the 30th anniversary of the fall of Saigon and the fall of Cambodia. I suppose quite a lot of people who were around will go back to Saigon and we'll have some sort of gathering there.'

If the relationship between correspondents reveals aspects of both co-operation and competition, how do these frontline journalists interact with their news desks?

Relations with the News Desk

What journalism lacks in term of formal rules and procedures, it gains through the claim to professional autonomy (Pedelty 1995, p. 89). All practitioners can readily produce a roll-call of correspondents they look up to because they 'told it straight', whatever constraints imposed by the powers that be. Journalists place a premium on their capacity to control their own work, to determine who to see and what to say about issues and events. In conditions of war, however, autonomy and independence are put under especially intense pressure, notably from government and military forces. Frontline correspondents are mindful of these pressures, though they tend to attribute impediments to their independence to their more immediate managers and sources. Hence it comes as no surprise that frontline correspondents are preoccupied with their relationship with their editors. More commercial, security or political forces that may dictate restrictions and compromise professional autonomy become personified as flaws in the character of specific editors (McLaughlin 2002, pp. 17–18).

Some frontline correspondents believe their editors back home have no idea what it is like at the front. David Williams, for instance, of the *Daily Mail* refers to 'crazy requests' he receives from London:

'They have no comprehension of what it's like on the road and they will ask for something which is just not a priority or is far too dangerous to try. Just maybe crossing a city – "Can you go and do something on the other side of Sarajevo?". It would be impossible. And you get a lot of very naïve requests from a lot of very naïve executives. But they're often given a request from the editor or somebody else, so they have to pass it on.'

But while needing autonomy, the frontline correspondent is also very grateful for the support from back home, be it in the form of equipment, money or escape from the front. Barbara Jones describes an aspect of her relationship with her employer:

'The last time I went back to Iraq there were a lot of hostages being taken. So I asked for a flak jacket and helmet and they sent them without a murmur. There wasn't time for them to send me the flak jacket before I went, so they sent another reporter with the flak jacket to meet up with me in Jordan. And if I called them at any time and said "I can't stand any more of this", they would fly me out straightaway.'

When a journalist is working under considerable pressure in a hostile environment, it is often the little messages of support that can make a difference. Sara Oliver says that her paper, the *Mail on Sunday,* was 'touchingly supportive', to the extent of sending lots of little gifts, such as sweets, magazines and wet wipes, while keeping her stocked with note pads and pens. Everything that she might require they did their best to send out. Her editor spoke to her at least once a week and sometimes a couple of times a week, which she found incredibly encouraging: 'Any reporter will tell you that they take a personal phone call from an editor very seriously. If he takes the time to speak to you, and to praise you or to thank you, it is very reassuring.'

Barbara Jones, a colleague of Oliver, is full of praise for the news desk:

> 'I did get brilliant support during the war in Iraq. Every week when I sent maybe two or three stories, I would get an email from them, which made it all worthwhile. Just before you settle into your sleeping bag to another night of tanks roaring past, and you check your email, there would be the email from my news desk saying "It's so well done and very nicely written" or "Brilliant story and, we're all thinking of you". So you know from your newspaper that they're pleased.'

This sort of psychological, as well as material, support for the reporter on the ground is obviously important and we discuss this further in Chapter 11.

An advantage of being in a war zone is that when the correspondent calls home, the news organisation will invariably drop whatever else it is doing and talk to its reporter. As James Meek remarks: 'It makes you feel important.' Relationships here are based on a series of negotiations. To frontline reporters, the priority is their judgement on the ground, against which may be what they feel are unrealistic requests of the news desk.

Jonathan Steele uses the case of Iraq to describe the negotiating process, a scenario related by many of the journalists to whom we spoke:

> 'There is constant communication with the desk about what one's plans are. If it's a quiet period, the desk may say, "Look, what about going down to Basra, we haven't had anything from Basra for two or three months." So, you would then respond to that and say, "Yes I think that's a good idea, there's nothing very much happening in Baghdad at the moment, it looks fairly quiet, I can't foresee any important events coming up, there aren't any big political meetings or anything special, so I'm going to go down to Basra for three days."
>
> On a more day-to-day basis, if there's a bomb in a city like Baqubah, they may say, "You ought to go and see what's happening about this bomb." And you might say, "Well, I don't think it's particularly important – it doesn't seem very different from the bombs we've had in other cities. It would take me an hour and a half to get there and an hour and a half to come back, that's nearly three hours. Could be a little bit risky – I'm not sure we're going to get enough out of it to justify it."
>
> But one's got to take into account the time difference; Baghdad is three hours ahead of London and many of these bombs go off in the morning. So, in practice, we take the decision before London's even got up. If I'm sitting in Baghdad at 9 o'clock in the morning and I hear that there's been a huge explosion in Baqubah, I will really decide, on my own, whether it's worth going there because it is still only 6 o'clock in London. I can't ring up my editor at 6 o'clock and wake her up and say, "Look, I was thinking of going to Baqubah,

do you think I should or not?" So I just have to make a decision and then luckily with our telephones I can phone at about 8.30 London time, which is 11.30 in Iraq and say, "I'm actually in Baqubah now because there was a huge bomb, probably two hours ago, and I decided to come up here. I'm on the scene and I'll be back in Baghdad later this evening and I'll send the story from there." Or I may even ring and say, "Look, you'll see on the wires, there's been a big bomb in Baqubah. I decided not to go because it seems very dangerous, it's not worth going, so I'm going to write it up in Baghdad." They basically have to accept my decision. Sometimes the logistics in certain time zones mean that the reporter has to decide in a vacuum.'

Kim Willsher of the *Mail on Sunday* describes her fight with one editor whilst she was on assignment in Bosnia:

'I had good and bad times with all of my editors. I had one editor who I had phoned on a BBC satellite phone in the middle of a field in Bosnia, which was being shelled, and I had spent a week with some British forces. I was the only reporter, with a colleague. We were the only team to have managed to do this – persuaded the British Army to take us, like a fly on the wall. We were so pleased at what we'd done. When people were asking questions about what the British troops were actually doing there, we felt that what we had done answered that question.

I called the editor on the satellite phone and he said to me, "I want you to write a piece on why this war isn't worth the life of one single British soldier." And I said "I'm very sorry but I can't do that." And he said, "What do you mean you can't do that?" And I said, "Well I don't agree, on that particular assignment." I'd spent one week with these soldiers, and I said to him, "They don't think that either, they think they're doing a worthy job and they feel it's right for them to be here and I'm sorry but I can't write that." And he said to me, "Could I write it?" And I remember saying, "Well, you're the editor, you can write whatever you like." And he said, "Can I write it and put your name on it because you're there?" And I said, "No, you can't because I don't agree with it – I don't agree with what you've just said." And remember this is all taking place with shells clattering down all over the place. And he slammed the phone down on me and he turned to the back bench and he said, "Bloody Willsher's gone native." I was in very bad odour with him for some time afterwards. I laugh and joke and say that I came back to London and I was on picture caption duty for the next few months. That's a slight exaggeration but I was certainly in bad odour with him. This was until we sorted it out.

It didn't stop me being sent again and it didn't stop me reporting it in a way that I felt it should be reported. And what was gratifying about this particular incident was that I got a letter signed by many of my colleagues – reporters who were there who heard about what had happened – and also by Army people who were there at the time, which says "Kim, we'd just like to thank you. There are a lot of misconceptions about this war in the UK, and a lot of people are asking what it's all about and why we are there. And there is a lot of misinformation. We'd just like to thank you for not adding to this, and for not doing what you were asked to do when you didn't believe in it." And I was very gratified by that.'

Recriminations or postmortems usually occur only after the frontline correspondent has left the conflict zone and returned home.

Most of the journalists to whom we spoke work for UK-based news organisations. The difference in autonomy for US-based reporters compared with that of their British counterparts was something remarked upon disdainfully by a number of British journalists. Julian Manyon clarifies the distinction:

> 'Increasingly, news is driven from the centre in the sense of actual story choice, but they then allow one considerable latitude and liberty to go and achieve that target by whatever means one so desires. So you do get considerable latitude in the way the story is constructed and the script. We don't have this rather disgraceful American television practice for script approval, by which the correspondent in the field has to email his script before it's recorded and it's then changed and sent back to him, effectively censored, and he then records it.'

Tim Lambon thinks it is outrageous that companies like ABC, CBS and CNN can hire somebody to go to a place and then not trust what they say:

> 'Nobody back in London would dare to say either to myself or Lindsey [Hilsum] what they thought we should be reporting. However, if they sent out somebody much younger or somebody with less experience, I'm sure that they would do. Just about all the American networks have what they call script approval, where the correspondent will go out and do the story but before they are allowed to voice the pictures and send the cut package back to Atlanta or New York or wherever, they will have to get approval for their script, and script approval is supposedly to make sure that their style is the house style. But I used to work for ABC and have been in Sarajevo and a lot of the time it wasn't anything to do with house style, it was to do with politics and with people wanting to have their say and put their stamp on it, even when they didn't know what the hell was going on in the place that they were commenting on.'

However, for the UK journalist, competitive pressures experienced by the news desk can sometimes override autonomy. Anton Antonowicz relates the one occasion whilst he was in Baghdad during 2003 where his office requested that he follow up a particular story:

> 'It was a Reuters picture of the little boy who lost his arms in Baghdad – Ali, the little fellow. He was very badly burned. I was very reluctant to do that story, simply because I hadn't seen the photograph. So the first time that I saw him was lying in the hospital bed, and this was a couple of hours after that picture was released. It was to me that that original quote was given by the doctor – "Why have you come to see Ali? We have hundreds of Alis" – with which one could only agree. There were many Alis in that hospital and in other hospitals around Baghdad by that time. It was awful to see this pathetic situation and luckily, as we know, he eventually survived. Trying to do something for him seemed to me more a priority than actually doing the story. We had a hundred Alis, but that picture became iconic, it was the lasting symbol, the lasting

image of that particular war. And no matter how much one might denigrate that in terms of what journalism means in the end, it means one single child in the middle of so many people who died. We have to say, well, okay, if that's the way people respond, then one has to satisfy that need of people – that, they're not interested in the others. They can only focus on one. And in the end you can't blame people for that.'

The human interest story is essential to how journalism views its readers, listeners and viewers and for the frontline correspondent especially it is a key motivator. As Antonowicz says:

'So Ali wasn't just Ali. Ali was a symbol, and that's the way in which these things happen. It's the same when you're writing a story. You don't say, "Thousands of bodies littered the battlefield last night." That doesn't mean anything. What you do is write maybe about a single drop of blood on an envelope, and almost like Hitchcock would, you then draw the camera back from that, further and further back. That way you have a lasting image, which will register with them. I wouldn't say it's a technique – it's story telling really, isn't it? It's just a way of conveying information in the most vivid manner.'

The final important relationship for the frontline correspondent is the one experienced with fixers and translators who are employed to assist in covering assignments. In the next chapter we explore these interactions.

8

FIXERS AND TRANSLATORS

> The most important member of any TV team in an unfamiliar war zone . . . is not the reporter or cameraman or producer or videotape editor, but the local contact with reality. To call these people interpreters is to undervalue them.
> (Martin Bell 1995, p. 85)

Frontline correspondents work with local translators, drivers, guides and journalists, who are often collectively known as fixers. These may be hired ostensibly for a certain purpose, but what is most desired is an amalgam of skills and abilities, high amongst which are enterprise, reliability and quick-wittedness. Thus somebody might be taken on as a driver, but their capacity to negotiate safe passage through paramilitary roadblocks is valued much more highly than their technical skill. Someone else may be employed to provide food, but might become a vital go-between because of his local connections.

Similarly, Suzanne Goldenberg emphasises that 'a good translator is crucial', but then she adds that 'the quality of their English is not as important as their ability to navigate through tricky situations, or their willingness to share their background knowledge and views on a situation'. Maggie O'Kane underlines the versatility of the 'best fixers [who] are the smart boys, the wide boys, the Del Boys . . . who need to talk, need to fix . . . who know how to get the black market petrol and how to get your electricity on'. They may be a 'bit crooked', but 'they know how to exist in a lot of different areas', and for this they are invaluable to the frontline correspondent.

Fixers are key personnel for news organisations because they can determine the difference between successful and unsuccessful coverage. Relationships between the frontline correspondent and the local fixer/translator/guide are often fraught with difficulties and dilemmas, and there is little research conducted about these people. But they are of inestimable and undoubted value to the work of conflict reporting.

Lindsey Hilsum claims that no foreign correspondent would do any work at all without translators, fixers and drivers: 'They are THE most important people.' John Sweeney too is effusive in his praise for the relationship:

> 'It's almost one of love. They are generally fantastic people whom I adore and I will pay them ludicrous amounts of money. I always try to give them more

than the going rate because they take terrible risks. I think they're fantastic . . . They're our eyes and ears. We don't pay them enough, we betray them too much and we leave them with terrible moral predicaments. You have this strange relationship. You fall in with these people, you look after them. They're desperately important to you for two weeks and then you forget them and then they go away.'

How are they recruited? Barbara Jones recalls her experiences in Afghanistan:

'We all flew in, it was all chaos. People went from London through Russia into Turkmenistan. It was a hellish, ghastly hotel and a lot of people got sick with dysentery. There was no clean water, the food was disgusting. There were thousands of journalists all converging in these hotels, which soon ran out of rooms. So we were all sleeping in the lobby. I had a room that had no water and no heating and I was really ill.

Every day we would go up to the Northern Alliance's office to try to find out when they would fly us in and of course they were charging us a lot of money and putting on these ancient troop carriers, these helicopters. And you would turn up and then you would stay there all day and then they would say, "No we haven't got any room". And then eventually on the third or fourth or fifth day we managed to get on one of these troop carrier helicopters. It was a turbo prop Russian built plane, but you didn't care by then. You got on the plane and you just found yourself a space and everyone had this sort of black humour. . . .

We flew into this funny little mountain town. The locals were people who hadn't got a penny and they wanted work. They had some rickety old jeep that they stole from the Russians when the Russians fled. And now they come along and they offer you their services. So you look around the vehicle to see if it's got decent tyres and find out if the driver can possibly understand you. And somehow or other you fix yourself up with a driver. So you pile all your luggage in and off you go. And we had four days driving through the Hindu Kush, which was a nightmare of my life and I wouldn't do it again for a million pounds. Jeeps went off the mountainsides, people broke limbs and it was an absolute nightmare.

Every night you stayed somewhere dreadful, usually with a load of ragtag soldiers cooking up some green tea on some ancient stove and smoking hash. And they've got all their RPGs and Kalashnikovs all over the place and you're trying to find a space for your sleeping bag amongst all this. You daren't eat any food because it's going to make you sick and you can't even get sick — there's no bathroom, there's nothing.'

Jones continues:

'Along the way, you would find other journalists and help them or they'd help you or you had a chat. And there was a very talkative, rather cheeky guy who always used to come up, particularly to the girls, and chat. And I asked him who he was working for and he said he was with some Japanese. I said, "Come and work for us instead." And he said he couldn't until we got to where we were all going, which was just outside Kabul. And when we got there I offered him double what he was being paid. Because at that stage, quite frankly, you don't care, you want the best. . . . I use him now.

I've been back to Afghanistan many times, and actually I brought him to Cape Town for a holiday to thank him. And that's how I got my translator. He's a fixer, he's part of the Northern Alliance command, so he knew everybody. And he's cheeky and he's likeable and he would persuade people. He got me into places like prisons where it was hard to get in, and he got me out of bad situations where it was hard to get out. So he's the key to everything – a good fixer and a good driver.'

Finding a good fixer can often determine whether a trip will be successful. So finding the right person is essential. Gavin Hewitt considers them hugely important:

'They understand nuances. You drive into an area which is dangerous and, however many courses you have gone to, you don't necessarily understand what's happening – what the mood is on the streets, how a mood can change very quickly. You are hugely dependent on your translator, your driver. I've been in situations before where the first person who speaks some English, and it could well be the taxi driver on the stand, I end up hiring him. You have to make a very quick judgement – have you picked up somebody who's reliable? I had a situation in Afghanistan with a driver we picked up. He was a very good man, having to explain to me that the people there were discussing whether to kill me.'

Bill Neely says that with a good local fixer, access can be available to people in places that normally would be inaccessible. But the choice of driver can be just as important:

'I know the occasions in my career when I've been very lucky and had a fantastic local fixer and it's made all the difference in the world. I've also known the times when I knew I didn't have the right person and I wasn't getting the right contacts and I wasn't getting to the right places. And so it's vital, I think, sometimes even something as simple as a good driver – sounds like nothing, doesn't it? The incident in which Terry Lloyd, Fred Nerac and Hussein Othman lost their lives was an example. I was a very close friend of Fred's, and I keep thinking would he still be alive today if his driver hadn't done what he did? There were two vehicles. They approached the Iraqis. The first vehicle saw the Iraqis and the driver turned around. The second vehicle containing Fred and Hussein did not turn around because it was ordered to stop by the Iraqis. The driver was from Kuwait and I think he may have been more prone to obeying authority than maybe a Westerner who might have thought, "Holy Shit, I've just got to get out of here fast." So even the selection of the driver can be very important.

When I was covering the fall of the Berlin Wall, I had a taxi driver, and one day, after about a week, we were looking for a big family who were going to travel . . . for the first time from East Berlin to West Berlin. The taxi driver and her extended family happened to be coming from East Berlin, and we ended up filming them for the rest of that day. It was four generations of people who were coming across from East Berlin to West Berlin and it was a wonderful, wonderful story, thanks to the driver.'

Fixers are often recruited through word of mouth recommendation from other journalists who have employed them. NGOs are another source of supply both on site and through offices in London for UK-based correspondents. With most journalists spending a limited time in the field, there is generally a pool of local drivers and translators on which to draw. However, efforts may be made by news organisations to monopolise the better fixers. James Mates explains that 'once you find good ones, you keep them throughout. If it goes quiet for six months, keep them on a retainer, make sure they don't go and work somewhere else'.

Technology has also changed the contact method. Jonathan Steele informed us that email is now commonly used: 'Drivers have emails, translators have emails and they get your address from somebody and I get emails saying, "Are you coming back to Iraq?" Or, "I'm willing to be your translator, I'll be free in August and September".' Steele relates that in some situations instead of employing a fixer driver they used taxis: 'In Central America there were taxis outside the hotel who were waiting and you went out to a taxi and negotiated a day rate with them.' It is mainly whilst working on the more complex stories like Iraq that journalists require a full-time driver, because they are taking more risks. Steele remarks:

'They need to be sure that the driver isn't working for some strange organisation that might take you hostage. So you've got to be confident that your driver is not only a good driver but honest and reliable and not going to betray you in some way.'

The huge number of journalists from all over the world converging on one place can set up a small economy with many job opportunities for locals who can act as translators, guides or suppliers of other services. Sara Oliver describes the situation in Afghanistan:

'People view it as an opportunity to make money and your basic unit of currency seems to become the hundred dollar note, which makes it incredibly expensive. It's very surreal. You're handing out hundred dollar notes and you're looking around this destroyed country and you're thinking, "What on earth are you going to spend it on? What do you think you're going to buy with it?" It's like Monopoly money, it's like pretend money. But conflict creates a weird economy all of its own. Conflict becomes the local industry and the local employer. And I'd be naïve and hypocritical if I said that the media didn't play a part in that. If you get hundreds of journalists from all over the world moving in to one small desert town, then food, water, accommodation, transport, security, communications are suddenly at an absolute premium. And you have nowhere else to go – it's not like being in London where if one hotel's trying to charge you way over the odds, you can go to one next door. Either you've got a goat hut to sleep in or you haven't.'

Sometimes the fixers are partial. In Afghanistan, for example, the BBC was given fixers by the Northern Alliance who were committed to the cause. According to Caroline Wyatt, it meant that the journalists had no idea whether these people were translating correctly. If proof were needed it came in the response from the interviewees. Wyatt relates:

'Funnily enough, everyone we went to speak to, even refugees who had come from somewhere else said, "No, we love the Northern Alliance. . . . The Northern Alliance is wonderful. . . . We couldn't live without them. . . . They should be in power." Gradually as the weeks went by, we got more local people, who spoke some English, maybe not perfect English but who were more honest and truthful.'

All correspondents needed to be alert to the trustworthiness of fixers. Some might be terrific at providing access to informants, but Adrian Monck warns that often 'they've got their own agendas and don't want you to meet certain people, and especially . . . in the Middle East, where I've worked many times, you often had someone working for you who's in the pay of the government'. Dan Edge likewise recalls that in Pakistan all the standard fixers were known to the military authorities, so 'hooking yourself up with that person is tantamount to throwing all your notes down in front of the Secret Services there'. The upshot is that, while fixers are essential, their reliability cannot be assumed.

Journalists develop strong relationships with some of their fixers and, due to the risks and dangers involved, a rapport develops. Kim Willsher outlines the dilemma they face when they are accompanied by a local person on an assignment:

'I was in Sarajevo during the time that it was being heavily shelled. There were snipers all around the hotel, and it was very difficult going out. We would put on flak jackets and stand alongside a local person who was working with us, who had no protection. We felt very, very uncomfortable about this because what you were saying was, "I've got this protection, my life's more important than yours", which is not how we felt at all. If you have very well organised television teams they will have armoured vehicles, with full teams of equipment. And they will have equipment for people who work with them. But when you're travelling as a two-person team – you with a notebook and somebody with a camera – then you're not carrying around spare jackets.'

In the Balkans, journalists would refrain at times from using their translators because of the inherent dangers. Jonathan Steele explains what happened:

'If you had a Serb translator and you wanted to go to an Albanian village, it wasn't safe enough to take them. And vice versa. If you had an Albanian translator and you went to a Serb checkpoint, as you inevitably did, the Serbs might say, "Who's this Albanian? Why's he in the car with you?" So partly to protect our translators when we went on these trips . . . we wouldn't take them, we would rely on finding people who spoke English or German and we would make do that way.'

Bill Neely recounts how he worked with a former BBC fixer in Kosovo:

'He was a Muslim but his father was a Croat. He had a Muslim girlfriend and just before the NATO bombing began in Priština, we helped him and his girl-friend get out of Kosovo into Bulgaria. And we got them a visa to come to Britain and we helped them in their attempt to get political asylum here . . . He didn't work with us because he thought this was an easy route to Britain, it just happened that that was the case. That was an instance where we were working with him, he was a Muslim, we were Brits, and Britain was about to bomb Kosovo. And we were working also with a Serb from Belgrade. And in fact the Serb from Belgrade helped the Muslim from Kosovo to get out; he drove him through one of the worst areas. So extraordinary friendships can be formed across all sorts of divides in situations like this.'

The relationship between journalist and fixer can become very close and, because of the degree of danger often present in areas of conflict, empathy can be heightened. Dependency, physical proximity and intensity of experiences are likely to breed intimacy between fixer and correspondent. It may also be in the interest of the reporter to 'develop a level of trust', says Gavin Hewitt, because 'if you haven't developed any relationship other than paying them a few bucks . . . they may not either share critical information, or indeed may not help get you out of a situation'.

The professional relationship often turns into a personal one, though its durability, and the precise characteristics it expresses, vary. As Gavin Hewitt observes: 'It's an artificial relationship. I'm here only for a short space of time [and] it's their country.' Consequently relations may not continue long after the correspondent departs. One can understand John Sweeney's *cri de coeur*: 'I care passionately about the man in Chechnya who got me into Chechnya and I can't remember his fucking name.'

On the other hand, Colin Baker's experiences in Central America demonstrate just how vital the fixer can be:

'I had a lot of trouble in Panama . . . but there was a lovely driver called Roberto, who's an example of how a taxi driver would get you at an airport and becomes much more than just a driver; it's his knowledge, it's his demeanour, his attitude, his alliances. And you very quickly learn to trust someone. And we did. We trusted him with our lives.

But we had some really nasty experiences where we were taken away . . . . We were released eventually, about midnight in Panama City and we had . . . been laundered during the daytime; taken from place to place, change of per-sonnel at the time, and we didn't think we were going to make it, when they had a mock firing squad. But, we came out of the police station and they flew us out in the middle of a gun battle, and I don't know how . . . we would be shot by the rebels, and it was the day that there was the attempted coup against Noriega. There was a sudden flashing headlight from way across the square, and we ran for it and it was Roberto. All day long he'd followed us and followed the convoy, wherever we'd been. And he knew we'd been in this building, where nobody else knew. And he just waited for us. He saved our lives really.'

Luke Harding believes the most important person is the driver – even more so than the translator. His experience in Afghanistan convinced him that a quick-thinking driver can be crucial:

'I was in the north of the country. We didn't know but it turned out that 500 Taliban foreign fighters had surrendered and were encamped on the outskirts of the city in the dunes. We drove straight into them and my driver spotted them. They were still armed and we immediately did a U-turn which was the right thing to do. But then he drove about another 200 metres and stopped and then we got out and talked to them. This is the difference between life and death and that was down to the driver.'

Perhaps the best-known episode of journalist–fixer relationship, one that was later portrayed in a feature film,[1] took place in Cambodia. Jon Swain was one of the few journalists who remained in Cambodia just as the Khmer Rouge was about to take power. Here he relives the horror of that time:

'Sydney Schanberg of the *New York Times* stayed behind in Cambodia, like I did, and the consequences were getting quite dire. Because he stayed behind, his Cambodian fix-it man interpreter, Dith Pran, who was extremely loyal to him, also stayed behind. The day that the Khmer Rouge took over we were captured and were going to be executed. We were put on a personnel carrier – the photographer, Schanberg, myself and Pran – and taken down to the waterfront to be shot. Pran got out and talked to the Khmer Rouge and persuaded them to let us go. He saved our lives and then we were all prisoners in the French Embassy.
    The whole city was being emptied and Cambodians were thrown out into the countryside to die. Some Cambodians jumped over the wall of the French Embassy because they thought the Westerners would protect them. But the Khmer Rouge forced the French to kick out all the Cambodians who were seeking refuge there and other Asians, Vietnamese as well. . . . We were in a terrible situation where Pran had saved our lives but we couldn't protect his.
    I doctored my passport, a second passport, to try and give him a British passport to see what he could do with that. Anyway, it didn't work. He went out into the countryside and he disappeared for nearly four years. He survived and he now lives in New York. But Schanberg felt incredibly responsible and it crucified him for those four years until he knew that Pran was safe. It's something I've never forgotten.'

Another example of fixers aiding journalists in trouble was provided by a translator for Caroline Wyatt when she was reporting from Afghanistan. Although Wyatt and her team could not take the person out of Afghanistan and back to safety in Moscow, he helped them to leave after another journalist had been killed by robbers in a house nearby[2]:

'The Taliban were coming into town and this young translator really did risk a lot; he went to the commanders and said, "The BBC want to leave this town and go somewhere that is safer." And he negotiated for us to leave because the Northern Alliance didn't want us to leave, because if we left, then everyone else would leave. And they lost about 100 journalists, who were paying them a lot of protection money so that their soldiers didn't come and loot our houses, and also to prevent the Taliban from getting into our houses. It's just the risk that the fixers take, because if they're paid $100 a day – and that's your normal annual wage [in Afghanistan] – they'll take that risk to feed themselves and their families, and we're not going to say no to their help. And it's a problem that you have ethically, which is, will I get this person into deep trouble?'

Frontline correspondents are conscious of difficulties that can be caused by their treatment of fixers who can easily be compromised in the eyes of their neighbours, yet condemned to remain when the correspondents leave. Bill Neely puts it cogently:

'We are very aware that we come into these countries and stay for a while, and then we walk away and we move on to the next conflict. And the people that we work with, who help us, usually have to stay and suffer the consequences – of not just what has happened there but what we have done in publicising this conflict. And those people may sometimes feel emboldened by our presence and working with us, and they may say things to people in authority that they wouldn't have said otherwise. Then, when we leave, they're punished for it in some way. In Iraq, translators are killed for working not just with Coalition forces, but sometimes with journalists.'

However, Neely then continues:

'I think, though, those people are grown-ups as well – we bear a responsibility when we hire them. There's no question about that. We once hired a woman in Kosova and worked with her for six hours. And we were attacked by the Serbs. She broke one ankle and fractured her foot and wasn't able to work for the next six weeks. I think we paid her for six months because, even though she'd worked with us for six hours, it was our responsibility. I had taken her to a place where we were attacked, she was injured, so we paid for her. But she willingly sought work with us. We willingly hired her, so there's responsibility on both sides. Even in Iraq, the translators who work with the Coalition forces, for example, never mind journalists, know what they're doing, they know that there's $100 dollars a day, or $200 a day. That's big money and they accept the risks.'

There is a growing awareness within the industry of the need to protect fixers and translators and to provide compensation when necessary. Mark Wood of ITN stresses the need for responsibility on the part of the news organisation:

'This is the constant issue. Reuters had this policy in Spain that if you hire somebody, whether it's a freelance journalist or cameraman or it's a translator, the minute you hire them, they are on your payroll and you are responsible for them. If they get killed, you have to make sure they're covered in insurance terms. One of the people we lost in Iraq was the news translator. He had worked for us for less than two weeks. We treated him exactly the same as we did every other member of the team, as if he had been working for the company for years. It means that the people at the frontline have to be very careful because every time they hire somebody, they're going into a commitment on the part of the company, so we do urge them to be very careful.'

The importance of responsibility extends to freelancers as well as fixers and translators. As news organisations become cautious in their deployment of staff journalists, the vacuum tends to be filled by freelancers. Wood recalls Ethiopia in the early 1990s:

'When I was at Reuters . . . we lost three people one day in Mogadishu in 1993. None of them were on the staff but they were all working for us on a freelance basis. We had a policy of not sending anybody into Mogadishu, but there was a great story there so people went in and filed – they volunteered and went in and reported back. And it's a constant problem – as soon as they are there working for you, you have responsibility towards them, as you should. Most responsible news organisations do. Not all of them, but most do.'

All the journalists to whom we spoke talked movingly about their fixers and translators. It reveals another intense relationship for the frontline correspondent in an already stressful situation. By way of illustration, Anton Antonowicz tells a 'heartbreaking' story of contemporary Iraq:

'There was a guy in Baghdad, who was, by mutual agreement, the loveliest man that any of us met while we were there. And he had been the Chief Steward for Iraqi Airways. And nothing was too much trouble for him. I remember one day him saying to me, "Anton, you're not eating well enough in this place, what would you like to eat?" And I said, "What I'd dearly love to have is just some decent chicken and some rice." And he said, "Okay I'll see what I can do." And he went away and he came back at 7 o'clock with all this food that his wife had cooked, and he came with his 16 year old son. And I was very angry with him. I said, "You're crazy. You're coming here, it's getting dark, you're taking terrible risks. I don't want you ever to do this again."

A few days later (he was by now working for a guy on the *Sunday Mirror*) . . . he said to him, "Look your clothes are stinking." He said, "Let me get them washed for you." He insisted. He took the clothes. We thought he was taking them to a laundry. He took them home and he washed them himself and ironed them. The following day he didn't come to work. Two days later his wife phoned, very worried, she hadn't seen him. And then the following day they discovered him dead, in his car. There were thirteen bullets in the car. He was still lying in the car dead, and the washing was on the back seat. He was bringing the washing back. And he'd been shot by the Americans coming into town. There was an underpass, and driving towards the underpass there was a little minibus in front of him, which had about 12 Iraqis in it. And they saw there was a roadblock in front – two armoured American Humvees I think they were, that were in the underpass. So you couldn't actually see them until you got there. And of course the first car panicked and started to turn, and then he turned, and the Americans opened fire on them and he died . . .'

Working in conflict zones is inherently dangerous and in the following three chapters we explore the problems of safety for frontline correspondents, their protection and training, and the ways in which they manage to cope with their experiences.

Notes

1   *The Killing Fields* (1984), directed by Roland Joffé, starred SamWaterston as *New York Times* reporter Sydney Schanberg, Julian Sands as Jon Swain and Dr Haing S. Ngor who played the part of Dith Pran.
2   Journalists face similar problems when trying to protect their interviewees. Caroline Wyatt outlines the problem in Chechnya and other countries:

> 'The people who helped us there or who were interviewed by us got into trouble afterwards. But they knew in talking to us how dangerous it was. And the same in Belarus and the same in the Ukraine. And in Chechnya, we said to people, "Are you sure you want to help us? Are you sure you want to be interviewed on camera? Are you sure you want to have your face put on screen? Are you sure you want your real name put up?" And most of the time they said, "Yes, for sure. I don't care what happens because I want the world to know what's happening."'

9

DANGER AND SAFETY

'There are a lot of people who, in this business, find it simply not for them to go out in the rough and tumble of the badlands of journalism.' (Jeremy Thompson, *Sky News*)

The thrill of writing an I-nearly-died-a-gruesome-death story is unbeatable . . . War makes you feel special; it makes you feel better than all the war virgins back home. But here's the downside: writing an I-nearly-died-a-gruesome-death story requires you to nearly die a gruesome death . . . And was it all worth it, for a fuck-you and a front page? (Ayres 2005, p. 265)

Reporting war is inherently dangerous. Some correspondents might be tempted to stay away from trouble in a comfortable hotel, but if they are doing their job properly – and as we have seen, there is a widely shared conviction about what that entails – then journalists must get amongst groups of people whose aim is to destroy one another. Combatants are heavily armed, wound up, and often resentful of those who are just there to write about it. Correspondents have a lot to fear – confrontations with drunken militias, stand-offs with angry soldiers, being hit by friendly fire, being seized by guerrillas, accosted by youths carrying AK47s, and even being driven at breakneck speed along unknown roads in the black of night (Adrian Monck, like others we interviewed, ranked traffic accidents a major concern 'for almost all journalists abroad [because] there are a lot of manic, odd people on the road').

Given such circumstances, it is scarcely surprising that many journalists are killed and injured while doing their jobs. Several hundred have lost their lives over the past decade. Looking back over 20 years, Gavin Hewitt thinks the job has got worse in this respect: 'It's become a very dangerous world . . . I don't think there's ever been a period when doing the job . . . has seemed so full of risk.' Julian Manyon, as with other experienced reporters, concurs, commenting that Iraq 'is very, very dangerous at the moment', now a place where journalists are seen by the 'anti-American insurgency' as targets.

The war in Iraq has highlighted the risk that journalists confront in covering conflict. Between March 2003 and July 2005, 52 journalists were killed on duty in Iraq.[1] Media workers, as we discussed in the previous chapter, who work with journalists in supporting roles as drivers, interpreters, fixers and guards have also been targets, with 21 killed during the same period (http://www.cpj.org/Briefings/2003/gulf03/iraq_media_wrkrs_killed.html).

According to the Committee to Protect Journalists (CPJ), during the decade 1995-2004, 341 journalists were killed while carrying out their work. While conflict and war provide the backdrop to much of the violence against the press, CPJ research demonstrates that the vast majority of journalists killed since 1995 were murdered rather than killed in cross-fire. In fact, according to CPJ statistics, only 68 journalists (20 percent) died in cross-fire, while 247 (72 percent) were murdered, often in reprisal for their reporting. The CPJ state that the remaining journalists were killed in conflict situations that cannot be described as combat – while covering violent street demonstrations, for example. Photographing and recording combat are among the most dangerous assignments and during this period 62 cameramen, photographers and soundmen were killed. The majority of them died in cross-fire in places such as Sierra Leone, Iraq, Yugoslavia and Russia. But others were deliberately murdered because of images they had captured (http://www.cpj.org/killed/Ten_Year_Killed/Intro.html).

The CPJ figures show clearly that local journalists covering crime, corruption and human rights violations continue to face the greatest risk. As the CPJ point out, even in Iraq, most of those killed have been local journalists. 'Covering combat is risky, but a much greater threat than a stray bullet are the murderers who kill journalists deliberately, using the generalised violence associated with war to cover their tracks' (ibid.).

The high profile of safety has undoubtedly increased apprehension on the part of news organisations whether or not the risk has increased. Thus Ben Brown is 'not sure it's more dangerous than it was in Vietnam or the Second World War', though as Jon Swain appositely comments, 'we're much more conscious now of danger'. Brown also stresses that 'we go to these places voluntarily'. Barbara Jones added an important perspective when she insisted that journalists 'don't have the right to be frightened when you've got 23 million people who are literally being targeted [in Iraq]'. Sean Smith also had little time for the sensitivities of reporters who 'don't have to be there' because they can always 'walk away'. He reminded us forcefully that the journalist's job is 'not as dangerous as . . . spending ten years as a Palestinian ambulance driver, which is very dangerous'.

Whatever risks the journalists may run, they can almost always get out if the going gets too tough – unlike the local people who have nowhere to go. As Robert Fisk wrote to us, 'It's the civilians trapped in wars – not well-paid journalists who can fly home Club class whenever they want – that suffer.' There can be no denying though, as Gavin Hewitt observes, that 'an element of risk . . . is implicit in the job'. There are certainly plenty of other forms of journalism where the pay is as good, the conditions better and the risks minimal. So how do frontline correspondents react to dangers at which most of us would blanch? Peter Sharp of Sky reflects:

> 'I was talking about this to my wife the other day. The simple thing is, you just know it's not going to happen to you. I know everyone says that. I was listening to some bomber command documentary the other day and the guy said exactly the same thing. Six hundred planes go out, well, you know someone's not going to come back.'

Convictions of immortality are no doubt helpful to the frontline correspondent, but Luke Harding feels that just getting on with the job in hand alleviates fear, generating a 'kind of adrenalin that sees you through in key situations [so] you don't need to think about it'. At the time, adds Harding, 'you're busy with getting the story . . . with the logistics of . . . filing' and this means 'you don't think too deeply'. Suzanne Goldenberg agrees: 'When I am in the middle of it, there is too much going on to notice that I am afraid.' But, she adds, sometimes 'I make up instant mantras that I repeat to myself in my head to reassure myself when I am walking somewhere dangerous, or about to drive somewhere dangerous'. The legendary photojournalist Robert Capa, who landed on the Normandy beaches on D-Day where he took some dramatic pictures amidst extraordinary mayhem, similarly comforted himself by chanting over and again a refrain he had picked up from the Spanish Civil War: 'This is a very serious business.'

Goldenberg also told us that 'with experience, I have come to realise that the reality of events is often less frightening than my imagination of them in advance', and others confirmed that experience helped them handle such difficulties. Thus Daniel Demoustier sees danger 'as something that you slowly grow up in'. He adds that 'the first time you confront it, that's a real big shock . . . Then you slowly get used to it more, and more, which is a danger because it's possible that you become too courageous, you think "I can do this"'.

Brian Williams of Reuters alludes to the lack of fear in youth:

> 'When you're young, you never believe you can die. You believe . . . the bullets are going to hit somebody else – they're not going to hit you. As you get a little bit older you become more cautious, because the actual bullet or bomb or the mortar shell can hit you. People who cover a lot of wars become very fatalistic. Your first war you regard more as an adventure with a belief that you're untouchable.'

Broadcast journalists and photographers are under pressure to achieve the dramatic shot and thereby put themselves in more dangerous situations than other reporters. David Zucchino of the *LA Times* recognises this:

> 'Print reporters have the luxury of staying a little further back and being on the edge because you don't necessarily have to witness everything. You can

piece it together by interviewing people. I'm very careful about the situations I go into. I don't take unnecessary risks but there are risks that are required of TV and still photographers.'

Cameras also mean that unacceptable behaviour is identifiable – a feature that means that photographers and cameramen are vulnerable to attack from those who have reason not to have their pictures taken.

Marie Colvin of the *Sunday Times* traces a change in journalists' status that has increased risks:

'So many journalists have been killed in the last few years. . . . We used to have almost an unofficial diplomatic status. We were seen unofficially as objective, and unofficially as neutral. And now we're actually targets.'

Colvin says that the increased danger has changed the relationship with her editor:

'What you're supposed to do is call in every day. I really hate doing it, and if you talked to my foreign editor he would say he pulls his hair out sometimes. But now that everything has become more dangerous, it certainly is better to always let your foreign editor know where you're going and you should call in once a day. And often you can't.

Once, when I was in Chechnya, I was under fire from planes for 12 hours. They hit the car I was travelling in. Luckily I had got out of the car, but I was stuck in this field. There was snow, so you had no covering, couldn't get out because there were mountains. The planes came back every hour . . . Obviously you can't use your satellite phone to call out, because a plane can zero in on that frequency. So I didn't call until I was sure they weren't coming back – and they came back about ten times. That's a decision you make on the ground.

I have a very good foreign editor, and usually we have discussions about the dangers and he will consult with the editor of the paper if it's something that's really dangerous. But they've both taken into account the fact that you're the person on the ground. You can't be working for them if they don't trust you.'

Jeremy Thompson of *Sky News* clarifies problems in covering conflict nowadays:

'There are vastly more people in the field. There's vastly more competition in the media. There are many more media out there. There's much greater pressure to deliver. The technology takes you close to the action and therefore raises the level of danger. There's an awful lot of inexperienced people out there who have no idea. I saw this in Southern Iraq last year [2003]. I just despair at the people who are whizzing up the road, and they're saying, "What's it like up there?" and I say, "Well, I wouldn't go there myself for these reasons." And they say, "Oh, oh, fine . . .".'

Thompson sees signs that journalists are no longer treated with the respect of independence and neutrality that they were previously.

'I first noticed that going by the board in the Balkans, and through the '90s, where even in Croatia . . . the combatants from either side were already getting themselves involved in copying our TV and press signs down the side of their vehicles and driving armed and shooting at each other, and then they were using ambulances. That continued right the way through that period, which meant that you didn't really have much protection. The Croats, the Serbs or the Bosnians – whichever bunch you got involved in reporting – quite easily assumed that you were the other side and you'd simply tried to give yourself some protection by putting "TV" or "Press" on. And that's one corrosion of our independence and an example of our greater involvement of being seen as combatants.'

Photographer Tom Stoddart warns of journalists who are 'crazy and want to make a reputation':

'There was a French journalist, a radio guy; he used to drive around in Sarajevo with "Don't waste your bullets, I'm immortal" written on his car. You look at it, you say, "You are crazy". He was shot by the Muslims. These kinds of areas attract really, really weird people and that is always dangerous. That's why, if we are working together, if there's a young guy there, you don't want to be with him. It's not my job to take some kid.'

Stoddart emphasises the importance of experience:

'Saying the wrong thing at the wrong time. Not understanding that to take a picture can be dangerous. Working somewhere like Gaza where the Palestinian kids would come up and greet you with an Israeli greeting, so then you respond in the same way, knowing that they're trying to test you out, that they think you're an Israeli spy. You can get into so much trouble with inexperience.'

It is also important to be with trusted colleagues. Stoddart explains:

'If you're with a friend, you would say, "Why don't we just stop a second here and wait?" because you know that he won't think you're being a coward. But in a group of people who hardly know each other, you have to be the bravest of the brave. I was in the third vehicle into Kosovo when they went into Priština with their forces . . . and that night, three guys from *Stern* were killed at a checkpoint and two of my colleagues from the *Daily Record* missed being killed at a checkpoint by inches. These are small things that you make the right decision, you make the wrong decision – you're lucky, you're unlucky. And they're important things; to survive.'

Jon Swain too underlines the dangers of inexperience:

'There is a danger if you're a very inexperienced journalist who's got the idea that he can be a war correspondent or foreign correspondent. Who comes under terrific pressure from his desk to perform and take risks, [but] he does not have the stature or the courage to tell his office that he's afraid of appearing to be afraid. And that's a very tricky situation, a very bad situation to get into. I tend to, more often than not, travel on my own with local people and not with groups of journalists. There is a herd instinct. You can build up a degree of competition where it becomes very difficult to stop. There was a tragedy in Sierra Leone a few years ago, when a very experienced journalist called Kurt Schork was killed, and a cameraman . . . killed as well. Despite their experience, they were in a car which got ambushed in a dangerous area outside the capital.'

Swain provides a scenario:

'Say you were sitting in the back seat and you're driving down this empty road at about 4 o'clock in the afternoon. Shadows are growing, bit of gunfire here and there, there's no government forces around. You're going straight into a real hostile area. You get . . . very, very twitchy. If you're sitting in the back of the car, you're not in control, and these are your friends, and you don't want to say, "Actually I don't like this". You all agree to what degree each of you can go, what your threshold of real fear is, or safety. Then you get into a tricky situation – you're just slightly desperate to get out of that car but you feel you can't say so. And then, someone shoots at the car and you're all dead.'

Danger can arise when least expected. Tim Lambon relates a time he was in Nicaragua, on the border with Honduras:

'This was back in '88. I was with the Contra guerrillas; we had just been walking for ten days into Nicaragua. There had been absolutely nothing. You'd see nothing, it had been completely peaceful. There had been beans and chickens all the way, very dry jungle and we had got absolutely nothing. We'd reckoned that this was turning into a stalemate between the Sandinistas and the Contras. So we got up that morning. We said to the people that we were with, "Okay we want to go back". They showed us an M41-A3, which is an anti-aircraft missile that the Americans had provided the Contras with. We filmed the guy with that a little bit, just so we had something, and then we turned around and we started walking back towards Honduras.
    We got to the bottom of a hill and suddenly there was a helicopter. It hadn't gone more than about a kilometre with us watching it from the cover of the trees, when the guy that we'd been filming a short time before had obviously taken out his weapon and shot the helicopter down. Then it turned into four days of absolute hell and [was] very, very dangerous. From being absolutely nothing for almost two weeks to suddenly becoming very dangerous, because that was the incident that kicked off the Sandinista offensive that had been building up against the Contras.
    It took the group I was with four days to get back to Honduras and all the way we were being harried. There were patrols on either side of us from the Sandinistas, we were having to avoid them. There were ambushes, there was all sorts of stuff. And by the time we got back to Honduras, out of the ten people in the patrol who were with me and my Italian colleague, there were only two left standing. The rest had either been killed or injured . . . There are times when it gets extremely dangerous.'

For women reporters, there are added dangers.[2] Jane Kokan, who worked in Ethiopia, was arrested at the airport:

'A couple of guys threatened to rape me. That was not a lot of fun and I was deported. I was there officially. I had a journalist visa and I did a piece on the politics, humanitarian aid. Then I had a couple of days in Addis Ababa. At that time, according to the Amnesty International report, there were more than 30 Ethiopian journalists in prison. I thought that would be an interesting little story, so I did some investigations. Somebody must have been following me is my guess, but that wasn't a lot of fun.'

John Irvine, who worked as a foreign correspondent in the Middle East for ITN, began to be worried about the safety of his family.

'The most danger I put myself in were some of the scrapes I got into on the West Bank in the first year of the Intifada when the Israelis were responding forcefully to many of the suicide bombers. I lived in Jerusalem. I have a wife and two young children. My children were at the Lycée Française in Jerusalem and the head of a suicide bomber who blew himself up outside the gate ended up in the kids' playground. My daughter brought home nails from his bomb a couple of days later and said, "Look daddy". And I thought, "What the hell am I doing here?" When the Israelis were pushing hard following these attacks in places like Ramallah, demolishing Arafat and the Palestinian Authority, some of the shooting situations, on reflection, were quite hairy. But at the time it was a big story and it had to be done and I wanted to get out with a TV camera and I wanted to tell it as up close and personally as I could.'

At one stage, the risks were deemed too high, so Irvine remained in Jerusalem.

'How can they micro-manage situations from thousands of miles away? Well, the truth is they can't. And what they base their judgements on are your TV reports and what other people are reporting. But I think this is one of the good things about ITN during the Iraq War. All the American networks left Baghdad: ABC, NBC, CBS were pulled away by New York two or three days before the war started on the grounds of safety. The organisations that stayed – the French, British broadcasters – left it up to individuals to decide whether they felt it was appropriate to stay or whether they thought it was too risky. That's exactly as it should be, because nobody can make the decision better than the person who's experiencing what's going on, on the ground.'

Orla Guerin of the BBC is also based in Jerusalem:

'Jerusalem is a strange place, and it's a strange existence, because you can have a bomb on your own doorstep. The last bomb in Jerusalem was at the end of my road, right opposite the filling station where I go for petrol every other week. But equally you can then have periods of calm where you feel okay about going out to restaurants, although, like many people who live in Jerusalem and the foreign media, I tend to do my eating and drinking in the east side of Jerusalem. That's the Arabs' side and there's less likely to be a suicide bombing. You think carefully about which restaurant will you go to. Will you go downtown Jerusalem? Will you go to the supermarket at peak hours, or will you go when it's less busy? You have to take those things into account. You try to reduce the risk where you can.

But I've always felt, in terms of living and covering the Middle East but also in terms of going off to assignments like Sarajevo, you have taken the risk when you decided to take the assignment, and everything that you're doing after that is for your own comfort and psychology.'

When journalists are on the ground, they have to know how to respond to dangerous situations. Jon Swain of the *Sunday Times* has experienced numerous terrifying situations:

'If you're really going to be executed or you think you are, you're probably quite frozen for the moment with complete fear, which is why some people get killed in very meek circumstances. They don't resist, they don't fight. I was kidnapped in Africa, in Ethiopia, so I thought I was going to get executed there. . . .

But the more recent incident – in East Timor, about three or four years ago – there was a moment when I thought that they were definitely going to kill us. And then we really made a break for it. We got out of the car and they started shooting the car. I think I was bolder at that moment about arguing the case to stay alive than in previous times.

A few years later in Kinshasa, the capital of the Congo, there was a very drunken Angolan major, who got very angry with me. It was just when President Mobutu had been overthrown and so there was a lot of fighting going on. He rounded on me. He was very drunk and he thought I was laughing at him because I was white and he was black. It became quite a racist thing. He got this Kalashnikov and I could see his eyes completely glazed with drink and drugs. I ended up being quite angry with him, which is not in my nature. It's very important in that sort of situation not to be aggressive, because aggression makes you noticed and you can easily be killed then. That tips things over the edge – you make people angry or you make people frightened of you and they react badly and kill you. But if you're too meek then it's easier for them to kill you because they feel it doesn't matter, you're nothing. You've got to find a tone which makes them think twice about killing you. It's a hard thing to do and I don't know if sometimes you can do it and sometimes you can't, but I think you've got to be aware of that.'

Swain continues to go back, drawing on his experience to reduce risk:

'That's what I've done for a long time. I hope I know how to look after myself. You build up a degree of experience which stands you in good stead, whatever the circumstances. Although a very dear friend of mine – Neil Davis, who was a fantastic cameraman – had more commercial experience in Vietnam than anyone I knew and he seemed completely invincible. He was killed in a silly little coup in Thailand, after the Vietnam War in 1980. He'd been through Vietnam, Cambodia, Angola, Beirut, Congo, everything. He was killed covering a little tinpot coup in the mid-80s in Thailand. So your luck can run out.'

Photographer Chip Hires was with Swain in Timor and he remembers the role of good (and bad) fortune:

'We got arrested by the army, local unit, and I thought they were going to kill us. They took our driver and blinded him, knocked out one of his eyes, and took our guide and he disappeared and never came back. And afterwards they killed a Dutch journalist. My real concern was that they were threatening to kill us, putting guns to our head and shooting them off next to our heads, and I just thought this is it. . . . They held us hostage. There were 300 of them. They stole all our gear. They broke up our car in the end and let us go away. But there was this Dutch journalist who was shot by the same group of guys, just about 10 minutes or 20 minutes after they let us go.'

Kim Willsher describes a hair-raising incident in Croatia:

'To this day, I don't quite know how we got out of it alive, because I was convinced that we were going to be killed. There were bullets pinging, they were quite clearly targeting us. There were three of us shouting in English and in Serbo-Croat that we were press. We made it quite clear that we were not tourists and obviously we had no weapons, we didn't fire back. We were not being aggressive but it was quite clear that the people that were shooting at us wanted to kill us. There were bullets pinging off the top of the stone wall just inches above our head and they were firing little rocket launch shrapnel grenades.
   We looked around and realised that there wasn't an awful lot that we could do. The road curved back on itself, it was single track. We couldn't get back to the car because every time we tried to move to the car, they shot at it and it was riddled with bullets. And we debated what we could do [whether to] jump over the wall on the other side. But we didn't know whether there was a huge drop and that would be even worse. So we just literally stayed where we were until it got dark and then crawled away on our hands and knees until we could get to a position where we thought we could no longer be shot at.'

Amongst some of the journalists a kind of fatalism was evident. Maggie O'Kane of the *Guardian* explains why she decided to stop reporting conflict:

'It's always been the most exciting job in journalism . . . I suppose I wanted to make sure I could keep on doing it. The thing that made me rethink was that a very good friend of mine, a photographer (not a war photographer) said to me, "You keep on doing dangerous things for long enough, there's a logic that you're going to get hurt in the end." And actually it's very rational – you increase the odds. I've seen the deaths of three journalists on the road from Islamabad into Kabul just after the liberation of Kabul. It became too big a lottery for me. Especially after ten years. I've been doing it since '89 and the words of my friend rang in my ear. In East Timor I've been very close. I've taken a bullet, it didn't hit me but it came close enough to pop my ear and I think that's very close actually.'

All conflicts and wars present dangerous situations for the frontline correspondents, all of whom recollect frightening events and incidents.

For example, Anton Antonowicz was in Kosovo when he came under fire from Serbian forces:

'I was on a hill with a checker, the Kosovo Liberation Army, KLA. I was look-ing down in Kosovo and this guy was saying, "There's my beloved Kosovo." We were going to the frontline, but we were on a hill and he stood up, which was not a good idea. And suddenly there was an explosion. What had happened was that the Serbs had seen us, and they fired a tank shell and it landed maybe about 20 yards from me. Luckily it went into the hillside, but there was a big explosion, lots of dirt and filth and I just threw myself on the floor and managed to avoid that. But then the only way of going to safety was to go towards the guns, and that was down the hill. So they were shelling artillery on us, mortars. Those were exploding around us, and then we realised that this hill was covered in mines.

In Baghdad it was much worse, because it was two months of fear. You didn't know what was going to happen. Were you going to get bombed by your own side when the fighting started? Were you going to be taken hostage by Saddam? Were you going to be the final human shield? Could you be gassed? You're with people that you couldn't trust at all – the Baghdadi offi-cials that were in charge of us. In a strange kind of way we were embedded, but we were embedded by the other side.'

Caroline Wyatt of the BBC was also in Kosovo:

'I drove into Kosovo alone with an Albanian driver after my team had gone in, because the BBC changed their minds – they needed an extra person. I had to go down a road that was full of armed Serbs who hate the BBC, who didn't want journalists in there. And I was in the car with an Albanian. And at one stage, the Serbs came to surround the car with their guns, and there was a German tank further up the road, which stopped, reversed, pointed their guns at the Serbs, the Serbs went back and we carried on down the road. Things like that are frightening because you don't know what they're going to do. They're drunk, they're probably stoned, they're aggres-sive, they hate the BBC. I'm a woman, I'm with an Albanian and other jour-nalists died on that road the same day. I was very lucky. I now look back and I think why did I do that? That was because London needed an extra live correspondent in Priština to talk about liberation. But it wasn't a safe way to do it. I shouldn't have gone with just an Albanian driver [and] without a flak jacket.'

Iraq has become a particularly dangerous place for journalists, especially for 'unilaterals' who make their own way round. However, even those embedded with the military remember tense situations. Chris Ayres of *The Times* relates an incident when he was 'absolutely terrified beyond belief, it was horrible':

'We came very close once to getting wiped out. We were ordered to move positions, and we got lost in the fog and got completely separated from the rest of the convoy. We had to stop by the side of the road and we just couldn't see anything. We were just stranded, and we felt certain that we were going to be captured. We had to stay there all night because it was getting dark and we just couldn't move any further.

Luckily there was a unit behind us and what they can do in a situation like that is that, instead of firing a round of ammunition, they fire white phosphorous, which lights up the battlefield. When the battlefield was illuminated, they saw 12 Republican Guard tanks heading towards us, ready to try and take us out. They said over the radio, "You've got 12 Republican Guard tanks coming towards you." We just couldn't do anything – the night vision goggles didn't work. I was sitting in the Humvee, listening to this exchange of information over the radio. It was terrible – you couldn't do anything, it was absolutely terrifying. It was so black you couldn't see anything because the air was thick with mud.

Eventually one of the commanders came on the radio and said, "We're going to send in a couple of F15s", which was extremely good news. But then he said, "They're going to be 30 minutes". We had to wait for these fighter jets to come from Kuwait to try to save us from these tanks. Then the artillery behind us started firing random artillery out in front of us to try and put the tanks off. On the 30th minute, these jets turned up and carpet bombed the tanks and destroyed them. It was probably one of the worst 30 to 40 minutes of my life by a long way. It was pretty intense. The Marines were pretty nervous about it, we really thought we were all going to buy it. It was horrible. But the next day when the smoke cleared and the mud had gone, everybody was so happy, it was unbelievable. We were just in the most elated mood you could imagine.'

Daniel Demoustier of ITN describes an incident from Iraq 2003 that ended in tragedy:

'We were not with the army. We crossed the border on the Thursday and we spent the night in the desert . . . When we got up in the morning, we succeeded in sending our stuff, and then I called London. I said, "Look guys, we're in the desert now, we are not far over the border of Kuwait. What do you want us to do?" We had so many teams – we had teams who were with the army, we had embedded teams, we had teams in Kuwait, we had teams everywhere. So it was a very big operation. And I wanted to find out what was going on. The official information was that Umm Qasr was taken by the Americans already. That was completely false propaganda information, because 10 or 14 days later we were still fighting in Umm Qasr. But then it was taken, and the logical place to go was Basra.

It was always our goal to go to Basra because we worked for British television and the British Army was, according to the military's plan, to go to Basra. We were on this enormous four-lane road that goes to Basra, and there was absolutely nothing happening. There was no fighting. There was normal civil traffic, Iraqi cars driving on the road. There was absolutely no sign of real danger where we were driving. Then the only danger we saw, from a distance, was Iraqi soldiers. That's when I made the decision – "Let's turn back now because we're not going to drive into Iraqi hands. That would be stupid." We immediately turned back a full U turn, 90 degrees. We were in two cars. I was driving the first car and Terry Lloyd was the person sitting next to me in the passenger seat. I had the second vehicle behind me, with Fred Nerac, my colleague, and Hussein Othman and our fixer. Hussein was driving the second vehicle.

When we did the U turn, I took some speed to get away from the Iraqis and then I looked in my mirror and saw that the car with Fred and Hussein had been stopped by the Iraqi soldiers. They had a car block. There was an Iraqi pick-up truck standing next to their car and they were stopped. So I stopped and waited. Then, after a few minutes we saw some people. I had very difficult vision because I could only use my mirror. I could not use the rear view because I had so much equipment in the car. After a few minutes the two cars behind me came closer and I started driving as well. Then the Iraqi car started driving next to me and they were smiling to me and signing in the direction we were going. At that very same moment the American tanks opened fire on us. We did find out that Fred and Hussein were probably taken out their car and put in the Iraqi car that was driving next to me, and that car was blown to pieces by the Americans. And my car was blown to pieces by the Americans, and I'm the only one who survived it. Of the three other guys, we only recovered the body of Terry Lloyd.'[3]

Colin Baker provides an angry critique of modern media and war in response to the death of Lloyd:

'I'll tell you why Terry Lloyd died and why other correspondents get killed in war. Correspondents like Terry Lloyd are killed in cross-fire between television managers, who . . . get other people killed because they want to increase the ratings. We had a ludicrous situation last year. There were 600 journalists trying to get onto a battlefield because they think it's wonderful, and they've never bloody been there before. And they want to get out and they want medals and they want to get home and tell people how it was.

And we have a media system in the West which wants to portray this in actuality and live. We have this thing about doing live-live-live with your neighbours – so there's somebody bonking on Channel 4 in a house, why not do it on a battlefield? And where are we going to take this to? And driving around a battlefield, a walk on top of your tank and playing it at the start and saying, "Hey look. There's guys getting killed up front, see if you can get any closer." I mean what are we doing here?. . .

Tour of Vietnam, a story was only news when it reached us, when it got out. Brave guys and girls who covered Vietnam, who'd go up country with the GIs, might have to go on the run for weeks with what they'd shot and try to get out if they had problems. They'd then try to get it back to Saigon. They'd then get their material out on a plane to Bangkok, which is where all the media processing facilities were, and then their film and sound film would go on a plane to New York. It would be developed and then after maybe three weeks, it got on air. And then you saw it, and that's when it became news. Now we actually want to see it *when it happens*. So people like Terry . . . have to go looking for it because maybe they feel threatened, maybe they feel the guy from Sky's got more gear than me, he's better prepared, he's got more ability, so I've got to really be lucky on this one, I've got to go looking for it. And you give me 600 journalists on the battlefield and more than 10% of them want to be heroes. Are they going to die?'

Bill Neely, also of ITN, describes the emotions within the organisation:

'We're a bit like a family. It's a cliché but when things like the death of Terry Lloyd and my friend, Fred Nerac, who died, even though officially he's still missing, when people like that die, it really affects the organisation in a very deep way. In relation to the last Gulf War, I think it made a lot of us stop and think about what we did, what we do, how we do it. The fact that Terry and Fred and Hussein Othman, the translator, died, and Daniel Demoustier, who was another friend of mine, survived, it makes us all think about exactly what we practise, how we do things.'

After the loss of life in Iraq, ITN management considered it too much to risk another life, so the editor decided to obtain news through agency cameramen on the streets of Baghdad. Bill Neely says that he would put a voice on the pictures provided by Iraqi cameramen.

'I would appear with Baghdad in the background but I would not go out to Fallujah. I would not try to get in with American infantry regiments on the streets. I would not risk anything. There are compromises, but there are compromises all the time in war reporting. It's the most challenging thing you'll ever do, because every minute, every hour is a compromise. I can see 50 yards down the road and then there's a corner. Do I go forward and go around that corner because I can't see what's round there? I might do it but I might get killed doing it. Is it worth it? Is it worth in the next two minutes me running up to the corner? You're always making decisions. Everything's a compromise.'

Anton Antonowicz witnessed the death of two journalists when US troops fired on the Palestine Hotel in Baghdad during the Iraq War (see Tumber and Palmer 2004, p. 44):

'I was in my room at that time. I was writing. It was just before 12 o'clock [midday]. Then suddenly there's this almighty explosion and I thought, "Oh God, now they're coming for us." I thought it was Iraqis, and everybody thought it was Iraqis, because we had heard mortars coming up from the other side of the hotel, which were . . . obviously Iraqi. And we saw those tanks on the bridge. You could see them from the room, the American tanks. And they were engaged in a fire fight. Two tanks and they were just firing one after another.
Suddenly they turned the barrel of the gun on one of the tanks towards our hotel. I suggested it might be a good idea if we got off the balcony at this stage. We came inside and that was about an hour or an hour and a half beforehand, and then suddenly there was this explosion. Then I went up to the room and there were two or three people lying on the floor. We carried them out and took them downstairs. It didn't look as though there was very much we could do for them, and the pathetic sight of the room, you can imagine, just shattered glass everywhere, all of the glass now red, just looking like rubies, dust everywhere covering cameras. What had been an ordinary working journalist's room was suddenly a place of death.
The following day I think it was, I went to that bridge and I talked to the people who'd done it. They just simply said that they saw two people up there, they were being shelled, and they thought that the hotel was being used as a spotting point for triangulation for the Iraqis to attack these two tanks. The simple fact is all the rest of the world knew that the Palestine Hotel was full of journalists. But they didn't. The American tank commander said he didn't, he wasn't aware that that was the Palestine Hotel. And to some extent I could believe him.'

Frontline correspondents inevitably encounter risks in their work. How they respond to these depends on personality, training and experience. But it is evident that on occasions – as in Iraq since the 2003 invasion – dangers are acutely high. Sometimes, too, their luck runs out.

Notes

1 This figure does not include journalists killed in accidents, such as car or plane crashes – unless the action was caused by aggressive human action – or journalists who died of ill health.
2 See *Women Reporting War,* a survey by the International News Safety Institute (INSI) www.newssafety.com/stories/insi/wrw.htm.
3 See also Demoustier's account from 2003 dictated by telephone to Mark Wood, Chief Executive of ITN (http://www.fred-nerac.info/ukartdesmout.htm).

10

TRAINING AND PROTECTION

'I'm not saying that you can't learn from training, you can. But the most important thing is experience.' (David Zucchino, *Los Angeles Times*)

A response to heightened concern for journalists' safety has been the development of training courses to prepare them for conflict situations. Where once young correspondents would learn their trade in the company of more experienced reporters, or even by just being in the field, in recent years specialist training courses have been introduced. These are usually organised by ex-military personnel.[1] Tim Lambon, producer cameraman for *Channel 4 News*, offers a history of 'hostile environment training courses' and an assessment of their usefulness:

'During the first Gulf War there was suddenly a big threat from nuclear, biological and chemical weapons, which the Coalition forces all said Saddam had and was likely to use. So before reporting in that desert, you had to undergo training with NBC. NBC training was not available commercially and you did the training once you arrived. [It was a] two-day course for the media, led by the military. The idea was that the media could then be taken to what was supposedly the frontline, in what they called a mobile reporting team – an MR team. There was also a bunch of people from the SAS around Hereford, who became AKE. And there was a bunch of Marine commandos who set themselves up in Hampshire as Centurion. Since then there has been the development of several others. These people all thought there was a market for ex-soldiers to do things with the press.

It's very interesting how it's developed, because after the Gulf War, we then had the Balkans. This was the first European war that anybody could get to – you could take a train from Vienna to Zagreb, or from Italy to Zagreb, and as long as you had a piece of headed notepaper from anything that you could have put together, even on desktop publishing in those days, you could get press accreditation from the UN in Zagreb. Then you could jump on a plane into Sarajevo without the slightest clue of what the bloody hell you were letting yourself in for.

I don't know what the figure was for the number of supposed journalists killed during that war, but I think it ran into over 120, 130. And that was because of the accessibility. The most unsuitable people went to this war and it was a serious fighting war. As a result of that, and people getting killed, the big broadcasters and newspapers, especially the Anglophone ones, suddenly started to get pressure from their insurance people. They said, "We're not going to insure you unless we have some reason to believe that the people that you're sending out there are suitable to be sent out there." So that's where the AKEs and the Centurions of this world stepped in.'[2]

The broadcasters have been at the forefront in paying for their reporters to attend these courses. Mark Wood, Chief Executive of ITN, outlines their policy:

'We insist that everybody going into a war zone now has proper hostile environment training. That has been the policy here for quite a while and it has to be refreshed regularly as well. I was previously at Reuters and we introduced it when I was Editor in Chief there as well. So I think there are a number of advantages which emerge. The basic training is helpful. The first aid training is very useful and a lot of the feedback that I've had over the years has been that that's been one of the most useful elements. If somebody is injured, people have an idea of what to do and what not to do.

But it really is more to familiarise people with dealing with environments in which they're caught by surprise or where there is gunfire and how to assess what the danger levels are. So it does help. Well at least it seems to, and I think most people who go on these courses think they do help. They probably also build in some reflexes, which can be useful. Like when to jump out of a car when it's under fire, what to do when you are ready to jump out, and what to do when you do jump out. Things that you might not know instinctively.'

Within ITN everyone going to a war zone had been on such courses recently. Wood also stresses the importance of using experienced people as much as possible (although in the recent Iraq War ITN lost four people, demonstrating that even experience and training cannot always guarantee safety). James Mates of ITN is one of the journalists who have experienced these courses and he explains:

'There are layers upon layers of protection that you can give yourself. One of those is just experience, which you don't get unless you first of all go somewhere without experience. So before you go anywhere, I think training courses are helpful. We at ITN do a five-day training course on hostile environments. Some of this is simply first aid but there are also things like mine awareness, how to spot trip wires, how to be aware of the dangers around you, how to know what a bullet can go through. So when you hear something and you dive behind a tree or a car or a wall, you know how much protection that will really give you. That's useful to open your eyes, especially for inexperienced people.

And then we also do a number of other courses that refresh that knowledge. For example, a four-wheel driving course, because obviously if you're driving in an armoured vehicle, that's four tons of vehicle. It could kill you if you don't know how to handle it. So, for an inexperienced reporter or even for a more experienced reporter, those courses are always useful. There's always one thing that you can learn, that you can walk away with, even if the rest is boring. You think you know it all, but if you learn one thing, it could save your life. Anyone who turns their noses up at those courses is crazy because they're useful.'

Mates continues to draw attention to the importance, in matters of safety, of journalists passing information amongst themselves:

'When you get to an area, journalists are pretty good at talking to each other about the risks involved. Where your personal life is concerned, we swap information in wars all the time, as long as you're not giving away any secrets.'

BBC journalist Orla Guerin talks about the routine character of the training:

'Before I started covering areas of conflict for the BBC, I was sent on a hostile environments training programme, which, from memory, was about five days. I was also sent on a battlefield first aid course. Subsequently, over the years, I've done refreshers of both of those courses. Prior to the Gulf War, I was sent on the military's chemical and biological hazards course, and you have to do that if you are going to be embedded with the military, although I had already done a BBC course in Israel two years ago on chemical and biological weapons. There is now a continuous practice of updating training. I've also been sent on a dangerous driving course and how to drive armoured cars – which was very useful, although I was already driving them in the field without any kind of official training.'

Sara Oliver of the *Daily Mail* is very positive about her experiences of the courses:

'Up until the Iraq War, there was no training or preparation at all. You just read as much as you could and tried to plan as best you could, which I have to say in retrospect now seems quite haphazard. Certainly the formal training that I received prior to going to Iraq has helped me in many jobs since and I'm sure will help me for the rest of my career. I went on a hazardous environment course, which involves escape and evasion – what to do in the event of kidnap, first aid. I enjoyed that very much. It taught me some stuff I had already just gathered, over the years, by experience. Other stuff was new to me and I think proved very useful . . . I think overall in terms of the nuclear, biological and chemical warfare training, it was excellent. And general preparations for army life, while not rigorous, certainly meant that we all looked less foolish than we might otherwise have done when we did arrive to set up home with the army.'

Despite being told things he already knows, Daniel Demoustier thinks the courses are very useful especially for first aid, not least because 'after ten years of war zones I had not the slightest idea how to put a bandage on somebody'. Indeed, for most of the journalists we interviewed, first aid was the most valuable part of the available training courses.

Before the 2003 Gulf War, David Williams spent two days on a course run by former British Army people:

'The one we went to was up in Cambridgeshire and it's run by a company called Objective. They've got a couple of former SAS people and some very distinguished soldiers. Theirs was an excellent course and it taught you about the impact of different bullets as well. So it's pointless hiding behind a certain type of wall if it's heavy machine gun fire, which will just go straight through. A lot of people wouldn't realise that – they'd just think they were safe. So the more courses of that type that people go on, particularly people going to conflict zones for the first time, the better. But you still learn very, very quickly when you're actually out in the field. Every conflict is slightly different.'

For Jeremy Thompson of *Sky News,* one of the most valuable elements of the training courses is that they can make reporters who have never been in the theatre of war more aware of what they're letting themselves in for, though this can never substitute for the real thing:

'It can be very useful in some basic awareness and remind people it's not a game and [that] it's potentially dangerous out there. There's no doubt that quite a lot of people have learnt skills that'll save their lives. People have learnt enough first aid to perhaps save a colleague in the field. I guess for my generation, we've done an awful lot of stuff before courses came into force. But for a new generation now it's much better to have them than not. But they can only teach you so much. It's only when you're under fire that you'll realise how well you can cope with these things.'

The awareness aspect was emphasised by Jerry Lampen when discussing the hostile environment course he was sent to by Reuters:

'It doesn't make you think you won't get injured or killed, but it does make you very aware of all the dangers that are there. It's more of an awareness course. When you are in those situations that get a little nasty, all of a sudden something pops up that you talked about or you discussed during those courses. Then on top of that we have the first aid courses which are very, very useful.'

However, like Jeremy Thompson, many journalists stress the value of experience as being the best protector in conflict zones. David Zucchino sums it up: ·

'I think the best training is just in-the-field experience. It's pretty hard in the classroom or training situation to impart the kind of wisdom and street-smart knowledge that people develop over years just from experience. It's the kind of profession where you really just have to go out and do it and that's how you learn. I'm not saying that you can't learn from training, you can. But the most important thing is experience.'

Nonetheless, Gavin Hewitt of the BBC thinks the courses have improved over the years:

'Initially I felt they had not had the experience of, for instance, how you go through a hostile roadblock, or what you do if you're being held by gunmen. They developed some good ideas, and people fed back information to those doing the training and gradually they became better. They did cover, for instance, not just war but also disturbances in the streets – that a rock can do you as much damage as a bullet. They made people realise that these are very, very dangerous places and that you need a very serious approach to them. They gave courses about how to get out of a minefield – nobody ever wanted to get into a minefield, but these were useful bits of information – and about booby-trapped mines.

Last year I went to a boot camp . . . for a week of training, and I also went for several days' training for chemical and biological attack – that was a new element, to get your mask on within nine seconds. That was part of the training for the Iraq War.'

Tim Lambon suggests that the approach of the courses has changed:

'They now understand us as journalists and how we work. The two-day refresher course I went on at Centurion was completely vehicle borne, which is how journalists work. Journalists get into a car and they drive to a place. They get out, they film and talk to people, they get back in the car, they go to the next place. And in a place like Iraq, moving around is the dangerous part of the job. Iraq is not a shooting war where you're going to get killed because there's a lot of lead flying around, like it was in Bosnia; there's no frontline as such, where you have to know what you're about when you're in an actual combat situation. Iraq is about personal protection, being aware of your environment and knowing when you're being followed – what to do in situations of possible kidnap.'

On the other hand, we interviewed journalists who were critical of existing courses. Vaughan Smith, freelance cameraman and founder of the Frontline Club, believes training within journalism is poor:

'You could argue that journalism in conflict zones is one of the most risky professions in the world. There's statistical evidence to support that. If that's the case, you would expect journalists to be the best trained in field craft, in surviving conflicts. That's not true at all. There's no way a journalist can compare to a soldier for training in a battlefield. Very few journalists have the training that an experienced aid worker has in conflict zones. It's a real problem. The industry has only just begun to address it. Television is leading the way and some of the industry's leaders are very conscious of the need for this. But at the same time, they don't understand it. The understanding of safety is appallingly poor. The argument on safety is normally about whether we should carry guns or not. Some do, some don't, some think we should, some don't. Americans like to carry guns, British people don't, on the whole. But there's no way of forcing people to do anything, because every company can have its own policy on this.'

Smith goes on to complain that:

'When it comes to actual practical improvement of safety, broadcasters are afraid of the cost. For example, we rely, as an industry, on ex-soldiers to train us. Now that is good but not good enough. Ex-soldiers don't often know about journalism. And journalists are normally suspicious of soldiers. So you have a problem there, where there's no sensible coherent resolution. The only reason we now have any safety is that, if you don't provide some sort of training, you might get sued. So the companies are worried about that. But added to that there are some individuals in the industry who generally wish their people to be safer.

People are in a blind panic about this because they don't know how to do it. Actually to improve safety you have to look at logistics. You have to have proper planning, you have to have good administration – all these boring things. But they don't understand how they relate to safety . . . I remember an instance, for example, where a producer took half a ton of bottled water over a pass in Afghanistan that was 14,000 feet high. Well of course it smashed and broke and froze and wasn't drinking water by the end of the trip. He didn't have the training or the knowledge to have a water purifying machine and to think that he should bring that instead, and a generator.'

Those journalists critical of the type of training provided include James Meek of the *Guardian*. He believes the key issue is that the instructors talk to them as if they were soldiers:

'We weren't really getting our money's worth because their advice ceased to be useful at the point when the chemical attack is taking place and you've put on your chemical suit. It seems to me, if you did a bit of thinking, the best advice for journalists at that point would be to leave the area as fast as they possibly could because they're not soldiers, they're not obliged to carry on fighting. The whole point about having a chemical warfare suit if you're a soldier, is that you carry on fighting: that even though the enemy has attacked you, it hasn't stopped you fighting the war. But journalists are in a completely different situation. And it's no good companies like Centurion coming along with these guys who've been in the SAS or the army who know all about chemical warfare for soldiers. I think it's rather a cheat for them to charge huge sums of money for journalists when they haven't bothered to do any research or take into consideration how journalists might react in that situation. And it may be that the best advice is simply to run away as fast as possible.

But then you've got the situation whereby you arrive in a civilian town in a contaminated vehicle – what is the best way in a civilian environment to dispose of contaminated clothes, contaminated car? What should you do? If you are, for some mad reason, going to attempt to continue to work in this environment, how are you going to operate a laptop? What's the best way to decontaminate a laptop? And what's the best way to decontaminate a TV camera? They hadn't done any research on this, and if there is ever going to be anything like this again, then they'll need to.'

Adrian Monck, formerly of ITN and Deputy Editor of *5 News*, echoes these sentiments on the value of the courses:

'I think a lot of them are bullshit, because what we used to do was that people would be trained by going out with experienced people. And these courses are run by soldiers who have very different needs and very different awareness of situations.'

Protection

Beyond learning from experience and undertaking the training courses, what do frontline journalists do to improve their protection? Kim Willsher of the *Mail on Sunday* recalls her experiences in the former Yugoslavia in 1991. Dubrovnik was being shelled and the war was just starting:

'It seems astonishing nowadays, but I went with just myself, no photographer, nobody else, no flak jacket, no helmet, no protection, nothing, just a notebook, and off I went. And it was pretty hairy at times. The journalists there, like myself, realised this was a very vicious war, like all wars. But it was very chaotic, very widespread, nobody seemed to know really what was going on or where. And shortly afterwards they sent out a photographer from the *Mail on Sunday*, who was another woman. We were quite unusual at that time – two women working as a team – and a lot of our male colleagues from other newspapers were rather concerned about what might happen to us. But we were very successful. We travelled around, we did what we had to do. But we had a very, very nasty situation where we ended up just outside Dubrovnik being pinned down by some Serbian forces. We ended up having to abandon our hire car, which was shot up, and hide behind a very low stone wall for about six hours being shot at.'

James Meek describes the occasions when he wears protective gear, indicating that there is no set rule and that on-the-spot judgement plays a big part:

'I've been in conflict situations where I have worn a flak jacket. I've been to places where I haven't worn a flak jacket. In the last war, I wore a helmet a lot, which I hadn't done before. Normally I think that wearing a helmet and a flak jacket makes you more of a target, it makes people more likely to shoot at you. But since most of the time that I was in Iraq during the active combat phase of the war, I was spending with Marines and they were all obviously targets anyway, I felt it was a good idea to wear a helmet, because the head is the most vulnerable part of the body. I wouldn't wear one in a guerrilla war and I would not normally wear a flak jacket either.'

But according to Kim Willsher of the *Mail on Sunday,* protective gear doesn't necessarily save you from injury or even death: 'You can wear a flak jacket and it does not stop you having your leg blown off.'

As well as protective gear, some journalists travel with unarmed security personnel. The BBC's Gavin Hewitt has travelled with ex-Special Forces:

'I've always been clear in my mind, they're not there as quasi-military protection because they don't carry weapons. They're there for their minds and their experience – it's how they read a situation. Much of safety is dependent upon correctly assessing a developing situation, it isn't about muscle or firepower. These guys don't go along with weapons. You hope that, having been in difficult situations themselves, they sense something that may happen before it happens, and that's really where their expertise comes in. But we're now in situations where journalists sometimes are the targets. There are people out there trying to kidnap or to actually kill us, and in those circumstances if you've got Special Forces people with you, it may not make a great deal of difference.'

According to Bill Neely, ITN only use people with whom they are familiar:

'In the last couple of years, there have been an awful lot of idiots and frauds coming forward saying "I was Special Forces, hire me." Occasionally they've been hired and within a day or two it's been proved that they're idiots. In Iraq ITN principally has one guy that we really trust, we like. He knows how we work, we know what he likes. He doesn't try and interfere with the journalism. He's good. I was very against having security men there because again I suppose I'm a bit of a rebel at heart. I want to choose my team, but these can be extremely dangerous situations and it can be useful to have an expert pair of eyes and someone that you can just ask, "It's very quiet, what do you think of this situation? Do you think we should go up there?" And they might say, "It's too quiet, let's just stay and wait another 15 minutes, let's see what happens." And that can be useful advice, whereas you ask a sound man, "What do you think?" and he might judge it differently.'

Some of the journalists have more experience than the soldiers they are accompanying on assignment. According to Neely, the Commanding Officer of the Marines that he accompanied during the Iraq war told him, 'You may very well have more combat experience than any of these guys.' He adds:

'Most of them had never been in a war zone before, and the same goes for security people, which is why we tend to narrow it down now to employ two or three on a rotating basis. The principal one that we employed has been in a lot of situations and we trust him and that's what it comes down to in the end, trust.'

Julian Manyon, a colleague of Neely's at ITN, has mixed feelings about the issue:

'The present Iraq conflict is overall about as dangerous, apart from Chechnya, as anything that I have covered . . . The wealthier companies have chosen to exercise their responsibilities towards their employees by using bodyguards. They go under the title of "security adviser" and they are generally former servicemen from elite British army units – in particular, the SAS but not exclusively so. These people are attached to us in Iraq at the moment, just one of them at a time, and are supposed to both advise us and accompany us out on stories. My feelings about it are very mixed. I don't like the idea of journalists having bodyguards and I like even less the idea of journalists having armed bodyguards. I'm in favour of, as we have in Baghdad, a largish and rather battered armoured saloon, which most people don't pay a blind bit of attention to. That gives us a degree of protection if shooting starts or a bomb goes off. I'm very much in favour of that. I'm not in favour of going around with armed bodyguards who look like bodyguards and tend to alienate the local population. And also if they're armed, they compromise the whole idea of what you're there for. We are there to hear people's opinions and to collect facts and to try to report them fairly.'

Mark Wood outlines ITN's policy:

'In Baghdad, like most media organisations we always have security people alongside our teams now. It's one of the big expense items. And the big debate in the last few weeks has been around whether the security men should be armed or not. CNN and others have set a precedent by saying they would have armed guards in Iraq. The British media in particular and the European media generally have been very reluctant to do it, taking the view that, if you're covering news stories, journalists shouldn't be armed and their minders shouldn't be armed. But I think the situation in Iraq is that travelling in and out is clearly so dangerous. One or two news organisations have started to review that. A lot of the security guards now won't work unless they are armed. So Iraq seems to be breaking all the records of being a particularly dangerous place to work. So far, we're still sticking to our policy that we don't want our journalists accompanied by armed guards, but that's on covering news stories. On travel in and out by road, we're leaving it to the security companies to recommend what they want to do. But we don't want our journalists accompanied by armed guards on news coverage.'

The BBC does much the same, as Ben Brown relates:

'What is new is the arrival of the safety advisers, who are ex-Special Forces, SAS guys, who, sometimes, are very useful. For example, we had a guy with us in Iraq, when I was embedded. He was really brilliant and he's an ex-SAS guy. He gave us a commentary on the battlefield as we went through it. And so we knew from his expertise what was happening, what the enemy was doing, where the dangers were. Sometimes they're not that much use because they don't really know any more about the situation than you do. Sometimes less, because I've probably been in more war zones than some of these guys.'

Jeremy Thompson of *Sky News* tells a similar story:

'Sky took on board a couple of guys from a private security company, both of whom interestingly had been in Iraq before when they were professional soldiers. But they had never been to Baghdad before. One went with one of our units and the other one was teamed up with me, but not until we were about two or three weeks into it. It was good, because he gave me a bit of reassurance. I'd just sensed by his demeanour, the way he carried himself, his 30 years' experience that he was not going to be able to stop an army, but he's going to sniff the air and tell you when he doesn't like it.'

Thompson makes it very clear, though, that he would not use armed advisers:

'I wouldn't let him be armed, and I think there's a great danger. There were quite a number of instances where the security [personnel] attached to journalists were armed. When I got back to Kuwait and saw telly for the first time, there was my old colleague from ITN days, and now with CNN, Brent Saddler, up with a whole convoy of CNN people getting involved in a fire fight with the

Iraqi militias on the side of the road, because he had armed security guys. I think that's madness and leads us down a terribly dangerous path.'

The newspaper journalists tend to take an antagonistic view of security personnel whether or not they are armed. But unlike the broadcasters, who work in teams, the newspaper correspondents usually work alone. This may, at least in part, account for different responses. Certainly James Meek believes the issue of safety and in particular the use of security personnel is becoming a problem:

'We're already going too far down the road of safety. The big danger now of journalism is not that it should be made safer but that it's perhaps become too safe, perhaps too obsessed with making journalists safe. It's only in the most extreme situations that a journalist should put on anything which is going to set them too far apart from the people that they're interviewing, like a helmet, or a flak jacket. But now in Iraq, you're in an extraordinary and very troubling situation where at least one major newspaper, the *New York Times*, on at least one occasion decided that it was appropriate to travel to an assignment with its own armed guard – not just one person with a gun, but a van containing security personnel. If you really, really feel that the only way you can go to do that story is by doing that, then you should not go and do it because if you turn up as a journalist and interview people with a handful of armed men, then you're not a journalist anymore, you're something else. I don't know what you are. It's intimidating and it's wrong and that is the way that this sort of obsession with safety is pushing us.'

Maggie O'Kane takes a similar view:

'There's a lot of different dangers with every conflict. Keeping yourself alive in Haiti is a bit different from keeping yourself alive in Bosnia, or from keeping yourself alive in Iraq. So don't ever sit up against a wall, don't hang around with armed guards. This pressure to salve the consciences of the executives in various newspaper and broadcasting institutions who pay vast contributions to security companies to supply armed guards [is] completely ill-advised and probably very, very dangerous for journalists. So I avoid armed people at all times unless I'm interviewing them or they're escorting me to other armed people. My theory is to try and be as low-key as possible, to blend as much as possible into the environment, and that's the basic grounds for safety as far as I'm concerned.'

Anton Antonowicz of the *Daily Mirror* describes the use of security personnel as a growth industry and it is something about which he is wary:

'I remember going back to Baghdad [during 2004] . . . and I was on a plane with a guy, ex-Marine. He was being paid £800 a day to work out there. He's English, he lives in Spain. He's a mercenary essentially. When we get to Baghdad, after a couple of days I see him, and he's going out to the restaurants to eat, which is crazy in this situation. I wouldn't do that. I'm only going to eat in the hotel. I'm not going to go out on the street by myself unprotected.

They're walking around with every kind of gun on them, looking like something out of the wild west, just annoying people really. They look as though they're invasive. This whole security operation reflects more the West's paranoia than it does the reality of the situation.'

Antonowicz prefers to survive on his wits, as he makes clear when he relates his experience of one of his assignments:

'If the *Mirror* said to me, "We want you to go for training in how to be an innocuous hostage," then I'll go and do that. But I think in the end so much of this is just commonsense. I found a very, very good thing is cigars actually. You offer somebody a cigar when they're being aggressive towards you, and the next thing, you find that you've struck up a relationship with them. I remember being arrested by the secret police in Turkey, when I was writing about the way in which the Kurdish children were being arrested and tortured. Then suddenly the secret police came and swooped on me when I was just standing on a street corner with an interpreter and a photographer. I pulled out a packet of cigars and opened it and they all stood back thinking I had a grenade. And I just offered them a cigar, and they were completely confused.'

Jon Swain also thinks the use of ex-soldiers can create problems:

'Although I respect those people, and it's their job to look after you, it can hamper what you're trying to do. They can say, "Well, we advise not to go down that road because you might get kidnapped." But there is a story at the end of it . . . If they say it's safe and you go down there and something happens to you, then their organisation is very culpable. At the end of the day you've got to look after yourself, you've got to work out your own security. Of course it's difficult if you're working in a team like in the BBC. But I'm just a one-man band. I usually travel on my own. I take my own camera sometimes. It's easier to make the decisions by myself than to make them for other people.'

There seems little doubt that 'hostile environment training courses' are here to stay, and they appear to be improving in terms of what they offer the journalist. In this regard they are a valuable supplement to the practical lessons correspondents learn from the experiences of doing their work in war conditions. No doubt, too, frontline correspondents will take measures to protect themselves as best they can in trying circumstances. Donning military equipment and even being chaperoned by former soldiers might be judged appropriate under particular conditions, though, as our interviewees observed, they can also pose problems for the practising journalist.

Moreover, Jon Swain, amongst many others, makes it clear that none of these measures can guarantee the safety of the frontline correspondent. And he highlights another aspect that is often overlooked, but which endangers him and his colleagues:

'The status [of journalists] has been eroded now because we're all Westerners, we're all white, we work for Western organisations. And particularly in the Middle East, we're targeted. It's very galling when you are trying to cover someone's conflict and you find yourself, like I did, in Ethiopia. I was kidnapped by some guerrillas. I was actually trying to cover their struggle. But they thought I was a spy, so I was their captive for three months. And that's pretty depressing because you're trying to shed some light on what they're doing, and they turn against you.'

All the training courses and all the protective kit in the world cannot guard the journalist against this threat.

Notes

1   The International News Safety Institute (INSI), which was set up in 2003, has published a 10-point safety code which urges news organisations to consider safety first before competitive advantage. It calls for all media staff to be given appropriate hostile environment and risk awareness training as well as protective health and safety equipment such as medical packs, helmets, respirators and flak jackets. It calls for adequate insurance for staff and freelancers, counselling for journalists traumatised by the horrors of conflict, and freedom for any media worker to refuse an assignment to a danger zone without penalty. Journalists themselves are not excluded from contributing to the new safety ethic: they are called upon to behave responsibly and not recklessly endanger themselves and their colleagues. They are reminded that journalists are neutral observers and should not carry firearms in the course of their work (www.newssafety.com).
2   See www.akegroup.com and www.centurion-riskservices.co.uk

11

COPING WITH FEAR AND DANGER

'You never feel more alive than when you're possibly about to die.' (Chris Ayres, *The Times*)

In this chapter we explore how journalists describe their fears and their ability to cope both on assignment and on their return home. As the issue of the physical safety of journalists has gained ascendancy on news organisations' agendas, so has the mental health condition of correspondents. Editors of the large news organisations, in particular, have become acutely aware of the possibility of post-traumatic stress disorder (PTSD) affecting their employees, and counselling and therapy are now readily available to those who may require it.

For some of the older generation of correspondents, the only way to avoid stigmatisation when encountering the syndrome was to avoid any discussion about it with one's editor, drink to tranquillise it and maybe talk about it with a colleague (Ochberg 2001, p. 12). The solution was simple: you accepted that your life was not normal and then you 'educated yourself about your own head' (Little 2001, p. 19). Other journalists suggest very unstable backgrounds and the lack of a strong sense of self as reasons for the symptoms of PTSD (Di Giovanni 2001, p. 8).

In his study of the effects of trauma on war journalists, psychiatrist Anthony Feinstein (2003) found that the issues raised most often and with the most spontaneity during the course of his interviews were divorced parents, dysfunctional military fathers, troubled families, and rudderless young men and women in search of identity and meaning. However, despite this, Feinstein found that 'there was a group of war journalists who experienced none of this turmoil. Their largely middle-class family backgrounds were uncomplicated and happy' (ibid., p. 78).

In our interviews with correspondents, we found that they all had a general appreciation of PTSD but they exhibited a widespread reluctance to take up any offers of help from their organisations. Instead we found a disparate range of responses to stress and the adoption of a variety of coping strategies.

Fear in the Field

Colin Baker of ITN describes the time he first went to Belfast as a young man:

'When I started, I thought it was cowboys and Indians, until you see what it does, and it chills us. And the first time you're really frightened, really, really scared and you think you're about to die, it changes everything.'

Photographer Chip Hires has similar feelings:

'Every time I went off to these things . . . I always thought, "Who knows if I'm going to come back in one piece?" I'm not a very brave guy, I was always scared to death, sometimes more scared to death than others.'

Freelance journalist Antonia Francis talks about the occasions of being afraid:

'Twice in Afghanistan, simply because we were being shelled quite heavily. But we had gone to the frontline to see that, so it was like a silly experience that we were seeking so I could write about it, and photographs could be taken. But in Nepal I was scared probably for about two months solidly out of the four months because I thought that we were being followed, not only by Maoist Secret Services but also by Government Secret Services. And we had a lot of tapes on us and I knew that the Maoists had an increasingly bad history of killing journalists. We were completely insecure, and every time we arrived in a village, we were told that the Maoists would probably slit our throats if we went to the next one. So every night I was thinking, "Well I'm completely alone, I can't go back, and if I go forward I might have my throat slit, and my insurance won't actually reimburse my parents." And that was a major overriding concern for me.'

Jeremy Thompson has seen journalists fail to cope with the situation:

'You try to get them out of it as fast as possible. There's no point in having those that don't cope. Nearly everybody is going to get scared at some stage, and there are some that don't appear to show it and that's worrying. There's no doubt there is a fear and an excitement all mixed in together. It's really a matter of how well you handle it. Some people get hooked, absolutely no doubt about it at all. Other people get completely put off and want to run the other way and get out of it. That leaves the rump of us in the middle. As sort of top line reporters, it's part of the job description. You're going to be expected to do that as long as you can handle it, as long as you don't get spooked by it, and as long as you can do your job. You've got to feel the emotion of the event, but you've still got to describe that emotion and relay it back. You are the medium through which people are going to experience a Madrid bomber, a Bali bomber, a war in Iraq, or a civil war in Central America. It's a matter of how well you can cope with the situation, assimilate the information you're seeing and tell that story, while passing on as much of the flavour and the colour of it and the reality.'

Jon Swain was affected by his experiences in Vietnam and this was the main reason why he wrote his book some 20 years after the war:

'Every conflict I was in, I related to Vietnam and Cambodia. I spent a long time there – most of my twenties – in a very extraordinary environment. It was very,

very intense and if you've been through that in your twenties, that's something which will always be with you. It really takes charge of your life. I was always very emotional about it. I'd get upset about those places and people I knew. I used to have nightmares . . . I know probably 11, maybe more, journalists, photographers, cameramen from Vietnam and Cambodia, who committed suicide. One shot himself, another guy jumped out of a window, another guy drowned himself in the Hudson River. They never found his body. No one can be unaffected by war.'

Brian Williams of Reuters has also worked in Vietnam and found a welcome change of assignment when he returned:

'I've had friends who never recovered from Vietnam, it just totally consumed their lives. I was lucky because after I'd finished in Vietnam, I was given a totally different assignment – I covered England cricket tours for six months. I was amongst this group of people who, not that they hadn't heard of Vietnam, but didn't give a damn about it. They lived in their own little world, and that was very good for me. I didn't realise it at the time but thinking back it was very, very good. I don't think employers often deal as well with people when they've finished covering a war. Sometimes employers should really make a conscious effort to save some people from themselves, to pull them out of the line of fire, if you like, and put them into something completely different and new.'

Chris Ayres of *The Times*, an embedded reporter during the second Iraq War (2003), returned early from his assignment:

'I think they [other journalists] felt I had genuinely betrayed some kind of code by admitting that I was scared by giving up the embedded position early and coming back. There was a feeling that I'd squandered the opportunity. It's bullshit because what I wrote was actually a lot more informative because it let people know exactly what it was like, as opposed to writing straightforward macho war stuff. That's not to say I didn't feel bad: part of me felt guilty, part of me felt that I should have stayed longer until the bitter end. I'd done two weeks out there and I felt as though I'd pushed my luck as far as I wanted to push it, and that I valued my life more than another story. I thought if I get killed fine, for me I'd die now, but that is going to ruin my parents' life, it will ruin the rest of my grandparents' life, it will fuck up my girlfriend for years to come, and I just thought it's about more than just me.'

Out of the Field

Sara Oliver of the *Mail on Sunday* makes the following observation:

'Somewhere like Beirut, where the conflict doesn't come to you, you can retreat from it at the end of the day. And Kosovo was like that, people lived in hotels towards the end. The strangest I've ever felt was coming home from Afghanistan. I felt very, very disorientated for more than two weeks. I felt very woolly-headed and sort of incapable, and very tired, very physically and mentally weary. I think that was simply a reaction to being in such an extreme place. That is the only time that I have returned from a job and not felt myself.'

Colin Baker of ITN describes how life seems to get harder for him each time he goes on assignment:

'You're a lot wiser and I would get more and more frightened each time. I'd wonder about spending too much time in a certain place. In Kosovo in the early days, I spent so many months in and out and I loved it really. It sounds awful, but I missed it sometimes. I used to go out in thunderstorms back in England, in Buckinghamshire, and at night time I'd start with my eyes closed and listen to the thunder and pretend there were guns going off, and I'd feel good.'

Chris Ayres had similar feelings after his return from Iraq:

'When I got back I did feel that sort of syndrome. I felt a bit bored. I wanted things to be a bit more dangerous for a while. I got a feeling that nothing was really that important. After you've been in a life and death situation for a few weeks, it makes you question everything. You make very big decisions about your life because you realise that life's pretty short. I couldn't get enthusiastic about a lot of things because I was just thinking well, it's so unimportant really.'

Ayres describes how he felt after returning from New York after September 11:

'I definitely had some kind of post-traumatic shock. It was horrible and it took me a long time to become normal, to recover. But Iraq didn't have that effect on me. I don't know why. I think it's because September 11 was unexpected, it was something that just happened out of the blue right in the middle of where you assume and expect everything to be quite safe. You don't expect to watch people jumping from 120 storeys in front of you when you get out of bed in the morning. Whereas if you go to Iraq, you're expecting bad things to happen. I was right under the building when they were all jumping out. I saw people die.'

Peter Sharp of *Sky News* thinks that there needs to be an interim period between working on the frontline and arriving back home:

'I can remember I was being shelled on the street in Sarajevo around 11 o'clock and I got a call saying, "You're out". And I was driven to the airport. There was a German Hercules going out. I was in a bath full of bubbles, with a large scotch and soda, at about half-past one in Italy. It was just bizarre, it really was. A lot of people have various thoughts about that. It is good in a way to stagger the trip back a little bit. I found Bosnia and Ethiopia very difficult. I came back from that, I'd done six weeks there, maybe longer. It was before we had satellite phones. It was a very punishing trip. Our convoy got attacked by MiGs and a village got wiped out. I can remember coming back from that and I was totally freaked out. Every time I saw an aircraft in the air, when I heard a helicopter, I don't jump, but I flashback on it.'

Lindsey Hilsum takes the same view as Peter Sharp:

'I find it quite good to have a bridge day in between. I went to Beslan with the school siege which was really horrible and upsetting, and we had a day in Moscow on the way back and that was really useful because that's a day where you're easing your way out. On the way out of Iraq, we have a sort of ritual. There's a very nice Italian restaurant in Jordan, in Amman, which we always go to. You have these little things which bridge you between the one world and the other. Then one has another life. I have a very nice house which is important to me and I have projects. I just built a new kitchen. It's another focus in life and if I'm somewhere really horrible, then I'm quite often thinking about designing my kitchen or changing the bathroom.'

When David Zucchino of the *LA Times* came back from the Iraqi invasion, he would wake up every night and be disorientated and jump out of bed:

'It took a week or two for that to stop. I would jump at a loud noise and be on edge because when you're in a combat zone, you're sort of hyper vigilant; you're just waiting for something to happen and you're in this high state of apprehension and anxiety. It takes a while just to let those senses down. My wife really notices when I come back that I'm very remote and very anxious for the first days until I get back into a normal routine. But it is hard to go back and forwards because it's two very different worlds.'

For the late Ross Benson of the *Daily Mail,* the sleepless nights led him to stop for a while:

'By the end of the '80s I really had had enough. I'd be waking up in the middle of the night, I was thinking about things and I stopped doing it for three or four years. Actually I think it was seven years. I gave my brain a rest and then you settle down. You've worked out what you think and your views and opinions change. They mature, they mellow, whatever you want to call it, then you go back and you do it again, if that's what you want to do. I don't think anyone really wants to do it, I just get sent, because there's a war, go to Iraq.'

One of the ongoing struggles in the correspondents' lives is re-adaptation. Jon Swain says:

'The idea of coming home is often nicer than the actual reality of coming home. Once you've had your bath and answered the phone, you find there are no messages on your answer machine, and I then think well, why am I here? On the other hand, you do need to have a normal life. I don't think you can report war properly unless you can relate it to normal existence, because it's very extreme.'

Photographers feel that they often suffer more than most because to get good pictures they witness more of the horrors. Jerry Lampen finds it difficult reintegrating:

'Photography is a very solitary profession where you have to make your decisions yourself; you have to press the button yourself. When you come home, you have to start to live in a normal pattern again and we just become very asocial. You have to watch your language, whether it's for partners or for your children, and it's very, very difficult. And when you come back from a conflict zone, it becomes even more difficult because you also have, on top of it all, your experiences. What is happening with me and most of my colleagues, friends, is that we talk a lot while we're there with each other and that already helps in the process of dealing with problems. I always like a week or two weeks, when I come back home. It takes me always a little while to function in a normal way again. I see friends and they ask how it was. You start telling them. I just tell it away from myself, and in the worse case, we can have help from Reuters.'

Marie Colvin, who lost an eye on assignment, describes her emotional state:

'I've found that I have gotten so depressed I didn't even want to talk to anybody. I just wanted to lie and read something – read a book of fiction. Or you just want to pull the covers up to your head until you're able to deal with the world. What I've realised is that we are all probably a bit too macho. It's a very macho culture, so you're not supposed to get depressed, you're supposed to just keep going. And I've realised for myself after 15 or 18 years, it's really started to impact on me. I just had to take time and say, "I'm depressed, I don't actually want to do anything." And my paper's been very good about that. They say, "Okay, you take a couple of weeks or months off." I don't know how you change that part of the culture, except that I don't know if we have to change it, because war correspondents might bitch but it's a very non-judgemental group. We all know what we've been through. Nobody is judged, unless you make something up.'

Colvin found support useful:

'I've done counselling in this last year, and I found it helped a lot. But I've also known war correspondents who have gone to counselling and it's been no help. It's finding the right person. If the counsellor is used to counselling women who are depressed because they missed the Prada sale, you're not going to get anywhere.'

Colvin admits that she went back to work too quickly after reporting from Jenin and coming under fire from Israeli tanks:

'When I feel the sound, when I hear the sound of a bullet having been shot, I can feel it much more physically. I can feel what it would feel like. And the expectation of pain is worse than pain, so that has made things more difficult. If you're shot, you deal with being shot. But if you have any kind of imagination, expectation is always much worse than reality. . . . I can't bear being a damaged person or being seen as being a damaged person, or in any way having anybody feel sorry for me. I really don't want that. So I immediately went back. It's only in the last year, after this war, that I've thought, "Okay, you've proved yourself, let's get back to the point where your brain can integrate experiences and not have to be running and running and running the whole time".'

Audrey Gillan was offered post-traumatic stress disorder tests by her employer, the *Guardian*:

'I don't feel that I'm really mentally scarred about last year. I think that might be because I never really saw any blood. I did see people die. I am concerned about going back – the mental impact later on. Journalists may find it hard to take up counselling because they're supposed to be hard.'

John Carlin speaks of writing itself as a means of coping. Constantly scribbling, formulating in words what he had experienced, was, for Carlin, 'therapy on the go' – a coming to terms with searing events. Similar was Dan Edge's self-treatment of 'yabbing loads, just talking, talking, talking to friends'. Kim Willsher echoes this. Her way of dealing with the horrors she witnessed was to talk to anyone who would listen.

'It just all came out. I would just tell anyone. I'd become a real Bosnia bore because I would just talk to my colleagues, to my friends. A lot of people, even my friends, even my family, couldn't really understand what was going on out there. I used to just talk and talk and talk, very often to get it out of my system and also to try and convince people – I don't know what difference I thought it was going to make – perhaps that this is why we should be doing something about what's happening there, this is why it's important, and this is why we do the job.'

Luke Harding of the *Guardian* believes the best therapy is to sit down with other similar kinds of journalists, 'talking to people who were there' over beers. Since it is 'sort of a macho trade', talking to someone outside the profession may be a barrier in understanding, one that cannot be crossed unless it has been experienced. Jeremy Thompson takes a similar view:

'It's a whole culture and a whole department's been spawned on the back of it. And it's probably not a bad idea. My wife always says, "For goodness sake, just stop somewhere on the way and have a few beers with your mates and don't come back immediately because you're useless." And it's true. She'll be communicating but I won't be quite taking it in. It's not a bad idea to go and let off steam somewhere, and tell the tales, because it's a little club and you've been involved in something that only you really know about.'

Caroline Wyatt of the BBC agrees:

'I think it changes you as a person more than anything. It changes your attitudes towards other people. It makes you less sympathetic with friends and family if they have a problem because wherever you come back from, you're thinking, "God, the people I've just seen have it a million times worse." I was probably more affected by Afghanistan and Chechnya than I think any other conflict, just because of the conditions you see ordinary people living in, struggling through, and the things they've suffered and the things they've seen are far worse than anything any of us will live through. You do come back changed but you do the same as you ever do; you go out for drinks with your friends, you have a laugh, you may talk about it but it's probably easier to talk about it with the people you were there with. And you end up having a much closer relationship with your colleagues, because you've been to the same places, you've done the same things, you've seen the same things, you've lived through them. You don't need to explain, they know how you feel, and it affects them in the same way. So you talk to them. But then when you meet other people, you tend not to talk about it.'

Lindsey Hilsum of *Channel 4 News* has developed her own ways of dealing with the horrors she witnesses by, for instance, channelling her energies into charity work:

'We're constantly being told we should be traumatised; people have been wanting me to be traumatised for years now and I absolutely and stubbornly refuse to be traumatised. You would be inhuman if you didn't think about these things – in Rwanda, in particular. Rwanda haunts me. I will never get away from Rwanda. I have Rwandan friends. Rwanda is there the whole time for me and you try and channel it. At the moment, I'm also doing some work with a charity which is trying to provide antiretroviral drugs to women who were raped during the genocide. You try and find a channel for those feelings of anger. People react differently to these things. My view is that I've seen a lot of really awful things, but I don't think I've done anything terrible, so I think that the psychological problems are the people who do these things, not the people who watch them. It's there all the time but I don't see why it should stop you living your life.'

Hilsum also eschews counselling support, but was quick to add that:

'It's nothing to do with being macho. I'm not interested in my psychological reaction and I'm not interested in some sort of well-meaning psychotherapist going "mmm". I might be interested in talking to somebody else who knows about Rwanda or about Iraq and discussing it. The point is not my psychological health. The point is the terrible things that go on in the world. That's what matters. You can't make the world a better place, but you can try and help individuals here and there. I believe in what I do in trying to bring some understanding of these situations.'

James Mates of ITN was also deeply affected by his experience in Rwanda. He uses the logistics of work to cope:

'I can relax straightaway. When you're covering conflict zones, you're under pressure, and there's always a background fear that it's a dangerous place. But for the most part I don't find it emotionally or mentally particularly stressful.

You're not normally seeing horrible gruesome things. When I come back I sleep 24 hours, enjoy some good food and some nice wine and I'm just glad to see the family again. You're happy that you've got some time off. You go away for a month, then you'll have two weeks off when you get back, and that's really what I look forward to – doing things with the children.

Then occasionally there are places that do put a mental strain on me. Rwanda was one of them. I saw some really horrible things, and it was a very, very stressful time. You were stuck in there for a month and couldn't get out because the civil war really erupted around you. Even so, the fact is that you're working all the time, you're not there as a tourist, you're not there thinking about it all the time in a deeply emotional way. You don't keep the unpleasant distant, but you've got to get your story out every day. The logistics are very, very difficult – even making a phone call can sometimes be hard, just to let the office know what you're doing. There's an awful lot to keep you busy and to stop you thinking about how horrendous it is.'

Barbara Jones of the *Daily Mail*, like Hilsum, found another way of dealing with the horrors she experienced:

'When I had five and a half months in Afghanistan I came back and I had a very bad time, crying all the time, wishing [I was] back there. There's something incredible about Afghanistan, the fortitude of those people and they are the most remarkable people. Africans are, too, but it really gets to you, Afghanistan. So I didn't deal with that very well. Getting my translator over here, I made that a mission. I promised him I would get him to Cape Town. He had no passport. I got someone in the Indian Consulate in Kabul on a satellite phone and they helped him get a passport and they got him a visa. I focused on that and I felt a little bit of Afghanistan had come to me and I got over it. I had sleepless nights. I wanted to sleep during the day and I was very tearful. I saw worse things in Iraq and I think you've got to use your anger or your upset – use it in your work, put it where it can do some good.'

From his own and other colleagues' experiences on assignment around the world covering the horrors of international conflict, Roger Rosenblatt (1994) suggests that most journalists react in three stages. In the first stage, they respond to atrocities with shock and revulsion, persuading themselves that the mere telling of the war story is valuable because the people who read it will know what they did not know, and some may act on that knowledge. In the second stage the atrocities become familiar and repetitive and many journalists, he says, get stuck in this stage, getting bogged down in the routineness of the suffering. 'Embittered, spiteful and inadequate to their work, they curse out their bosses back home for not according them respect; they hate the people on whom they report' (Rosenblatt 1994, pp. 14–15). The third stage sets in after years of observing the varieties of destruction of which people are capable. Everything feels sadder and wiser, worse and strangely better.

Back Home

'There's the BBC World Service introduction music to the news. They call it divorce music because you're going to get divorced if you hear it all the time' (Lin Hilton, photographer).[1]

Frontline correspondents are often away from their families and friends for lengthy periods. How does reporting conflict affect their personal and social lives? It would be easy to contrast the tranquillity of home life with the wear and tear of the frontline correspondents' work, contrasting succour and support with exhausting and searing labour. There is much truth in this, but we need also to acknowledge the excitement and energy that comes with war reporting which draws many journalists to it. There is even a genre of writing about war – from Michael Herr's *Dispatches* to Jon Steele's *War Junkie* – that conceives war reporting as a form of addiction. James Meek reports that the work is 'often compared to a drug' and admitted that 'the adrenaline rush' was 'difficult to reproduce away from it'. Not surprisingly, then, there is something in many frontline correspondents that draws them back to 'where the action is', where they are 'recording history', no matter how contented and comforting their domestic circumstances might be. There is a tension between home life (it could be dull and make one yearn to be back on the job) and being in the field (it could be arduous, hard to tolerate, debilitating in the extreme, making one hunger for home). Reporting war is exciting, even if tolerable only in bursts, which are when return trips home for rest and recuperation come in.

Many of the journalists to whom we spoke were happy to return to 'normal' everyday life. They found it restful and reassuring. Others, however, could find home very mundane. Jane Kokan, for example, finds it hard hearing people having normal conversations:

'You think, how pathetic – talking about the price of cherry tomatoes in Sainsbury's or talking about which fabulous restaurant they went to in London and which celebrity they saw. To me that's so lame. I think that's so sad that's all they seem to have to talk about. I guess when you're looking at really nitty-gritty life situations, people staying alive in a war zone, political activists operating in a police state, you think, that's really living, that's real life, that's survival. You go through a bit of a culture shock. It's strange to be able to go into Sainsbury's and Safeway and get normal milk or normal food and not have to worry. I don't have to drink goat milk, or camel milk.'

For many, the domestic support systems are very important. Sara Oliver describes hers:

'I travel an awful lot for my job and that does impact on your personal life. But my family are incredibly supportive and incredibly proud. We have little rituals if I'm going away somewhere unpleasant. I put a bottle of champagne in my mother's fridge and tell her that we'll drink it together when I get home. And we always do, always. If I'm away they write to me as best they can and obviously now we have emails, so that's great and I ring them.

I'd been away in Iraq for about six weeks and I got a letter from my mother and she'd pressed a flower out of the garden, and I was lying in the middle of this hellish town. We'd had no mail for 16 days and the mail caught up with us and there were lots of parcels and letters for me. One of them was from mum and this flower fell out and I actually burst into tears because I missed her − not her but what she stood for, the comfort of home and security. But then you remember that you've chosen to do this. My friends are very encouraging and very supportive, and they look after my life when I'm away. My boyfriend is an army officer and it's lovely to be with somebody who understands that side of my life completely, and I know that he finds the same thing.'

Photographer Tom Stoddart describes the effect on his relationship:

'No doubt about it, there is a price to pay. I remember in Sarajevo, in the Holiday Inn, it was always being shelled. We started dinner downstairs in a basement. I'd been trying to get a call through to my girlfriend for hours and then you pay someone to do it, like the guy at the desk. After about four hours, he came down, and said, "Tom, your call for London is through." This was right in the middle of a firefight, big explosions. I was sitting down behind the desk and my girlfriend was on the phone, and I said, "I'm not coming back this week" and she said, "What do you mean? We're having dinner on Friday night at the so and so".'

The work can be all-engrossing and, as such, might jeopardise relationships. Jane Kokan, for instance, tends to put emotions into work rather than energy into relationships, something that can cause 'regret that you're too busy even to date. You put relationships on the back burner, or you don't invest in them, you don't spend the time on them'. A broadcast journalist to whom we spoke expressed something similar. She split up from a boyfriend mostly because she kept going to war zones:

'He didn't like it, and he kept saying, "No, you have to ask me if you can go, and I don't want you to go." And I kept going. And I never asked him and he got upset and couldn't cope with it, and that was very sad. I could understand that it was hard to cope with, and you're not there for people when you want to be. I missed his birthday every year because I was in Chechnya, the next year I was in Afghanistan, the year after I was in Iraq. So for three years running, I just wasn't there, and I feel bad. But clearly I didn't feel bad enough to be there and say no to work and no to going. There's just something that I can't explain that drives you to go. It's part of the job definitely but it is a choice, and they asked me if I wanted to go to Iraq, so I said yes. I wouldn't have missed it for the world. I mean it sounds ridiculous but . . .'

New technology, particularly satellite phones, makes contact with friends and family back home somewhat easier. As one journalist explains:

'I rang my parents once a week and my boyfriend every other day just to say I'm okay, and if you've heard about the journalist being killed, it wasn't me. I can understand it's really tough, but my parents are great. I know they're worried but they don't communicate that worry to me. They just say be care-ful. It was different with my ex-boyfriend. I went out with him for five years from the first war I did, which was Kosovo. I thought he'd be used to it after five years but I think it got harder every time for him. It's maybe one reason why we didn't have kids together because the job doesn't really allow you to. Or you give up the job to have the kids and I'm not yet prepared to give up the job to do that. I'm getting to that stage. I'm 37, so if I do want to have kids, then it's the next five years. If you can choose between covering wars and having children, then I'd probably rather have children.'

Uwe Kroeger of ZDF finds email a useful tool for communicating:

'At the end of a long day, you sit down and write an email to your friend or partner. In former times, you didn't have that – you would have to write it down in your diary. But email is so tempting because it's so easy and it's a new way of communication.'

Some of the more experienced journalists have found ways of balancing work and home. We end this chapter with the words of Colin Baker, who relates his own successful homecoming routine:

'I always seem to come back on Sunday nights, which are good nights to come back on. I'd phone up from Heathrow and she'd [my wife] open the cot-tage door and I'd throw my bag in. I wouldn't go in the house, and she'd come out, and we'd go to the local pub where we had so many good friends. It's just a country pub, and nobody would talk to me about my job. I was very well protected – they'd nod, smile and drink, send me a drink over and just say good to see you back. That was it. I used to have a few drinks, maybe a bite to eat and go home. And she'd go to work the next day and the house was just quiet, deserted, absolutely deserted. I'd get up and couldn't get into gear. I couldn't get moving. I'd maybe walk around the garden and cut across the fields, feel-ing a bit like a hermit, wondering what to do next. No one to relate to, no one to talk to. I had nothing to worry about, really, nothing to worry about at all.'

Note

1 The BBC Worldservice is now more easily available to listeners in the UK following the growth of digital and cable services.

PART III

Conclusion

12

INFORMATION WAR AND JOURNALISTIC PRACTICES IN THE 21ST CENTURY

The demolition of the Berlin Wall in 1989 and the dismantling of the USSR two years later released a wave of optimism around the world. Soviet communism had turned from a dream of liberation into a nightmare of oppression and inefficiency. Its almost bloodless collapse gave heart to democrats everywhere. The Soviet Union's demise ended the Cold War, breaking the 'balance of terror' that had long prevailed between the United States and the USSR and the 'mutually assured destruction' by nuclear missiles that was its corollary. It also brought to a finish the organisation of the globe in terms of opposing capitalist and communist blocs and their respective satellites. The outlook then was of one world living in harmony, agreed upon basic values of democracy and freedom. There remained only one superpower, the USA, and this was regarded – with all due qualification – as a force for good, committed to democratic ways and unsurpassed in its capacity to improve living standards. The immediate prospect was of a major 'peace dividend', the cessation of war, and the advancement of democracy round the world.

But war has not disappeared with Soviet communism. Conflicts have persisted and new ones erupted during the 1990s. Even while the Soviet system was disintegrating, the first Gulf War was being fought following Iraq's seizure of Kuwait. Soon afterwards the Balkans began to implode, leading to civil war and the break-up of the former Yugoslavia, and with a loss of life in Europe unseen since the days of the Second World War. In the Middle East the Palestinian Intifada, suicide bombings and uncompromising reactions from the Israeli military, meant that much public attention remained fixed on this festering problem. Chechnya has been the most serious of several conflicts fought inside the remnants of the former USSR. Following the September 11 assaults on mainland America, United States military forces together with their allies invaded Afghanistan in 2001 and Iraq in 2003. These two wars, accounting for relatively minimal casualties on the part of the invaders, resulted in tens of thousands of dead Afghan and Iraqi people. Other conflicts have continued to prevail in places such as the Sudan and Indonesia, as well as between India and Pakistan over the disputed territory of Kashmir.

Alongside these conflicts, terrorism has increased since the 1990s. Terrorist attacks have long been a feature of the world. Nationalist movements such as Irish republicanism, which spawned the IRA, and Basque separatism (ETA), have maintained campaigns over a period of more than 30 years. But some of the post-Cold War terrorism is of a markedly different character, giving no warnings of attacks, targeting civilians rather than military or government targets, and endeavouring to maximise casualties. This form of terrorism is couched in a religious ferocity that eschews negotiation. The 3,000 deaths as a result of the 9/11 attacks on the Twin Towers and the Pentagon, the 200 tourists blown up in a Bali nightclub in 2002, the 191 people murdered when Al Qaeda-inspired terrorists bombed train commuters in Madrid in 2004, and the 52 killed in London on the 7 July 2005 attacks all testify to a new enemy. The world has not lived up to the great expectations of 1989.

Neo-liberalism

The end of the Cold War, signalling the failure of command economies and collectivism *tout court*, also unleashed neo-liberalism. As historian Mark Mazower (1998, p. 405) argued, 'the real victor in 1989 was not democracy but capitalism'. With the Soviet system ended, barriers to marketisation were removed and the neo-liberal ascendancy was assured. Led by pro-market governments, deregulation and privatisation advanced rapidly during the 1990s, eagerly supporting transnational corporations which increased their activities worldwide. Important differences remain: European social democracy continues to be distinctive; the Anglo-Saxon practices of the British put them somewhat apart from the continent; China's authoritarian communist marketisation, and Japanese protectionism, are each in some ways different from the more rampant *laissez-faire* orientation of the United States. Nevertheless, the ending of the Cold War has announced the triumph of core organising principles and practices around the world. These include the following characteristics:

- The ability to pay is the major criterion determining provision of goods and services;
- Provision is made on the basis of private rather than public supply;
- Market criteria – i.e. whether something makes a profit or loss – are the primary factor in deciding what, if anything, is made available;
- Competition – as opposed to regulation – is regarded as the most appropriate mechanism for organising economic affairs;
- Commodification of activities – i.e. relationships are regarded as being amenable to price valuations – is the norm;
- Private ownership of property is favoured over state holdings;
- Wage labour is the chief mechanism for organising work activities.

These are idealisations of what happens in practice, but wha indisputable is that these principles have spread round the glob accelerated pace in recent years. They constitute what one might c echo Fernand Braudel, the consolidation of *business civilisation*. They adapted extensively and intensively, enveloping places from which th have been excluded such as Russia and China, and penetrating deeper into relatively undeveloped areas such as childcare, personal hygiene and education (Robins and Webster 1999).

This shift has been accompanied by a profound transformation in ways of life. These changes have been expressed in three major forms.

1 The remarkable development of *Information and Communication Technologies (ICTs)* that have been insinuated into most aspects of modern life, from medical treatment to personal entertainment, office organisation to political campaigning, education to factory production. The marriage of computing and communications has enabled the spread of a network society around the globe, leading to, in principle as well as in practice, real-time action on a planetary scale. This is witnessed by the everyday routines of transnational corporations or even email exchanges between individuals across continents (Castells 1996–98).

2 The growth of *mobilities* across a vast range of realms (Urry 2000). This concept encompasses the mobilities of people, of products and of ideas, including the extraordinary growth of travel in recent years (from tourists to migrants), the production of products across huge distances, and the constant movement of ideas and information in the form of journalism, music or Internet exchanges.

3 The continued and quickening development of *globalisation*, in which the ongoing interpenetration and integration of life takes place across the world. It is vital that globalisation is perceived in the context of the outcome of the Cold War: indeed, it is 'Cold War victor's history conceptualised in a wider frame' (Reynolds 2000, pp. 3–4) in so far as it proceeds, by and large, on market terms. It is equally important that a central paradox of globalisation be acknowledged: at least tangentially, it draws the world together into a single unit while simultaneously it divides the world. At one level, this means that decisions taken in one more powerful location have consequences in other less powerful spheres, largely by and for the privileged region. At another level, it means that people around the world have become more aware of divisions. For instance, Eric Hobsbawm points out in his autobiography that 'nothing is more impressive to someone of my age [born 1917] than the extraordinary discovery, since 1970, of the First World by the peoples of the Third World' (Hobsbawm 2002, p. 363).

Capitalism nowadays is *systemic* in the sense that it pervades the globe. Oddly enough, however, it is also less amenable to control than hitherto.

Order is ensured, goes the now conventional argument, by adherence to market principles, the assumption being that capitalism is more or less self-regulating. Accordingly, liberalisation, privatisation and deregulation are leitmotifs of neo-liberalism, in which a thoroughly marketised society can generate more employment opportunities than a firmly regulated one, demonstrating superiority of performance over more collectivist economies. However, a price demanded by market societies operating in a highly competitive global capitalist system is fast adaptation, high turnover of staff and insecurity of occupations, hence a lack of control in terms of work assurance for many employees. Manuel Castells makes a related point when he suggests that today's 'new economy' is at once a 'hardened form of Capitalism in its goals, but it is incomparably more flexible than any of its predecessors in its means' (1998, p. 338). It is a world of permanent turbulence, one that is systemic and systemically volatile. Global capitalism is a condition of permanent effervescence manifested in innovations – of organisation, investment and management – that radically change production, processes and even products. The outcome is continuous upheaval.

Existing within this global capitalist system are important transnational bodies, in particular the United Nations, the International Monetary Fund and the World Bank, who play key roles in managing global affairs, with the latter two dedicated to advancing marketisation and removing regulatory controls wherever feasible. The globalisation of market practices, the enormous expansion of transnational corporations (Dicken 2003), and the accompanying immediacy of information flows has led to a situation where the one-time major controlling body – the nation state – has been weakened. It has lost leverage over economic matters especially, and even political options need to take a more global perspective (Held et al. 1999). Indeed, nations, however essential they may be in a range of activities from education to medical attention, are increasingly regarded as 'merely complicating factors' (Hobsbawm 1994, p. 277) in a globalised capitalist system that is strikingly competitive and fast moving. It is a period of remarkably rapid change in which the historically critical controlling agency, the state, is diminished.

The Nation State

Despite this inexorable process of globalisation, the nation state still matters. It has enormous consequence for individual citizens. The particular case of the United States is dramatic evidence of this, and one discussed at length in Chapter 4. The United States has interests around the globe and a huge military presence. Within the military sphere the USA is incontestable but in other aspects there are identifiable limits to its power. Politically it is considerably more powerful than all other nations but still

it cannot guarantee to always 'win' in global affairs (*vide* the unsucc
attempt by the United States to assemble a convincing 'coalition
willing' to assist in its invasion of Iraq in 2003). Economically, the
faces distinct challenges from competitors, notably from the Euro~~ean
Union and in the rising economic might of China. Culturally, the USA
clearly has a good deal of 'soft' power, but the failure to persuade the rest
of the world to embrace wholeheartedly the values, policies and habits of
America – in many respects the very opposite is the case – is marked.

Globalisation has not yet ended the nation state even though it has
eroded some of its sovereignty. In many states, a strengthening of security
agencies, especially in the face of concerns about illegal migration, criminal
activity and, most worryingly, terrorism (Ball and Webster 2003) is occurring. Further, many peoples aspire to a nation of their own, on grounds
that this will provide a means for effecting change for their benefit.
Globalisation can provide some nations with a greater leverage by providing recognition on a world stage, and through the use of globalised technologies increasing the reach of nations. The continued formation of nation
states, for example in the former Soviet Union and the Balkans, as well as,
to a lesser degree, in the devolved governments of Scotland and Wales in
the United Kingdom, is testament to the drive of peoples to exercise control
over their lives, perhaps especially in a world of global activities.

But however many new states are formed, and however much people
aspire to have a country of their own, they must come to terms with
increasingly borderless activities, whether in the instantaneous movement of capital, the provision of goods and services by transnational corporations, the heightened rate of movement of citizens (and non-citizens)
as travellers, tourists or migrants, or in the complex exchanges and adaptation of varied lifestyle habits. Territorial sovereignty remains the *sine
qua non* of the state, but this is much more porous than hitherto, and it is
hard to imagine a serious reversal of the deep-seated changes announced
by globalisation.

This haemorrhaging of the nation state's powers has been both symptom and cause of an extraordinary acceleration of changes in recent
decades, especially since the late 1980s.

The Acceleration of Change

The Industrial Revolution and its consequent changes, however disconcerting to our predecessors, were as nothing compared with the pace and
profundity of changes in recent decades. The term 'Industrial Revolution'
was coined late in the 19th century, but the changes it brought about,
though continuous and persistent, took decade upon decade to permeate
the wider society (Landes 1969). Today, the expectation is not only of change
in our lifetimes, but of radical change in little more than a decade. This

permeates most aspects of life, from travel to reproductive technologies. Computerisation, notably the coming of the Internet, and the ubiquitous PC, is but one important index of this transformation. The radical de-industrialisation of the advanced capitalist societies since the 1980s, has seen in the UK the virtual disappearance of the British coal-mining, automobile, steel and shipbuilding industries. It has also led to the erosion of established occupational communities and the growth of new jobs such as software engineer and telephone call centre operative. In addition, it has been accompanied by a radical transformation of the physical environment as old industrial centres are demolished and cities reconstructed with the building of modern office complexes and regenerated with the establishment of new cultural centres.

This conjoining of globalisation and accelerated change brings deep uncertainty and anxiety, both at the level of the self and of the wider society. There is a characteristic lack of stability on every level in the postmodern world of globalised capitalism. Intimate relationships are more fragile, employment is uncertain, moral commitments unhinged. The great advantage of living in the world now is the ability to refuse to accept things as they are, and by not having to bow to destiny and fate that characterised the lot of humankind for millennia. Now hitherto incurable illnesses may be treated, unsatisfactory relationships abandoned, traditional moralities refused, inhibiting ways of life rejected . . . The prospect now is that old ways of doing things can be re-engineered, that even the self may be re-invented.

There is a personality type that fits with this ethos: cosmopolitan and open to others and their different ideas, adaptable to change, responsible for his or her own life and lifestyle. Such an outlook is characteristically sceptical of moral and cultural absolutes and is keen to tolerate and embrace alternatives, whether it is a matter of rethinking work practices, sampling fashions and cuisine, or in interacting with other ethnic groups (Lasch 1995). However, the great disadvantage of life today is the pervasive anxiety it brings. We are free to choose, but there are no longer secure bases for choosing the 'good life' (Bauman 1997). Long-held certitudes – from one's occupational craft to one's parenting abilities, from religious belief to political faith, from one's sexual identity to class outlook – are cast into doubt by the combination of access to other points of view and the constant change of so much of life today. Some, generally the economically and educationally privileged, greet this constant change as an opportunity. Others, however, usually the less well-off and those lacking in cultural capital, find it disturbing and a threat (Lasch 1991).

It is illuminating to link these observations to the diminishment of the state. The modern world was created – almost invariably through wars, both civil and external (Giddens 1985) – largely on the basis of nation states that brought with them considerable security, even some certainties. Once these nations were established, obligations and rights as well as emotional attachment came alongside. Nation states also, especially in Europe, came into being with relative ethnic homogeneity (Mazower 1998), creating 'national communities' around groups sharing common descent and culture, en route often expunging and always oppressing minorities. In Europe this was notably the Jews (Naimark 2002). A result was that members of one state were definitely not of another sort – Englishmen, for instance, were certainly not French, with their strange cooking, affectations and suspect Catholic religion (Colley 1992).

A good deal of this remains still. For instance, it is a sobering thought that, with just four exceptions (Spain, Belgium, Britain and Switzerland), all European countries are still today 80 percent mono-ethnic (Mann 2005, p. 507). But it is possible to gain insight into the weakening of the state by reflecting on the ties of identity that pertained in most nations until recently. These required from citizens a preparedness to guarantee frontiers, often by serving in armies at war, against others who threatened periodically the integrity of the nation. An accompaniment was what Zygmunt Bauman (2005) has called 'heroic nationalism': an unwavering patriotism, a commitment to the nation as one of singular importance especially in times of stress. Such heroic nationalism persists in one especially advanced nation, the United States of America, where terms like 'patriot', 'duty' and 'military sacrifice' remain acutely resonant for reasons we discussed in Chapter 4.

But in most advanced societies outside of the United States, heroic nationalism holds less of an appeal. There is a heightened awareness of the artificiality of national frontiers, there is consciousness that other cultures are equally rich, a knowledge that all nations invent traditions to inculcate commitment amongst their members, and also the plain fact of working day to day with and amidst diverse cultures. All this feeds a sceptical outlook that finds excessive patriotism faintly ludicrous. To such people, *civic nationalism*, where belonging to a nation means living, paying taxes, receiving education and rights of abode, trumps *ethnic nationalism*, where genuine belonging means endorsement of national ideals and beliefs. Certainly some degree of national attachment is a requirement of harmonious living (Goodhart 2005), but in countries like Britain, nationalism is on the ebb, with a fierce, even belligerent nationalism largely restricted to a reactionary minority. Amongst the most nationalistic, those who embrace ethnic conceptions of the nation are those also ill at ease with globalisation and rapid change (Kumar 2003).

Globalisation has brought change to once distant and poor parts of the world with a vengeance. The global marketplace brings profound challenges to traditional ways of life at an unprecedented pace, and it comes into a world of unremitting poverty for many. Peasant life is being destroyed because it is antipathetic to capitalism: peasants are self-sustaining, unwilling to innovate, inept and unreliable wageworkers, inadequately educated and poorly adapted to the market. Perhaps most telling, since employment in cities yields a better-rewarded way of life, the offspring of peasants yearn to be away (Worsley 1984). Little of this is comfortable for the peasantry. They – as well as other traditional orders – are challenged on all fronts: on their ways of working, on their family structures, even on their religious adherence. Many are of course inspired by change, especially the young, seeing in globalisation an escape from their penury. These drive the unrelenting migration of the skilled as well as the unskilled, those with and without the right documents and credentials, that has so remarkably increased worldwide since the 1980s (Castles and Miller 1998).

Amongst many people, then, globalisation and change can be deeply disconcerting, an assault on beliefs and traditions that are regarded as sacred and beyond challenge. It is here that fundamentalism, an assertion of certainty in an uncertain world, may thrive. This is not exclusive to the poorer parts of the world, but is mostly found where conditions are especially propitious for its spread among the disadvantaged and disconcerted. Fundamentalism may be found everywhere, for example in Born Again Christian organisations inside the United States where literal interpretations of the Bible provide rules for living, or in Deep Ecology movements in Western Europe, where subordination to Nature is the imperative of life. But it is also evident in peripheral regions where it can provide comfort for the insecure and destabilised.

Many fundamentalist organisations advocate an ascetic withdrawal from the world in order that undiminished attention can be devoted to a pure doctrine. They present little or no threat to social order and will make some pragmatic arrangement with the worldly life. However, in some forms, fundamentalism can lead to militant resistance, even military action in the name of absolute beliefs.[1] One expression of this comes in the form of ethnic nationalism, the assertion of 'my country right or wrong', with evocations of long-held myths ('our people have always been here, living like this'). Ethnic nationalism has long played a part in the establishment of nations (Mann 2005). When leaders appeal to an organic vision of a nation as 'one folk', as they continue to do today in parts of the world, it may be accompanied with ethnic cleansing, whereby minorities are stigmatised, forced into exile and frequently killed. The former Yugoslavia saw this expressed ferociously with a loss of more than 250,000 lives during the 1990s.

Fundamentalism is always territorially situated, and often makes claims for a place for its own folk. However, in recent decades fundamentalism with universal aspirations has emerged. It is a version that refuses the Western secularised ways of life, railing against the 'Great Satan' of America especially, and insisting on the rectitude of its version of the Koran. Terrorists of the loose-knit and for some inspirational network of Al-Qaeda[2] – which does *not* reject Western technologies such as the satellite phone and semtex, though it uncompromisingly opposes secular capitalism – are the leading edge of such 'enemies without states' (Giddens 1994). It would be an egregious mistake to imagine these are entirely placeless fundamentalists. Hence countermeasures need to take into account the origins of these people and their grievances. But there is no gainsaying that, with such 'enemies without states', there is little to negotiate since their hostility is implacable and murderous in intent.

Information War

It is in this context of turbulence that one may situate the spread of Information War. This is war capable of pursuance only by affluent and defence-oriented nations and especially by the United States or the NATO alliance that it dominates. It is war that does not require the mobilisation of the wider population to fight. Since a professionalised military is equipped with virtuoso weaponry, especially missiles and aircraft, which provides vastly disproportionate advantage, there is little need for the wider populace to be engaged in the war effort. Information War is unlikely to be fought between nations with this military capability mainly due to the widespread acceptance of the global market system and the diminishing of the former territorial concerns which previously motivated war. Instead, Information War is conducted, for the most part, in areas where there is marked turmoil and in cases where ethnic cleansing results in large-scale murder, as in Kosovo in 1999. It has also been practised in the Persian Gulf, where the United States has pursued a 'rogue nation' that it fears will combine with terrorist groups against its interests. Enormous asymmetry ensures that possessors of Information War weaponry will quickly vanquish an enemy, so long as it can be identified, and that post-war conditions do not demand lengthy occupation by forces vulnerable to guerrilla attack. Though Information War is monopolised by a limited number of countries, 'weapons of the weak' (Mann 2003) such as explosives and the Kalashnikov rifle have proliferated, not least courtesy of the collapse of the former USSR and the marketisation of arms dealing (Castells 1998, ch. 3), factors that have 'transformed the prospect of violence *anywhere* on the globe' (Hobsbawm 1994, p. 560).

Irrespective of the wisdom of the US invasion of Iraq in the name of its declared 'war on terror', it is clear that a key feature of Information War is the mobilisation of the public as spectators rather than active participants. In Part I of this book we emphasised the formidable task this is today (even inside that exceptional nation, the United States). Nowadays when – and even before – Information War breaks out, there is an astonishing amount of coverage ensuring that the public is saturated in information about the conduct of assaults, the casualty rates, and various factions involved. So sustained and wide-ranging is this information flow that Oliver Poole, an embedded journalist in Iraq, is correct to insist that people in Europe and even in the United States 'had a far better idea of what was going on in Iraq [in 2003] than the average soldier who was actually there' (Poole 2003, p. 116). This massive amount of reportage and comment provides audiences with an intense means of engagement with war, yet it is engagement at a distance and it is an engagement experienced with much argument and disputation. Despite this, the public is vital to the military endeavour, not least because at some point or other, appeals to the legitimacy of the war in terms of 'our way of life' are always made.

This needs to be located in what one might term a growing *globalisation of consciousness*. We alluded to this a moment ago when we observed how much harder it is today to be unaware of the abject circumstances of the world's poor because of social movements, adeptly using advanced technologies and communications skills, working to ensure that we are made conscious of conditions however far removed from them in terms of physical distance and standards of living. The globalisation of consciousness more generally signals at once the spread of technologies such as satellites and television that distribute round-the-clock news, entertainment, music and sports programming, but also the messages that migrants carry with them as they travel, as well as the symbolic import of clothes and cuisines. The globalisation of consciousness means that, however uneven and complex is the process, increasingly we have a world in which people have knowledge of others – of their lives, conditions and beliefs. This by no means leads to a uniformity of outlook, but it does mean that, more and more, round the world there are shared reference points, common issues of discussion and awareness of the meanings of symbols.

We suggested earlier that a growing awareness of human rights and democracy is intimately connected to this globalisation of consciousness. This awareness has received impetus from the collapse of communism, from the radical legacies of the anti-Stalinist Left (Eley 2002), and from the progress made by democracies around the world in recent decades. It sometimes leads to calls for military action to restrain anti-human rights actions and undemocratic regimes (Cushman 2005). News media are key participants in this heightening of consciousness, as Seib recently concluded: 'the strongest and richest nations do not have the moral right to avert their gaze from injustices they could halt or at least limit', so much so that 'the journalist's most important role . . . [is] to be the witness who arouses conscience' (Seib 2002, p. 121).

Frontline Correspondents

It is because Information War massively increases the mediation of war that we focused in Part II of this book on the frontline journalists who report on it. These men and women are essential contributors to the public understanding of the war. They operate in conditions of danger and discomfort, where threats to their safety are commonplace and ugly experiences are routine. They risk being shot at and bombed, even of being kidnapped and held to ransom and possibly worse. They have to function in inhospitable locations where something as mundane as pot-holed roads and incompetent driving can present significant risks. The dangers encountered by foreign correspondents are nothing like so grave as those for local journalists (Pedelty 1995), but they are considerable and suggest a degree of passion that motivates the frontline correspondent.

John Carlin told us that, early in his career during the 1980s, when he was reporting for *The Times* from Central America, the 'rules of the game' were that combatants 'did not kill journalists, especially [those] from prestigious newspapers'. In other locations conditions became much less hospitable for the foreign correspondent. Iraq by 2004 had become a deadly location for reporters, as Tim Lambon relates:

> 'The hostile environments courses prior to the [Iraq 2003] war were teaching if you get abducted, just act the grey man. Don't resist, do whatever they tell you, follow through with it, negotiations will take place, you'll be released. Now they're saying if somebody tries to abduct you, you take whatever chance you can to get away.'

Frontline correspondents operate under stressful conditions. Increasingly they are trained for this by organisations staffed with ex-services people who have knowledge of field conditions, first aid and hostile environments. Advisers with military experience that helps ensure the journalists' safety may even accompany them into the field. Journalists have developed ways of coping with the pressures ranging from compulsive writing (*'therapy on the go'*, in the words of John Carlin), to talking incessantly with intimate friends, to treating themselves with good food and wine when back home. It was noticeable how few were willing to take advantage of the professional counselling services made available by their employers.

It is striking, too, that, just about uniformly, these journalists refused the title 'war correspondent', finding it limiting, somehow presumptuous, and often an uncomfortable reminder of a macho type that is seen as no longer relevant to serious coverage of conflict. As Luke Harding put it, 'Ernest Hemingway is long gone'. Or as Colin Baker explains, 'I'm just a correspondent who's been to war, [who does] not like being called a war correspondent'. Most of his colleagues shared this sentiment.

These journalists inhabit the same globalising and fast-changing world outlined in Part I of the book. Working for well-resourced organisations, they benefit from technological innovations, notably the satellite videophone and laptop computer that enable them to send pictures and text from the remotest areas with ease and immediacy. These technologies have a downside in making the journalists always connected to their organisational headquarters and therefore liable to be bombarded with requests from the centre for 24/7 continuous reportage, which prevents them getting out of the hotel and into investigative mode. As Ben Brown commented, this rolling news 'is a complete monster, which requires endless feeding'. The permanent connection of field reporters to the news headquarters is leading, as Julian Manyon warned, to the situation where 'increasingly news is driven from the centre'. In addition the Internet provides correspondents with the rapid capability to research background materials as well as to see what rival journalists are reporting. It also enables the subjects of the reports to read what was said about them with disconcerting immediacy.

Information War correspondents operate in a milieu of vague borders and lines of combat, when they may be reporting from inside 'enemy' lines (as, for example, Baghdad) and where contesting sides are unclear. They spend relatively short periods of time inside the war zones, where they rely on local fixers to get access to informants and supplies, as well as to interpret and provide background information. These fixers, the 'unsung heroes', as Sky's Peter Sharp described them to us, are 'the people we always leave behind'. Today's correspondent is less persuaded by appeals to 'my country right or wrong'; moreover there are likely to be many other correspondents in the combat zones from a variety of nationalities, so any unthinking reflection is likely to be contested.

The military go to considerable lengths to constrain and channel what the reporter sees and produces. The embed alongside the US and British forces in Iraq in 2003 is only the latest attempt by military forces to gain greater control over what is reported. On this occasion it seemed that embeds, once given over to a military unit, were able to do their job pretty well unencumbered (cf. Atkinson 2004). Oliver Poole, embedded with the US Third Infantry Division, echoed several of our interviewees when he observed 'amazement at the amount of freedom I was given to wander around and ask whatever questions I liked to whoever I chose. There was no minder and no censor' (Poole 2003, pp. 12–13). Audrey Gillan confirmed this from her own experiences as an embed: 'I wasn't a propaganda tool in any way; they didn't tell me to write stuff and they didn't tell me any lies.' What we learned from our interviews with frontline correspondents is that there is considerable self-awareness about the limitations of the embedded journalists. Some frankly refused to countenance what they regarded as an inherently limiting role, but others made a judgement that set against *de facto* censorship the access that being an embed allowed.

Frontline correspondents contribute a vital role in conditions of Information War. The military forces endeavour to enlist them in the war effort, to limit them to filing stories of derring-do and of brave men and women doing a tough but worthwhile job away from home. Some embeds are prepared to play this part. However, for the most part the reporters have more laudable goals, not least to 'tell it like it is', to get the story and tell it straight. As Orla Guerin said, resonating many of our respondents: 'You want to feel that you're getting at the truth.' Kim Willsher added that: 'You want to bear witness to what has happened; you want people to know what is happening in those places.' Barbara Jones echoed this when she stated that: 'We're gathering information, not for the military or for the government, but for the truth.' This is a vitalising and admirable, though not a novel, aspiration for frontline correspondents; for instance, Peter Arnett recalled that throughout a 40-year career that began in Vietnam 'I believed that . . . truth was the greatest goal I could aspire to' (1994, p. 321). It is a quality that finds support amongst journalists in a theory of democracy, that the public have a right to know what is being done in their name. It is also, as we have observed, something that military forces also find hard to ignore, since it risks media coverage that queries the legitimacy of the military action itself.

Aspirations to report truthfully are couched in the language of objectivity. We – and the correspondents themselves – know that objectivity is a weasel word (Knightley 2000). Legendary correspondent James Cameron (1978, p. 72), for instance, long ago asserted that 'objectivity was of less importance than the truth', a distinction that would cause considerable consternation among many reporters. In the abstract, 'telling the truth' may mean reporting in a disinterested, detached and comprehensive manner. However, in the practice of journalism it is more a matter of striving to get things right by reliance on sources that can be cited and evidence that can be confirmed by an accredited authority. In this sense it becomes a 'strategic ritual' (Tuchman 1972) that is manifested in practices and procedures; the journalist reporting that 'x says this' and 'y says that'. Inside a military unit as an embed, it is hard to imagine how the inescapable reliance on the limited sources available could even approximate to objectivity.

Nonetheless, frontline correspondents are well aware of the limitations both of being an embed and of an excessive focus on the drama of war in action. As Dan Edge told us: 'All an embed can cover is the mechanics and modalities of how a modern war is fought . . . but that's a miniscule percentage of what war reporting needs to be about.' Edge is by no means alone in his assessment. Pictures taken from atop a fast-moving military vehicle, with terse voice-over from a reporter, all recorded in real time, are likely to be deemed newsworthy. David Zucchino, who joined with US soldiers in Abrams tanks as they sped into the centre of Baghdad, was candid about the limits of this reportage:

'What we didn't have access to is the decision-making at the Pentagon and at the National Security Council and at the White House . . . and that's really the most important story – how decisions are made and what the rationale is . . . And part of the problem is the secrecy of the administration and the sort of duplicitous nature of a lot of . . . what they were doing, a lot of the claims they were making.'

The embed Chris Ayres, more blunt, concluded that, though he was about as close to a frontline as could be imagined today, 'my battlefield perspective . . . was about as useful as Baghdad Bob's.[3] My mum knew more about the war than I did' (2005, p. 258). Another journalist, Oliver Poole, 'constantly had to resist the temptation to generalise about what was going on across Iraq as a whole from the evidence available from my own isolated viewpoint' (Poole 2003, p. 259). Others recognised that the limitations of being embedded with troops, and even being a unilateral, restricted them to a particular time and place. This meant that they relied on the central news organisation collating different reports and putting together the jigsaw to produce a complete picture. This led James Meek, himself an embed, to complain that 'I felt I missed the war because I hadn't seen it on TV' (quoted in Greenslade 2003). Indispensable though frontline correspondents are to public knowledge of war, their perspective, no matter how assiduously it cites available sources, is not in itself the whole truth.

A focus solely on action can indeed be a distortion. There is the added difficulty that, in circumstances in which combatants are all conscious that the mediation of the conflict can be of major significance, all sources are unreliable. As Dan Edge put it: 'There are fewer and fewer corners of the world where one's sources and interviewees are not hypersensitive to the power or lack of power of the media. And that informs everything they say.' The journalist's job is made that much more difficult when he or she is reliant for information on those who have an agenda. Sources endeavour to persuade the journalist that their perspective is the correct one, conscious that media play a key role in contemporary conflict. At other times, sources bypass journalists, going directly to news media, especially to propagate their view. Nothing more vividly illustrates this than the production of hostage videos through 2004 in Iraq that were put out on sympathetic websites.

It is the frontline correspondents who act as the major definers of reality as regards war for the huge audiences back home who receive their reports through television, radio and the newspapers. These correspondents co-operate and compete with their peers in unscripted but calibrated relationships, manifesting camaraderie while striving to get out their own reports ahead of those of the others. As Orla Guerin put it: 'Though competition exists . . . you watch out for people in other organisations [because] you do not want to see any journalist hurt.'

Despite the frontline correspondents' words being the usual starting point for news, the copy they file is by no means untouched before it reaches viewers, listeners and readers. Editors in news organisations can play a crucial role in framing and contextualising what the frontline correspondent sends through. In both activities the views of other participants (for example, government officials, party spokespeople, military experts, political commentators), as well as other sources of information (for example, other reports from the theatre of operation, statements from combatants) are important elements of any product that goes out on air or appears in the press. This manufactured process involving many more hands than those solely of the frontline reporter is familiar to media analysts.

However, a developing phenomenon, likely to be of increased importance in future, is the emergence of bloggers, those who put accounts, evidence and/or comment on the Internet (Drezner and Farrell 2004). One may distinguish at least three ways in which bloggers contribute to the mediation of war:

1 *Bloggers as witnesses* who report from particular locations, the most renowned of whom in 2003 was architect Salam Pax, the 'Baghdad Blogger', who kept an online diary to tell of his experiences inside the city as it was bombarded. Such blogs, as with emails direct from scenes of conflict, can become newsworthy and even news making. There are other blogs from witnesses, for instance milblogs (military weblogs), where participants circulate stories of their experiences in the field. Direct emails back and forth to friends and family can also, if more widely circulated, become contributors to news. Such sources of information can play an important role on occasions, notably at times and at locations of conflict when regular journalists are not present. Here lightweight video equipment, digital cameras and even mobile phone photography can make a contribution, as was evident in the hundreds of digital images taken by soldiers and guards at Abu Ghraib prison that were leaked to the media in May 2004 and have subsequently caused incalculable damage to the American effort to persuade opinion that they invaded to liberate Iraq (Hersh 2005).

2 *Bloggers as commentators* have grown rapidly over recent months as Internet connectivity reaches larger majorities of the population. These appear to be read more avidly by journalists than by the rest of society (Gibson 2005), and by virtue of this they may increase their importance in the news-making process. This category is itself wide, ranging from commentators promoting items that are overlooked by mainstream media to those bloggers who can make news by correcting reported versions of events. A renowned example of the latter was the way in which bloggers, after discrediting his evidence, forced CBS anchor Dan Rather to apologise in 2004 for a report on George W. Bush's service in the Texas Air National Guard.

3 *Bloggers as amplifiers of news*, notably by extending discussion and debate in the blogosphere. Both this and the second category appear to have played a role in the recent American presidential election in the denigration of Senator John Kerry over military medals awarded for his part in the Vietnam War, and in the rise and fall of Howard Dean as Democrat contender. Though extravagant claims have been made for these developments (Gillmor 2004), one does not need to embrace notions of 'citizen reporters' or the 'end of journalism' to agree that they contribute appreciably to an already complicated information environment.

on

on War, for those people inhabiting advanced parts of the globe, about mediated experiences. 'Shock and Awe' was the name given ᴊᴜ the US-led campaign during the invasion of Iraq in 2003. For the invading forces this attack was assisted by massive technological advantage over the enemy, while for those on the receiving end it brought death, massive casualties and rapid defeat. But Information War also involves communication. When conflict breaks out, even before it starts, there is an enormous upsurge of information from, about and beyond the war zone. Frontline correspondents play a central, but not solo, role in the presentation of what is often spectacle – vivid pictures of explosions, aerial images, cities lit up at night by tracer fire – to audiences around the world whose actual experience of war is far removed from combat. Audiences are presented, through virtuoso technologies, with astonishing pictures and sounds from the theatre of war.

Propaganda and persuasion are very much in evidence at every stage of this process. The winning of hearts and minds is of vital importance to the fighters of Information War. However, whatever the level of planning that goes into these efforts to massage public opinion, the ambiguities and complexities surrounding the informational dimensions of conflict nowadays make endeavours to control it always tenuous. If it were not so, how might one begin to account for the effects of the images that appeared of Abu Ghraib prison in Baghdad in the Spring of 2004, images that have undermined the case for the overthrow of Saddam Hussein, and have sullied the name of the United States?

In conditions of armed conflict, there is always the 'fog of war', the unpredictability of events and an associated lack of clarity as regards information. The confusion of battle makes it hard to ascertain precisely what is occurring. However, it is the wider information environment pertaining today that is more responsible than the battle for the chaos. First of all, frontline journalists are not easily controlled or manipulated to act as conduits for combatants and their leaders. They have a strong disposition towards 'telling it like it is', they cling to notions of 'objectivity' and they have access to versatile equipment that allows them to report quickly and immediately back to their news organisations. Furthermore, the boundaries between fighting forces are often confused, and, perhaps more important, journalists are such a diverse group that once-powerful appeals to support 'our boys' have weakened. Moreover, while embeds are severely constrained by virtue of their locations, news organisations now receive an enormous volume and variety of information. What gets into a finished programme or news report may be quite at odds with any single journalist's report.

What is also emerging, assisted by the growth of new media though by no means restricted to technological developments, is what Craig Calhoun

(2004) has described as a *transnational public sphere*. This is not an equal playing field for contesting forces. However, it is one that is considerably more diverse than that available during the era of Industrial War, when national media systems projected images and carried reports in support of the nation's fighting forces. It is an information domain where Al Jazeera, CNN and the BBC all co-exist (Miles 2005), where claims and counter-claims may be encountered from a variety of disputing quarters, where images are posted that may be profoundly antipathetic to all sides in the confrontation. It is a domain where the digital camera and the Internet web site can play a key role in defining reality. It is one where even the weaker forces – who are acutely conscious that the media are globalised phenomena – can stage dramatic events through careful use of video cameras and the Internet. Such ambiguity and complexity come with the territory of Information War. The virtuoso weapons of war ensure massive asymmetry between combatants, but the media features are also crucial in the waging and long-term success of Information War. And these are much harder to predict or contain.

Notes

1   Fundamentalism as a response to uncertainty can only serve as a generalised background explanation for conflict. In particular cases, matters are contingent on, for instance, the personalities of actors, the socialising they undergo, availability of weapons, and responses to events and policies. Our argument therefore is that increased uncertainty, upheaval and instability are the necessary, but not sufficient, conditions to account for fundamentalism taking the form of armed action. In this regard Michael Mann (2003, p. 182) makes a valid point when he complains that the term 'fundamentalist' may throw too much responsibility on to those who resist imposed change. We would add that such conditions are not without precedent. Harold Lasswell (1935) presented his 'insecurity hypothesis' in the 1930s to account for the emergence of fascism in Europe, pointing to mass unemployment, hyperinflation and the collapse of faith as reasons why people were driven towards the certainties of fascism.
2   Since Al-Qaeda instigated the International Islamic Front for Jihad Against the Jews and Crusaders in 1998, almost 5,000 people have been killed and over 12,000 wounded in more than 30 major attacks in 16 countries. *The Human Security Report 2005* also notes that 'international terrorism is the only form of political violence that appears to be getting worse', with 'a dramatic increase in the number of high-casualty attacks since the September 11 attacks on the US in 2001' (p. 2). See http://www.humansecurityreport.info/
3   Baghdad Bob, also known as Comical Ali (Muhammad Saeed al-Sahhaf), was the Iraqi Information Minister for Saddam Hussein during the 2003 US invasion of Iraq, disparagingly named because of the divorce from known reality of his assertions.

REFERENCES

Adie, Kate (2002), *The Kindness of Strangers*, London: Hodder.

Adie, Kate (2003), *Corsets to Camouflage*, London: Coronet.

Alagiah, George (2001), *A Passage to Africa*, London: Time Warner.

Albrow, Martin (1996), *The Global Age: State and Society beyond Modernity*, Cambridge: Polity.

Allan, Stuart and Barbie Zelizer (2004), *Reporting War: Journalism in Wartime*, Oxford: Routledge.

Arico, Santo L. (1998), *Oriana Fallaci*, Carbondale, IL: Southern Illinois University Press.

Arnett, Peter (1994), *Live from the Battlefield: from Vietnam to Baghdad, 35 years in the World's War Zones*, London: Corgi.

Arquilla, John and David F. Ronfeldt (eds) (1997), *In Athena's Camp: Preparing for Conflict in the Information Age*, Santa Monica, CA: RAND.

Artz, Lee and Yahya R. Kamalipour (2005), *Bring 'Em On*, Oxford: Rowman & Littlefield.

Atkinson, Rick (2004), *In the Company of Soldiers: A Chronicle of Combat in Iraq*, London: Little, Brown.

Ayres, Chris (2005), *War Reporting for Cowards: Between Iraq and a Hard Place*, London: John Murray.

Ball, Kirstie and Frank Webster (eds) (2003), *The Intensification of Surveillance: Crime, Terrorism and Warfare in the Information Age*, London: Pluto.

Bamford, James (2001), *Body of Secrets: Anatomy of the Ultra-secret National Security Agency*, New York: Doubleday.

Barber, Benjamin (1995), *Jihad versus McWorld*, New York: Times Books.

Barber, Benjamin (2003), *Fear's Empire: War, Terrorism, and Democracy*, New York: Norton.

Bauman, Zygmunt (1997), *Postmodernity and Its Discontents*, Cambridge: Polity.

Bauman, Zygmunt (2005), *Liquid Life*, Cambridge: Polity.

Beaumont, Peter (2004), 'Fear drives reporters to rooftops', *Observer*, 24 October, p. 6.

Bell, Martin (1995), *In Harm's Way: Reflections of a War-Zone Thug*, Harmondsworth: Penguin.

Bell, Martin (2003), *Through Gates of Fire: A Journey into World Disorder*, London: Weidenfeld & Nicolson.

Bennett, W. Lance and David L. Paletz (eds) (1994), *Taken by Storm: The Media, Public Opinion, and U.S. Foreign Policy in the Gulf War*, American Politics and Political Economy Series, Chicago: University of Chicago Press.

Berkowitz, Bruce (2003), *The New Face of War*, New York: Free Press.

Blair, Tony (2001), Speech to Labour Party Conference, Brighton, October 2.

Blair, Tony (2004), Speech at Sedgefield, March 5.

Bobbitt, Philip (2002), *The Shield of Achilles: War, Peace and the Course of History*, Harmondsworth: Penguin.

Boltanski, Luc (1999), *Distant Suffering: Morality, Media and Politics,* Cambridge: Cambridge University Press.

Bowen, Jeremy (2004), 'Now we're the target', *Guardian,* June 14.

Brysk, Alison (ed.) (2002), *Globalization and Human Rights,* Berkeley, CA: University of California Press.

Calhoun, Craig (2004) 'Information Technology and the International Public Sphere', in Douglas Schuler and Peter Day (eds) *Shaping the Network Society,* Cambridge, MA: MIT Press, pp. 229–52.

Cameron, James (1978), *Point of Departure: Experiment in Biography,* London: Panther.

Carruthers, Susan L. (2000), *The Media at War,* Basingstoke: Macmillan.

Castells, Manuel (1996), *The Rise of the Network Society,* Oxford: Blackwell.

Castells, Manuel (1996–98), *The Information Age: Economy, Society, and Culture.* 3 volumes, Oxford: Blackwell.

Castells, Manuel (1998), *End of Millennium,* Oxford: Blackwell.

Castles, Stephen and M.J. Miller (1998), *The Age of Migration: International Population Movements in the Modern World,* Basingstoke: Macmillan.

Chalaby, Jean (ed.) (2005), *Transnational Television Worldwide: Towards a New Media Order,* London: I.B.Tauris.

Cohen, Eliot A. (1996), 'A Revolution in Warfare', *Foreign Affairs,* 75(2): 37–54.

Colley, Linda (1992), *Britons: Forging the Nation, 1707–1837,* London: Pimlico.

Collier, Richard (1989), *The Warcos: The War Correspondents of World War Two,* London: Weidenfeld & Nicolson.

Conetta, C. (2003), 'The wages of war: Iraqi combatant and non-combatant fatalities in the 2003 conflict', Project on Defence Alternatives Research Monograph 8(20) October; www.comw.org/pda

Cooper, Robert (2004) *The Breaking of Nations: Order and Chaos in the 21st Century.* London: Atlantic Books.

Curtis, Liz (1984), *Ireland: the Propaganda War,* London: Pluto.

Cushman, Thomas (ed.) (2005), *A Matter of Principle: Humanitarian Arguments for War in Iraq,* Berkeley, CA: University of California Press.

Diamond, Larry (2003), 'Universal Democracy?', *Policy Review,* 119: 1–28.

Dicken, Peter (1998), *Global Shift,* 3rd edition, London: Paul Chapman.

Dicken, Peter (2003), *Global Shift: Reshaping the Global Economic Map in the 20th Century,* London: Sage.

Di Giovanni, Janine (2001), in Freedom Forum, 'Risking more than their lives: The effects of post-traumatic stress disorder on journalists', 12 April. At www.freedomforum.org

Di Giovanni, Janine (2003), *Madness Visible,* London: Bloomsbury.

Dimbleby, Jonathan (1975) *Richard Dimbleby.* London: Hodder and Stroughton.

Drezner, Daniel W. and Henry Farrell (2004), 'Web of influence', *Foreign Policy,* November–December. At http://www.foreignpolicy.com

Economist (2003), 'A Nation Apart', November 3.

Elegant, Robert (1981), 'How to lose a war', *Encounter,* 57(2): 73–90.

Eley, Geoff (2002), *Forging Democracy: The History of the Left in Europe 1850–2000,* Oxford: Oxford University Press.

Farsihi, Farnaz (2004), 'From Baghdad', September 30 email available at http://www.commondreams.org/views04/093015.htm

Feinstein, A. (2001), in Freedom Forum, 'Risking more than their lives: The effects of post-traumatic stress disorder on journalists', 12 April. At www.freedom forum.org

Feinstein, Anthony (2003), *Dangerous Lives: War and the Men and Women who Report it*, Toronto: Thomas Allen Publishers.

Ferguson, Niall (2004), *Colossus: The Price of America's Empire*, London: Allen Lane.

Ferrari, Michelle and James Tobin (2003), *Reporting America at War*, New York: Hyperion.

Filkins, Dexter (2004), 'Under fire in Baghdad', *New York Times*, October 10.

Frank, André Gundar (1998), *Re-orient: Global Economy in the Asian Age*, Berkeley, CA: University of California Press.

Freedom Forum (2001), 'Risking more than their lives: The effects of post-traumatic stress disorder on journalists', 12 April. At www.freedomforum.org

Friedman, Tom (2000), *The Lexus and the Olive Tree*, London: HarperCollins.

Garrels, Anne (2003), *Naked in Baghdad*, New York: Farrar, Straus & Giroux.

Garton Ash, Timothy (2004), *Free World: Why a Crisis of the West Reveals the Opportunity of Our Time*, London: Penguin.

Gibson, Owen (2005), 'The bloggers have all the best news', *Guardian* [Media Section], June 6: 12–13.

Giddens, Anthony (1985), *The Nation State and Violence: Volume Two of a Contemporary Critique of Historical Materialism*, Cambridge: Polity.

Giddens, Anthony (1994), *Beyond Left and Right*, Cambridge: Polity.

Gillmor, Dan (2004), *We the Media: Grassroots Journalism by the People, for the People*, Beijing; Sebastopol, CA: O'Reilly.

Goodhart, David (2005), 'Britain's glue: the case for liberal nationalism', in Anthony Giddens and Patrick Diamond (eds), *The New Egalitarianism*, Cambridge: Polity, pp. 154–70.

Gray, Chris Hables (1997), *Postmodern War*, New York: Guilford Press.

Greenslade, Roy (2003), 'Fighting Talk', *Guardian*, 30 June: 6.

Griffiths, Richard (1988), *Fellow Travellers of the Right: British Enthusiasts for Nazi Germany 1933–39*, 2nd edn, Oxford: Oxford University Press.

Halberstam, David (1979), *The Powers that Be*, New York: Dell.

Hardt, Michael and Antonio Negri (2001), *Empire*, Cambridge, MA: Harvard University Press.

Harvey, David (2003), *The New Imperialism*, Oxford: Oxford University Press.

Havel, Václav (1999), 'Kosovo and the end of the nation-state', *New York Review of Books*, 29 April.

Hedges, Chris (2002), *War Is a Force that Gives Us Meaning*, Oxford: Public Affairs Unit.

Held, David (1995), *Democracy and the Global Order: From the Modern State to Cosmopolitan Governance*, Cambridge: Polity.

Held, David (ed.) (1996), *Models of Democracy*, 2nd edition, Cambridge: Polity.

Held, David and Anthony McGrew, David Goldblatt and Jonathan Perraton (1999), *Global Transformations*, Cambridge: Polity.

Herr, Michael (1991) *Dispatches*. New York: Vintage Books.

Hersh, Seymour M. (2004a), 'The gray zone', *New Yorker*, 17 May.

Hersh, Seymour M. (2004b), 'Torture at Abu Ghraib', *New Yorker*, 6 May.

Hersh, Seymour M. (2005), *Chain of Command*, London: Penguin.

Hertsgaard, Mark (2003), *The Eagle's Shadow: Why America Fascinates and Infuriates the World*, New York: Picador.

Hess, Stephen (1996), *International News and Foreign Correspondents*, Washington, DC: The Brookings Institution.

Hirst, Paul (2001), *War and Power in the 21st Century*, Cambridge: Polity.

Hobsbawm, E.J. (1994), *Age of Extremes: The Short Twentieth Century*, London: Michael Joseph.

Hobsbawm, E.J. (2002), *Interesting Times*, London: Allen Lane.

Horne, Alistair (1988), *Macmillan: Volume 1, 1894–1956*, London: Macmillan.

Horne, Alistair (1989), *Macmillan: Volume 2, 1957–1986*, London: Macmillan.

Hoskins, Andrew (2004), *Televising War*, London: Continuum.

Human Security Report: War and Peace in the 21st Century (2005), University of British Columbia: Human Security Centre. Available at www.humansecurityreport.info

IFJ (2003), 'Justice denied on the road to Baghdad', available at www.ifj.org

Ignatieff, Michael (2000), *Virtual War: Kosovo and Beyond*, London: Chatto & Windus.

Ignatieff, Michael (2002), 'Nation-building lite', *New York Times*, 20 July.

Ignatieff, Michael (2003), 'The burden', *New York Times*, 5 January.

Ignatieff, Michael (2004), 'The year of living dangerously', *New York Times*, 14 March.

IISS (International Institute for Strategic Studies) (2002), *The Military Balance 2002–3*, London: Oxford University Press.

Johnson, Chalmers (2004), *The Sorrows of Empire: Militarism, Secrecy, and the End of the Republic*, New York: Metropolitan Books.

Johnson, Peter B. (2003), *Roving Reuter Reporter 1959–61*, Norfolk: The Tagman Press.

Kagan, Robert (2003), *Paradise and Power: America and Europe in the New World Order*, London: Atlantic Books.

Kaldor, Mary (1999), *New and Old Wars: Organised Violence in a Global Era*, Cambridge: Polity.

Kaldor, Mary (2003), *Global Civil Society: An Answer to War*, Cambridge: Polity.

Kamalipour, Yahya R. and Nancy Snow (eds) (2004), *War, Media and Propaganda*, Oxford: Rowman & Littlefield.

Katovsky, Bill and Timothy Carlson (eds) (2003), *Embedded: The Media at War in Iraq*, London: The Lyons Press.

Keane, Fergal (2005), *All of These People*, London: Harper Collins.

Keane, John (1998), *Civil Society: Old Images, New Visions*, Cambridge: Polity.

Kellner, Doug (2002), *Media Spectacle*, London: Routledge.

Kellner, Doug (2004), 'Pre-emptive strikes and the war on Iraq: a critique of Bush administration unilateralism and militarism' (mimeo).

Kennedy, David M. (1999), *Freedom from Fear: The American People in Depression and War, 1929–1945*, New York: Oxford University Press.

Kennedy, Paul (1988), *The Rise and Fall of the Great Powers: Economic and Military Conflict from 1500 to 2000*, London: Unwin Hyman.

Knightley, Phillip (2000), *The First Casualty: The War Correspondent as Hero and Myth-maker from the Crimea to Kosovo*, London: Prion Books.

Knightley, Phillip (2003), 'History or bunkum?' *British Journalism Review* 14(2): 7–14.

Kumar, Krishan (2003), *The Making of English National Identity: Englishness and Britishness in Comparative and Historical Perspective*, Cambridge: Cambridge University Press.

Kupchan, Charles A. (2002), *The End of the American Era: US Foreign Policy and the Geopolitics of the 20th Century*, New York: Vintage.

Lacquer, Walter (1980), *The Terrible Secret: an Investigation into the Suppression of Information about Hitler's 'Final Solution'*, London: Weidenfeld & Nicolson.

Landes, David (1969), *The Unbound Prometheus: Technological Change and Industrial Development in Western Europe from 1750 to the Present*, Cambridge: Cambridge University Press.

Lasch, Christopher (1991), *The True and Only Heaven: Progress and Its Critics*, New York: Norton.

Lasch, Christopher (1995), *The Revolt of the Elites and the Betrayal of Democracy*, New York: Norton.

Lasswell, Harold D. (1935), *World Politics and Personal Insecurity*, New York: McGraw-Hill. Available at http://www.policysciences.org/worldpoliticsand-personalinsecurity/wppi_contents.htm

Lipset, Seymour Martin (1996), *American Exceptionalism: A Double-Edged Sword*, New York: Norton.

Little, Allan (2001), in Freedom Forum, 'Risking more than their lives: The effects of post-traumatic stress disorder on journalists', 12 April, www.freedomforum. org.

Loyd, Anthony (1999), *My War Gone By, I Miss It So*, London: Doubleday.

London, Louise (2000), *Whitehall and the Jews, 1933–48: British Immigration Policy and the Holocaust*, Cambridge: Cambridge University Press.

Luttwak, Edward (1996), 'A post-heroic military policy', *Foreign Affairs*, 75(4): 33–44.

Mandeles, Mark D., Thomas C. Hone and Sanford S. Terry (1996), *Managing 'Command and Control' in the Persian Gulf War*, Westport, CT: Praeger.

Mann, Michael (1986), *The Sources of Social Power, vol. 1: A History of Power from the Beginning to A.D. 1760*, Cambridge: University of Cambridge Press.

Mann, Michael (1993), 'Nation-states in Europe and other continents: diversifying, developing, not dying', *Daedalus* 122(3): 115–40.

Mann, Michael (2003), *Incoherent Empire*, London: Verso.

Mann, Michael (2004), Speech to the Friedrich Ebert Foundation, 13 May.

Mann, Michael (2005), *The Dark Side of Democracy: Explaining Ethnic Cleansing*, Cambridge: Cambridge University Press.

Marr, Andrew (2004), *My Trade: A Short History of British Journalism*, London: Macmillan.

Massing, Michael (2003), 'The unseen war', *New York Review of Books*, 50(9): 16–19.

Massing, Michael (2004a), 'Now they tell us', *New York Review of Books*, 51(3).

Massing, Michael (2004b), 'Unfit to print?', *New York Review of Books*, 51(11): 6–10.

Matloff, Judith (2005), 'Women reporting war – the three challenges'. Accessed at www.newssafety.com/stories/insi/wrw2.htm

Mazower, Mark (1998), *Dark Continent: Europe's Twentieth Century*, Harmondsworth: Penguin.

McCullin, Don (1990), *Unreasonable Behaviour*, London: Vintage.

McLaughlin, Greg (2002) *The War Correspondent*. London: Pluto.

McNeill, William (1982), *The Pursuit of Power: Technology, Armed Force and Society*, Chicago: University of Chicago Press.

Miles, Hugh (2005), *Al-Jazeera: the Inside Story of the Arab News Channel that Is Challenging the West*, New York: Grove Press.

Morrison, David and Tumber, Howard (1985) 'Strangers in a Strange Land: The Foreign Coreespondents in London', *Media, Culture and Society*, 7(4): 445–70.

Morrison, David and Howard Tumber (1988), *Journalists at War: the Dynamics of News reporting during the Falklands*, London: Sage.

Morton, Oliver (1995), 'Defence technology: the information advantage', *Economist*, 10 June.

Mowlana, Hamid, George Gerbner and Herbert I. Schiller (eds) (1992), *Triumph of the Image: The Media's War in the Persian Gulf – A Global Perspective*, Boulder, CO: Westview Press.

Naimark, Norman M. (2002), *Fires of Hatred: Ethnic Cleansing in the 20th Century*, Cambridge, MA: Harvard University Press.

Nef, J.U. (1950), *War and Human Progress*, Cambridge, MA: Harvard University Press.

Norris, Philippa (ed.) (1999), *Critical Citizens: Global Support for Democratic Government*, Oxford: Oxford University Press.

Novick, Peter (2000), *The Holocaust and Collective Memory*, London: Bloomsbury.

Nye, Joseph S. Jnr (2002), *The Paradox of American Power*, New York: Oxford University Press.

Ochberg, Frank (2001), in Freedom Forum, 'Risking more than their lives: The effects of post-traumatic stress disorder on journalists', 12 April. Accessed at www.freedomforum.org

Oettinger, Anthony G. (1990), *Whence and Whither Intelligence, Command and Control? The Certainty of Uncertainty*, Cambridge, MA, Program on Information Resources Policy, Harvard University.

Omaar, Rageh (2004), *Revolution Day*, London: Viking.

Owen, John (2001), 'Training journalists to report safely in hostile environments', *Nieman Reports*, 55(4): 25–27, The Nieman Foundation for Journalism at Harvard University.

Pedelty, Mark (1995), *War Stories: The Culture of Foreign Correspondents*, New York: Routledge.

Politkovskaya, Anna (1999), *A Dirty War*, London: The Harvill Press.

Ponting, Clive (1999), *World History*, London: Chatto & Windus.

Poole, Oliver (2003), *Black Knights: On the Bloody Road to Baghdad*, London: Harper Collins.

Power, Samantha (2002), *A Problem from Hell: America and the Age of Genocide*, New York: Basic Books.

Rampton, Sheldon and John Stauber (2003), *Weapons of Mass Deception*, London: Robinson.

Reynolds, David (2000), *One World Divided: A Global History since 1945*, Harmondsworth: Penguin.

Roberts, L., R. Lafta, R. Garfield, J. Khudhairi and G. Burnham (2004), 'Mortality before and after the 2003 invasion of Iraq: cluster sample survey', *The Lancet*, 364(9445): 1–8.

Robertson, Geoffrey (1999), *Crimes against Humanity: The Struggle for Global Justice*, Harmondsworth: Penguin.

Robins, Kevin and Frank Webster (1999), *Times of the Technoculture: from the Information Society to the Virtual Life*, London: Routledge.

Robinson, Piers (2002), *The CNN Effect: The Myth of News, Foreign Policy and Intervention*, London: Routledge.

Rosenblatt, Roger (1994), 'Rwanda therapy: battle-scarred journalists heal', *The New Republic*, 210(23): 14.

Ruthven, Malise (2004), *Fundamentalism: The Search for Meaning*, Oxford: Oxford University Press.

Schechter, Danny (2003), *Media Wars*, Oxford: Rowman & Littlefield.

Schlensinger, Philip and Tumber, Howard (1994) *Reporting Crime: The Media Politics of Criminal Justice*. Oxford: Clarendon Press.

Schiller, Herbert I. (2000), *Living in the Number One Country: Reflections from a Critic of American Empire*, New York: Seven Stories Press.

Seaton, Jean (1987), 'Atrocities and the media', in Jean Seaton and Ben Pimlott (eds), *The Media in British Politics*, Aldershot: Avebury.

Seaton, Jean (2009) *Carnage and the Media: The Making and Breaking of News about Violence*. London: Allen Lane.

Sebba, Anne (1994), *Battling for News*, London: Hodder & Stoughton.

Seib, Philip (2002), *The Global Journalist: News and Conscience in a World of Conflict*, New York: Rowman & Littlefield.

Seib, Philip (2004), *Beyond the Front Lines: How the News Media Cover a World Shaped by War*, New York: Palgrave Macmillan.

Shanor, Donald R. (2003), *News from Abroad*, New York: Columbia University Press.

Shaw, Martin (1991), *Post-Military Society: Militarism, Demilitarization and War at the end of the Twentieth Century*, Cambridge: Polity.

Shaw, Martin (2000), *Theory of the Global State: Globality as an Unfinished Revolution*, Cambridge: Cambridge University Press.

Simpson, John (1998), *Strange Places, Questionable People*, London: Pan.

Simpson, John (2001), *A Mad World, My Masters*, London: Pan.

Simpson, John (2002), *News from No Man's Land: Reporting the World*, London: Pan.

Simpson, John (2003), *The War against Saddam: Taking the Hard Road to Baghdad*, London: Pan.

SIPRI (2002), *SIPRI Yearbook 2002: Armaments, Disarmament and International Security*, Oxford; Oxford University Press.

Smith, Anthony (1998), *Nationalism and Modernism: A Critical Survey of Recent Theories of Nations and Nationalism*, London: Routledge.

Steele, Jon (2002), *War Junkie*, London: Corgi.

Steele, Jonathan (2004), 'How do you cover events like this?', *Guardian*, 26 April.

Stewart, Ian (2002), *Freetown Ambush*, London: Vision.

Sylvester, Judith and Suzanne Huffman (2005), *Reporting from the Front: The Media and the Military*, Oxford: Rowman & Littlefield.

Taylor, Philip M. (1992), *War and the Media: Propaganda and Persuasion in the Gulf War*, Manchester: Manchester University Press.

Teather, David (2004), 'The war on bias', *Guardian*, 23 August.

Todd, Emmanuel (2004), *After the Empire: The Breakdown of the American Order*, translated by C. Jon Delogu, London: Constable.

Toffler, Alvin and Heidi Toffler (1993), *War and Anti-War*, Boston: Little, Brown.

Tuchman, Gaye (1972) 'Objectivity as Strategic Ritual: An Examination of Newsman's Notions of Objectivity', *American Journal of Sociology*, 77(4): 660–79.

Tumber, Howard (1997), 'Bystander journalism, or the journalism of attachment', *Intermedia* 25(1): 4–7.

Tumber H. (2005), 'Journalism and the war in Iraq', in S. Allan (ed.), *Journalism: Critical Issues*, Maidenhead: Open University Press, pp. 370–80.

Tumber, Howard and Jerry Palmer (2004), *Media at War: The Iraq Crisis*, London: Sage.

Tumber, Howard and Marina Prentoulis (2003), 'Journalists under Fire: subcultures, objectivity and emotional literacy', in D. Thussu and D. Freedman (eds), *Reporting Conflict – War and the Media*, London: Sage, pp. 215–230.

Tunstall, Jeremy (2006), *The Media Were American*, New York: Oxford University Press.

Urry, John (2000), *Sociology beyond Societies: Mobilities for the 21st Century*, London: Routledge.

Vulliamy, (ed.) (1994), *Seasons in Hell: Understanding Bosnia's War*, London: Simon & Schuster.

Wasserstein, Bernard (1979), *Britain and the Jews of Europe, 1939–1945,* Oxford: Oxford University Press.

West, Bing and Major General Ray L. Smith (2003), *The March Up: Taking Baghdad with the 1st Marine Division,* London: Pimlico.

Wheeler, N. (2000), *Saving Strangers,* Oxford: Oxford University Press.

Whitehead, Laurence (2002), *Democratization: Theory and Experience,* Oxford: Oxford University Press.

Worsley, Peter (1984), *The Three Worlds: Culture and World Development,* London: Weidenfeld & Nicolson.

Wright, Evan (2004), *Generation Kill: Devil Dogs, Iceman, Captain America, and the New Face of American War,* New York: Putnam.

Zelizer, Barbie and Stuart Allan (2002), *Journalism after September 11,* London: Routledge.

Zinsmeister, Karl (2003), *Boots on the Ground: A Month with the 82nd Airborne in the Battle for Iraq,* New York: Truman Talley Books.

Zucchino, David (2004), *Thunder Run: The Armored Strike to Capture Baghdad,* New York: Grove Press.

LIST OF INTERVIEWEES

Anton Antonowicz; Chris Ayres; Colin Baker; Yannis Behrakis; Ross Benson; Ben Brown; John Carlin; Rory Carroll; Dan Chung; Marie Colvin; Daniel Demoustier; John Downing; Dan Edge; Antonia Francis; Audrey Gillan; Suzanne Goldenberg; Orla Guerin; Luke Harding; Gavin Hewitt; Lindsey Hilsum; Lin Hilton; Chip Hires; Halim Hosny; John Irvine; Barbara Jones; Jane Kokan; Uwe Kroeger; Tim Lambon; Jerry Lampen; Julian Manyon; James Mates; James Meek; Adrian Monck; Bill Neely; Paul O'Driscoll; Maggie O'Kane; Sara Oliver; Peter Sharp; Sean Smith; Vaughan Smith; Jonathan Steele; Tom Stoddart; Jon Swain; John Sweeney; Jeremy Thompson; Brian Williams; David Williams; Kim Willsher; Mark Wood; Caroline Wyatt; David Zucchino.

In addition to the interviewees we also received advice and comment from Mark Brayne; Robert Fisk; John Owen and Stuart Purvis.

INDEX